CANADIAN IMMIGRATION LAW AND POLICY: THEN AND NOW

OTHER BOOKS IN THE COLLECTION

Political Law in Canada

Canada's Parliament: A Primer

The Senate of Canada

The Recognition of Two Official Languages in Canada

Drafting, Interpreting, and Applying Legislation

Federalism in Canada: Evolving Constitutional, Political, and Social Realities

The House of Commons of Canada

UNDERSTANDING CANADA

CANADIAN IMMIGRATION LAW AND POLICY: THEN AND NOW

Mario D. Bellissimo

INSTITUTE OF PARLIAMENTARY AND POLITICAL LAW
INSTITUT DE DROIT PARLEMENTAIRE ET POLITIQUE

Irwin Law
An imprint of University of Toronto Press
Toronto Buffalo London
utorontopress.com
Printed and bound by CPI Group (UK) Ltd, Croydon, CR0 4YY

ISBN 978-1-5522-1719-1 (paper) ISBN 978-1-5522-1720-7 (PDF)

Library and Archives Canada Cataloguing in Publication

Title: Canadian immigration law and policy : then and now / Mario D. Bellissimo. Names: Bellissimo, Mario D., author. | Institute of Parliamentary and Political Law (Ottawa, Ont.), issuing body.
Description: Series statement: Understanding Canada collection | Includes bibliographical references and index.
Identifiers: Canadiana (print) 20240356799 | Canadiana (ebook) 20240356837 | ISBN 9781552217191 (softcover) | ISBN 9781552217207 (PDF)
Subjects: LCSH: Emigration and immigration law — Canada. | LCSH: Emigration

---

We wish to acknowledge the land on which the University of Toronto Press operates. This land is the traditional territory of the Wendat, the Anishnaabeg, the Haudenosaunee, the Métis, and the Mississaugas of the Credit First Nation.

University of Toronto Press acknowledges the financial support of the Government of Canada and the Ontario Arts Council, an agency of the Government of Ontario, for its publishing activities.

Canada Council for the Arts Conseil des Arts du Canada

ONTARIO ARTS COUNCIL
CONSEIL DES ARTS DE L'ONTARIO
an Ontario government agency
un organisme du gouvernement de l'Ontario

Funded by the Government of Canada Financé par le gouvernement du Canada

Canada

To Polina, Elisabetta, Alexandra, Maria,
Joseph, and Mary, who inspire me daily and
make all things possible.

Contents

Foreword

Canada is a country comprising a composite population. The Indigenous were the first inhabitants of this land. Colonizers from France and the British Isles came next, to various parts of what would eventually become the Dominion of Canada. Starting not long following the British conquest of New France and lasting until now, individuals, families, and groups of people have come to this land with the intention of establishing themselves here, remaining for their own as well as their succeeding generations' lives, building their futures here, and developing the country. Immigration is one of the inherent characteristics of Canadian society and of the body politic. The absorption of generations of contributors to the country is no longer merely an accepted social tradition. It has also become an economic necessity.

Immigration is inadequately understood if its points of reference are derived merely from articles in the daily press, newscasts (however serious), or worse yet, passing notes on social media. The fact of immigration is now framed by constitutional provisions and federal and provincial statutes. It is applied by large bureaucracies interpreting the law, generating policy, and carrying out procedures. At various times, this is a topic of intense political discussion on the national scene. Genuine understanding of the subject matter requires a comprehensive text aimed at citizens desirous of knowledge.

The reader should put this book in perspective, as immigration is not a stand-alone subject. Its most basic convergence is with demography. No state, however welcoming, can accept all those who solicit entry. The relevant law must be drafted so as to enable Canada to select those who it believes will make a useful contribution. Immigration also overlaps with education, health care, housing, employment, and economic development. The arrival of migrants both fills vacancies in the workforce and generates demand for further goods and services. The actual rules of the immigration system should thus be read and understood in their most comprehensive context.

Thick textbooks more suitable for students of law and public administration, as well as for those hoping to become immigration consultants, are already in circulation. What Mario Bellissimo presents here is an explanation that is both complete and eminently readable.

This book should adorn, first, the bookshelves of parliamentarians called upon to deal with immigration as one of many issues of Canada's national life and who have to familiarize themselves rapidly with this among a variety of other subject matters. It should also serve as a summary for public servants and officials new to the immigration portfolio. Yet more to the point, this book should be of help to two groups. It should be in the back pocket of those, all around the world, who seek to attain the status of immigrant to Canada, as it can serve as a passport of understanding for them. Finally, this book is suitable for the shelves of Canadians who are already part of the national family and who seek to review the facts of this important function of government.

It is not sufficient that those of us already here declare for others: "Come to Canada!" It is better to show them the way.

Gregory Tardi, DJur.
Editor, Understanding Canada Collection
March 2023

Preface

Much of my life has been dedicated to the practice and study of immigration, citizenship, and refugee law. Immigration no doubt is an enduring facet of the evolution of humanity and has deeply informed the course of history. Immigration has always been crucial to the development of Canada. For me, once introduced to the area of law, my passion grew from my immigrant background and the fascination of persons leaving everything behind and beginning anew. Growing to learn the powerful role an immigration lawyer plays in the process and how you can change people's lives began a life-long passion I enthusiastically hold to this day. I, along with many committed individuals over the years, have been privileged to represent incredible people at every stage of the immigration process and court level and make a real difference.

I have learned that to understand Canada is to begin to understand its complex relationships with diverse groups of migrants that have made Canada their home over hundreds of years. Immigration is a topic most Canadians can relate to, can speak to, because it is part of our personal journey unless one is indigenous to Canada. Though, despite the commonality for most Canadians, immigration does not translate into a monolithic view of its history, role, and future bearing on Canada. The path to Canada's current immigration program was not lateral or always progressive.

Naturally, Canadian immigration is inextricably tied to the delicate societal, economic, and political tapestry of the broader world, so it comes as no surprise that racism, power imbalances, and exclusion not only infiltrated Canadian immigration but shaped its "colour" and scope. Regrettably, this has led to periods where Canada closed the door, for example, to Jewish migrants attempting to flee the horrors of the Second World War and even imprisoned and deported many because they shared an ancestry with those with whom we were at war. Xenophobia and racism fueled the socio, political, and even the legal evolution.

The drivers and tensions that have long existed in immigration law and policy between the "perceived" responsibility to protect resources and the "citizenry of the day" tempered by the need to grow as a country fueled in large measure by economic demand persists. The decisions reflect Canada's "shared" values, power dynamics, and political choices then and now.

This book, in a concise yet comprehensive way, surveys important immigration touchpoints since Confederation, speaks to current immigration law and policy, immigration inadmissibility law, and the future of immigration processing, including the use of artificial intelligence (AI). The book is an excellent resource for hundreds of additional sources, jurisprudence, and policy.

Reading about Canadian immigration law can help readers better understand present-day dynamics in Canadian society and immigration law and policy. Understanding the different permanent and temporary resident pathways both in law and policy helps readers (journalists, students, legal professionals) become familiar with different status holders in our society. Appreciating who is not eligible for entry to Canada tells us as much about our immigration legal and socio-policy framework as does those who are permitted entry.

Exploring the pathways for immigrants in Canada can also help readers grow empathy and understanding for those who have had to navigate the immigration process. This can help foster greater compassion and inclusivity in Canadian society.

Recognizing the emerging use of AI can provide insights into the benefits and potential challenges of using AI in the immigration field, which will be a large part of the future of Canadian immigration delivery. Reading about immigration history and law can help develop critical thinking skills by encouraging readers across society, from academics to government to professional organizations, to foster different perspectives and revisit assumptions. This can help individuals become more informed and engaged citizens.

Analyzing Canadian immigration history with respect to its genesis, its tainted history, and demographics, to list a few topics, are crucial in understanding the complex aspects of Canada's immigration past, present, and future.

In all, *Canadian Immigration Law & Policy: Then and Now* is an excellent resource for those with an advanced grasp and those who are just beginning within this field. The intention is to make this content as concise, transparent, and accessible as possible, to engender and enable a deeper appreciation and dialogue of past and current immigration law and policy while envisioning what the future of Canadian immigration may look like and how the law may and should respond.

Mario D. Bellissimo, LL.B. C.S.
Toronto, Ontario
25 March 2023

CHAPTER ONE

Immigration: The Canadian Way

> The business of the law is to make sense of the confusion of what we call human life — to reduce it to order but at the same time to give it possibility, scope, even dignity.[1]

Introduction

The immigration experience is multi-faceted. Different pathways to Canadian immigration status, for example, reflect the disparate roads to becoming a future Canadian. The term "refugee," for one, is often conflated with "immigrant." Yet, a refugee and/or a refugee claimant follows a vastly different path, if successful, to immigration status. Canadian-born citizens, naturalized citizens, and landed immigrants all have different rights and obligations in law. Thus, when I discuss an "immigrant" in the context of Canadian immigration law and policy, I am not necessarily referring to refugees and citizens. Both encompass separate areas of law not addressed directly in this book. However, a recognition of refugees and citizens and the conflation of terms are important to our discussion because they contribute to challenges in understanding our immigration history and law.

For one, the conflation of different terms can propagate fallacies that may have serious consequences on policy development, media coverage, or racial and ethnic relations throughout Canada. Indeed, understanding Canada's immigration "people" story requires many lenses. Canadian immigration law and policy inevitably did not and cannot today exist outside of the ebbs and flows of international crisis, conflict, and need. Nor could it predict every outcome and have the law speak to the same with clarity. Ultimately, examining the roots of "to Canada" migration law is a fascinating exercise. One that can only be surveyed here in a broad way, to explore the Canadian experience. The Canadian way.

Pre-Confederation Migration

Generally, demographer Kingsley Davis identifies two key factors as the underpinnings of migration. First was the ability of early humans to adapt to any number of conditions. Second was the burgeoning diversity of cultures — born of population growth — from which inequalities developed between different groups. While the first factor "gave us the key to the door of any room on the planet," the second "gave us reason to use them."[2] Migration has been at the core of many great events in history, both as a cause and an effect. Religions have spurred on pilgrims and settlers; wars have left refugees in their wake and made new land available for conquerors; political upheavals have displaced millions; economic innovations have drawn workers from across the globe; and environmental disasters have forced survivors to replant elsewhere.

Prior to the recent, more diverse wave of immigrants, the focus of Canadian immigration had been to populate Canada with Western Europeans.[3] This focused inclusion of certain types of people often meant the exclusion of others through the normalization of explicitly racist policies.

While some people were simply restricted from entering the country, others were forbidden.[4]

Movement of immigrants into what would later be known as Canada in 1867 was largely unrestricted in the 1800s. Prior to the American Revolution, the primary immigrants to Canada were those of the Anglo-European (British, Scottish, Irish) and French backgrounds, who began settling in Canada from the 1600s.[5] In the seventeenth and eighteenth centuries, the first immigrants who entered Canada were 42,000 United Empire Loyalists, who came as political refugees displaced by the American Revolution and settled.[6]

In the nineteenth century, the great Irish potato famine led many Irish to immigrate to Canada, making the Irish the first group of overseas immigrants.[7] With the arrival of the Irish came the new social, cultural, and religious values that significantly differed from those of Anglo-Canadians, who were mostly Protestants. The Irish migrants felt the impact of being different. As a result of this Irish settlement, though, the French and the Irish were able to form a Roman Catholic minority in Canada. Toward the late nineteenth century, on 1 July 1867, the enactment of the *Constitution Act* united the three separate colonies of Canada, Nova Scotia, and New Brunswick into a single Dominion within the British Empire, called Canada. The cusp of the twentieth century saw Canada's first step toward defining immigration laws. Much of the early legislation left the handling of persons with criminality to the sole discretion of immigration authorities with little, if any, opportunity to appeal or judicially review the findings of the department.

Legislative Underpinning

From the very beginning of our country, the federal and provincial governments have shared jurisdiction (power) over immigration law. Interestingly, perhaps a reflection of priorities in 1867, in the *Constitution Act, 1867*[8] immigration was referred to in the title of the concurrent jurisdiction provision as "etc.":

> *Concurrent Powers of Legislation respecting Agriculture, etc.*
> **95** In each Province the Legislature may make Laws in relation to Agriculture in the Province, and to Immigration into the Province; and it is hereby declared that the Parliament of Canada may from Time to Time make Laws in relation to Agriculture in all or any of

> the Provinces, and to Immigration into all or any of the Provinces; and any Law of the Legislature of a Province relative to Agriculture or to Immigration shall have effect in and for the Province as long and as far only as it is not repugnant to any Act of the Parliament of Canada.

The wording has not since been amended. Immigration was and remains one of the few areas of explicitly concurrent jurisdiction (along with agriculture and old age pensions) in the *Constitution Act, 1867*.[9] Over time, provinces have played a larger role in immigration law and policy, but the federal government remains the chief authority in the delivery of immigration programs.

At the outset extreme power was conferred on the federal government with absolute authority over all immigration and enforcement powers. Not surprisingly, over time, like other burgeoning common law jurisdictions, ministerial and enforcement powers became increasingly subject to individual rights. The means used to implement the policy choices of the day often reiterated the need to respond to international developments. How this tenuous balance was maintained in Canada presented one of the greatest failures in our history as will be explored below. While the checks and balances of democracy are imperative in every legal field, the need for proper legislative review and debate and careful judicial scrutiny became ever more essential given the profound personal and societal implications at play in the immigration context.

Post-Confederation Migration

In 1869, Frank Oliver, a former newspaper publisher who sat as a Liberal Member of Parliament (MP) between 1896–1917, took one of the first steps toward defining immigration laws. Given that emigration and the population of the West became national concerns, a transcontinental railway was promised alongside the promise that immense farmland was available in Western Canada. Facilitation of this commitment led to the introduction of the first large-scale immigration wave, and the first *Immigration Act* in Canada was passed in 1869, with the purpose of ensuring the safety of European immigrants[10] who chose Canada. Based on the time's social values and ideology, the ideal settlers were, in descending order, British and American agriculturalists who were followed by French, Belgians, Dutch, Scandinavians, Swiss, Finns, Russians, Austro-Hungarians, Germans, Ukrainians, and Poles.

Close to the bottom of the list came those who were, in both the public's and the government's minds, less assimilable and less desirable, for example, Italians, South Slavs, Greeks, and Syrians. At the very "bottom" came Jews, Asians, Roma people, and Black people.[11] Discrimination based on race, ethnicity, and class was openly prevalent.[12]

In 1885, the Royal Commission on Chinese Immigration was appointed[13] because the government had to balance their ethnic anxieties against the needs of industrialism. The *Chinese Immigration Act of 1885*[14] was passed to satisfy the need for inexpensive labour, and Chinese people began immigrating to Canada while paying a head tax of $50 to enter Canada, which rose to $500 per person in 1903.[15] With the influx of "undesired" Europeans and Chinese, the agricultural and economic development of Canada was flourishing.

However, in 1906, the *Immigration Act* was amended to introduce restrictive immigration policies, including the deportation of immigrants. Regrettably, racist anxieties only grew, leading to the *Gentlemen's Agreement* between Canada and Japan in 1908,[16] which was targeted at reducing Japanese migration to Canada. Simultaneously, the *Continuous Journey Regulation* was also passed, restricting Indians from immigrating to Canada[17] by legislating that one must reach Canada without stopping along the way.

Specifically, it was in 1908 that Wilfrid Laurier's federal government made the amendment to the *Immigration Act* of 1906. The amendment was in response to then Deputy Minister of Labour Mackenzie King's findings that an undesirable Asian (at the time, referred to as Oriental) influx was attributable to high immigration from Hawaii. He recommended that Ottawa should severely limit the admission of Japanese newcomers as well as new settlers from India. As such in 1908 the "continuous journey regulation" came into effect and remained until 1947 — thirty-nine years.

Pursuant to this regulation, all intended immigrants to Canada were required to travel to Canada by continuous passage from their country of origin or citizenship on a through ticket purchased in the said country. Since no shipping company offered direct services from India to Canada or from Hawaii to Canada, both Indian and Japanese immigration were eliminated.[18]

The regulation did not go unchallenged. The most notable challenge to the regulation is known as the *Komagata Maru* incident on 23 May 1914, when 376 East Indians (including twenty-two landed immigrants of Canada) arrived in Vancouver in the *Komagata Maru* steamer. In the end, after weeks of depriving the passengers of food and water and a test case before an Immigration Board of Inquiry, all except the returning residents were redirected to India, found to be in violation of the continuous journey regulation. Although exceptions over the thirty-nine years were permitted the legislation is a significant blight on Canada's immigration history.

By 1910, Frank Oliver enacted changes to the *Immigration Act* that barred a broader spectrum of people and increased government power in immigration selection and deportation of persons who would not be fit to settle in Canada. Notably, in that year, the descendants of previously enslaved Black people, who were now persecuted Black farmers in the United States, were looking to migrate to central Alberta for a more prosperous life.[19] Although these policy changes in 1910 were not explicitly racist, these amendments were racially charged.

At the surge of the First World War, despite the needs of the Canadian military, the heightened unease and mistrust surrounding foreign-born Canadian citizens led Britain and Canada to send foreigners back to their countries, especially if they were born on enemy soil.[20] After the First World War, Prime Minister Robert Borden and the Conservative Party of Canada addressed these feelings of uncertainty by introducing amendments to Canada's immigration policy through the *Act to Amend the Immigration Act*.[21] Until the establishment of its own citizenship and immigration legislation after the Second World War, Canada relied on other statutes, particularly legislation from the United Kingdom, to determine its immigration policy.[22]

Section 13 of the *Act to Amend the Immigration Act* expanded on the factors that would warrant prohibiting hopeful immigrants from entering the country. The provision provides insight into the stark reality of the time. It read:

> [B]ecause such immigrants are deemed undesirable owing to their peculiar customs, habits, modes of life and methods of holding property, and because of their probable inability to become readily assimilated or to assume the duties and responsibilities of Canadian citizenship within a reasonable time after their entry.[23]

At the time, the government also introduced new grounds for the revocation of "British subject" status.[24] These included the demonstration of disloyalty to the Crown by act or speech,[25] communication with the enemy,[26] and even residing outside of the British Dominions for seven years.[27] The broadened revocation powers were coupled with the apprehension that subsisted.[28] Citizenship revocation between 1947 and 1977 saw some additional ebbs and flows, depending on the administration of the day.

At the end of the Second World War, Canada focused on making industrial and economic strides to compensate for the impact of the war.[29] Massive industrial projects required a larger workforce than was readily available in Canada, leading the government to allow more foreign workers to enter the country.[30] While the acceptance of so many foreign workers is often seen as a pivotal shift in the history of Canada's approach to immigration policy, it should be noted that at the same time as European workers entered Canada, thousands of Canadians with Japanese roots had their citizenship revoked and were subsequently deported. What is most striking about this is that many of these Canadians had never been to Japan and were in fact born in Canada.[31]

It is clear from both the assimilation criteria and denationalization/denaturalization of Canadians with ties to Japan that much of the paranoia that existed in Canada regarding immigrants and immigration policy was (albeit implicitly) to maintain cultural homogeneity and "whiteness" in the country.[32] It is important to note that the intensified sensitivities surrounding immigrants was not only a symptom of the war in Canada, but also in countries including the United Kingdom, the United States of America, and Australia.[33] The loss of millions in a few decades was in opposition to the urgent need to rebuild and restore after wartime. Also, Jewish migrants, as noted, were denied refuge from the atrocities of the Second World War.

Consequently, even though the wars had also exacerbated the fear of foreigners and their ability to assimilate, the need to rebuild and reposition economies to recover was prioritized.[34] This resulted in an unprecedented movement of people hoping to build new lives across the war-torn world.[35] An opportunity for thousands that likely would not otherwise have been available.

With the passage of time, it was evident that more open immigration policies would be the way forward in Canada. Canadian citizenship, however, was not legally recognized until 1 January 1947, prior to which all persons born or naturalized in Canada were considered British subjects. The *Canadian Citizenship Act* of 1 January 1947 specified the requirement of becoming a Canadian citizen. In 1977, a notable change came with the enactment of the *Citizenship Act*, which, for the first time, recognized dual citizenship. Between the 1960s until the tail-end of the 1980s is the period some academics consider to be the de-ethnicization period.[36]

In 1966, the Pearson government outlined an immigration philosophy that highlighted the basic premise of entry and exclusion based upon potential adaptability. Individuals inadmissible due to criminality, security, or human rights violations were viewed as lacking adaptable qualities. In 1967, a change in geopolitical sentiments led to the establishment of the point system, which sought to eliminate racial discrimination in Canada's immigration policy.[37] In turn, 1971 became a historic year in Canadian immigration history, being the first official year that most immigrants coming to Canada were of non-European ancestry.[38]

Globalization seemed to have spearheaded the need for an international human rights regime that would codify the conduct expected of leading nations across the world. Specifically, in the aftermath of the Second World War, it became evident to the world that Jewish migrants might have survived if Canada or other countries had offered genuine protection. The Second World War therefore served as a sobering time in immigration history because it led to the international recognition of human rights and set a solid policy basis for refugees. This, coupled with the consistently increasing need for workers in Canada, helped pave the way for Canada to adopt a more progressive immigration outlook. Immigration law and policy necessarily followed suit.

During the 1970s, immigration and population policies were officially reviewed. Both a Green Paper on Immigration Policy and a report to Parliament (1975) by a Special Joint Committee of the Senate and the House of Commons were prepared. Almost all the committee's recommendations were accepted by the Liberal federal government. In 1976, these recommendations became the *Immigration Act*, which comprised the most comprehensive legislative framework to date.[39]

By the late 1990s, Canada firmly cemented its reputation as an immigrant-friendly country that proudly featured multiculturalism.[40] The attitude across countries such as the United States of America, the United Kingdom, and so on, also saw a more open approach to the idea of immigration, as it had become more prevalent following the Great War era. This is why, despite the considerable progress that was made by way of the 1977 *Citizenship Act*[41] (which eliminated all grounds for citizenship revocation except for where naturalization was the result of false pretenses), 11 September 2001, at 8:14 a.m. Eastern Standard Time, ushered in a new trajectory for immigration and citizenship revocation policy and immigration law generally.

A Tainted and Complex History

Canada's immigration history is rife with explicit examples of discrimination because of race and national origin. I canvass a few to provide a line of sight into how the law and prejudices intertwined. Notably, the denial of refuge to our country involved many groups over many years. Although the focus here for the most part is on immigration law and policy that was racist and discriminatory, refugee law and policy unfortunately did not fare better. With respect to immigration law and policy, the Chinese head tax, the internment of racialized populations during the Second World War, the "continuous journey" legislation targeting migration from Asia, and the characterization of Black migrants as "unsuited to the Canadian climate" are a few of the most striking examples.[42]

Inadmissibility however, was not restricted to race but included the "feeble-minded, an idiot, or an epileptic," or someone "who is insane" in the 1906 *Immigration Act*.[43] The *Immigration Act* of 1952 created tiers of immigrants and discriminatory prohibited classes to include "idiots, imbeciles or morons," the "insane," "psychopathic personalities," persons with "epilepsy," and those who were "dumb, blind or otherwise physically defective."[44] The Act continued to allow the government to place quotas on the entry of "less preferred" migrants. The impact of these measures is felt today.

Indigenous Peoples

No discussion of Canada's legal progression in the immigration context can ignore that while the law was being developed to admit and regulate the entry of newcomers, concomitant laws were developed to displace and marginalize those that were Indigenous to the land. Indeed, Canada is often perceived as being on the right side of history: as a tolerant, benevolent country. Prime Minister Justin Trudeau's 2022 Christmas message, for example, emphasized these very points:

> As we celebrate those unique traditions that reflect Canada's diversity — let's remind ourselves how fortunate we are to live in a country of peace. A country where families can live out their faith and be proud of the communities they represent. And as we look ahead to the new year, let's continue to stand together as we build a better future for all Canadians.[45]

However, this singular perspective of Canada and its history minimizes the burden carried by Indigenous peoples. The Truth and Reconciliation Commission of Canada, created to confront the memory of the Indian Residential Schools system, points out that "the central goals of Canada's Aboriginal policy were to eliminate Aboriginal governments; ignore Aboriginal rights; terminate the Treaties; and, through the process of assimilation, cause Aboriginal peoples to cease to exist as a distinct legal, social, cultural, religious, and racial entities in Canada."[46] Thus, it was the policy of the Government of Canada to create a relatively homogenous cultural community through a process of cultural genocide — that is, through the systematic destruction of traditions, values, language, and other elements that make one group of people distinct from another.[47] This policy was manifested through the unlawful seizure of territories, the forced transfer of populations, and the banning of languages and cultural practices.[48]

Historian John Milloy furthers this point by explaining that "Aboriginal traditions, ritual life, social and political organization [and] economic practices [were] proscribed as obstacles to Christianity and civilization."[49] The contemporary Canadian identity, therefore, was fostered through a targeted approach to immigration: despite "the absence of a formal immigration policy or administration . . . strategies of recruitment contained a certain vision of what immigrants should be and do; that is, Europeans were recruited for settlement, with the promises of land ownership."[50]

Indeed, Prime Minister Macdonald described the government's responsibility to "Indians" as one of "guardianship as of persons underage, incapable of the management of their own affairs."[51] Unsurprisingly, it was under the crudely named *Indian Act* that the

Indian Residential Schools system, and all the horrors that followed, was institutionalized.

Chinese Canadians

In the early 1880s, Canada allowed Chinese migrants to enter the country as the state required workers to help build the Canadian Pacific Railway (CPR). This railway system was a crucial project to Confederation as it meant a cheaper, faster, and more convenient way of transportation. Chinese migrants were brought by ship from China and began working on the CPR from the West coast, while European workers began on the East coast.[52] Unfortunately, while navigating dangerous terrain on the job, many Chinese migrants became injured or died due to malnutrition, accidents, and cold weather conditions. Beyond work conditions, Chinese workers were maltreated compared to European labourers.

For example, during the construction of the railway, Chinese migrants were asked to work intense hard labour with extended hours in comparison to White workers.[53] In addition to labour, Chinese migrants were paid 40–50 percent less than European labourers. Chinese migrants were paid $1 per day and were expected to use this to pay for their work gear and food, while others were paid $2 to $2.50 and were provided with the essentials. By the end of 1882, the railway was completed with the help of 9,000 railway workers, of which 6,500 were Chinese migrants.[54] When the CPR was completed, many Canadians did not want the Chinese Canadians to reside in Canada and wanted them to leave the country. At the time, Canada was predominantly White, and many citizens feared that these Chinese Canadians would repopulate with other White Canadians and poison its "purity." It was at this time when Prime Minister William Lyon Mackenzie King passed an immigration policy that would restrict and discourage Chinese migrants from entering Canada.

Stephen Winter provides an in-depth analysis of the redress that the Canadian government has made to Chinese migrants in regret of the *Chinese Immigration Act* that included a discriminatory head tax.[55] In 1885, the *Act to Restrict and Regulate Chinese Immigrants into Canada* was imposed on all Chinese migrants to discourage their entry to Canada.[56] This Act included a head tax that initially required $50 for entry; however, in 1901, this then increased to $100 and then to $500 in 1903, which was extremely difficult to afford as, in those times, this amount of money was double many individuals' annual wages.

Prime Minister Wilfrid Laurier stated, "In my opinion, there is not much room for the Chinaman in Canada"; therefore, the reasoning behind imposing this tax was unjustifiably racist on all grounds.[57] Such a statement propagated exclusionary impressions based on underlying racist and discriminatory beliefs. Winter writes that the "head tax derived about $23 million from approximately 81,000 Chinese immigrants," which the Canadian government felt was still insufficient to prevent further immigration from China.

Therefore, in 1923, the *Chinese Immigration Act* was imposed, denying immigration from most Asian countries. Furthermore, in amending the original *Act to Restrict and Regulate Chinese Immigrants into Canada*, Winter explains these actions not only negatively affect Chinese migrant families financially, but the "racist immigration legislation communicated a status of ethnic undesirability."[58] In addition to the Act preventing Chinese migrants from finding work and their ability to provide for themselves and their families, the policy was morally degrading to their cultural dignity. Furthermore, this Act created many divides within families due to external stressors such as financial burdens and verbal and physical harassment relating to racism.

Similarly, Mayo Moran and David Dyzenhaus analyze historical Canadian immigration policies, identifying the damage it left on many Chinese migrants.[59] Moran and Dyzenhaus argue that if a government places a head tax on immigrants of all ethnic backgrounds, national origins, ages, or wealth when coming into the country, then by theory, this is acceptable. However, due to the Act strictly including only Chinese migrants, it was immensely racist on all grounds.[60]

On 6 February 2006, the Conservative government announced the current redress program, which provided $20,000 to those affected by the Chinese head tax.[61] In addition to the payments made to Chinese migrants, $24 million was invested in the Community Historical Recognition Program and $10 million in the National Historical Recognition Program to educate the public on how the *Chinese Immigration Act* was discriminatory.[62] However, this one-time payment or "one certificate, one payment" was a financial approach that did not satisfy many Chinese Canadians as the financial debt the head tax caused for the first generation of children was immense.[63] Furthermore, the Chinese head tax caused deeper issues related to dignity that needed to be addressed by the Canadian government accepting moral responsibility. This transpired in addition to an apology made to all Chinese Canadians on 22 June 2007, as well as $34 million directed to programs that promoted awareness among all Canadians about the physical, psychological, and moral damage Chinese migrants faced during the *Chinese Immigration Act* era.[64]

Internment of Italian and Japanese Canadians

Although not by virtue of immigration legislation, after Italy joined the Second World War as an ally to Germany in 1940, more than 600 Italians were interned in camps under the authority of the *War Measures Act* and the *Defence of Canada Regulations*, with 31,000 Italian Canadians declared "enemy aliens."[65] Specifically, the Canadian government was permitted "to detain without charge, seize property from, and limit activities of Canadian residents born in countries that were at war with Canada."[66] Most of the Italian Canadians who were interned were men, although some women and children were also detained. They were forced to leave their homes and businesses and were taken to detention camps in remote areas of Canada, where they were held without trial or charges for the duration of the war.[67] Conditions in the internment camps were harsh, and internees were often subjected to forced labour and poor living conditions.

The internment of Italian Canadians had a significant impact on the community, causing many to lose their homes and businesses and suffer discrimination and prejudice after the war. In 1990, the Canadian government officially acknowledged the injustice of the internment and apologized to Italian Canadians for the harm done to them.[68]

Simultaneous to the internment of Italian Canadians, on 7 December 1941, Japan bombed Pearl Harbor, leading Canada to declare war on Japan and initiate the internment of Japanese Canadians.[69] The internment was carried out by the Canadian government between 1942 and 1949 and was based on the belief that Japanese Canadians were a potential security threat to Canada. Specifically, following the attack on Pearl Harbor in December 1941, the Canadian government began to view Japanese Canadians with suspicion. Even though the vast majority of Japanese Canadians were Canadian citizens or permanent residents, they were seen as a security risk due to their ethnic ties to Japan.[70] In February 1942, the Canadian government issued an order-in-council that authorized the forced removal of all Japanese Canadians from a designated "protected area" along the British Columbia coast.[71]

Japanese Canadians were given only a few days' notice to pack up their belongings and leave their homes and businesses. They were forced to sell their property at a fraction of its value or leave it behind, and many lost everything they had built up in Canada. For an immigrant, this loss is devastating. To exacerbate their pain, Japanese Canadians were then sent to internment camps in remote areas of British Columbia and other parts of Canada,[72] where they lived in substandard conditions. Today, the internment of Italian Canadians and Japanese Canadians is recognized as a dark chapter in Canadian history and serves as a reminder of the importance of safeguarding the rights and freedoms of all people, regardless of their ethnicity or background.

Black Canadians

Since the beginning of the transatlantic slave trade, Black people have been living in Canada. From a historical standpoint, very few arrived directly from their ancestral homeland in Africa. Therefore, the term "African Canadian" is used to identify all descendants of Africa regardless of their birthplace. The term "Black Canadian" is also used, but it is employed in a more general sense. The earliest arrivals to Canada were enslaved people who were brought from either New England or the West Indies. Most Black migrants who came to Canada between 1763–1900 were from the United States as they were fleeing enslavement.

The intersection of Black Canadians and immigration is intricate, but the last thirty years of this history has begun to finally receive important attention. It has been described as "crimmigration." The Canadian context is no exception to the "crimmigration" process. The passage of the *Immigration and Refugee Protection Act* (*IRPA*) in November 2001[73] introduced several new tools to increase the security of the border, including front end security screening of refugee claimants, clearer grounds of detention of incoming migrants, deportation of those individuals already in the country determined to be inadmissible because of serious criminality, and fewer rights to appeal for foreign nationals in this later group. While the government steadfastly maintained that these provisions were not the result of an "overreaction to a few isolated incidents," the tabling of this legislation followed two highly publicized events in Toronto: the death of Georgina Leimonis during the *Just Desserts* shootings and the death of Todd Baylis.[74] The media identified the perpetrators of the offences in the events noted as Black, Jamaican men. The media further stated that these individuals were *not* citizens of Canada and that they were not legally in the country.

The need to remove "dangerous" Black, Jamaican men was oft-repeated in the promotion of Bill C-44, the genesis of what would later appear in the *IRPA* that dates back to 1994. For example, then Member of Parliament (MP) Art Hanger stated the following in supporting the new enforcement initiatives during debates of the Bill:

> First is the much publicized case of Clinton Gayle who is suspected of the murder of Constable Todd Baylis. Mr. Gayle came to the country legally. Mr. Gayle had a removal order issued against him. Mr. Gayle evaded that deportation order not by running and not by tying up the system with appeals. Rather, Mr. Gayle avoided removal because his file was lost. Mr. Gayle avoided capture and removal because the system was over worked, because priorities for removal were confused. It is more likely than not, although we will never know, because someone dropped the ball.
>
> . . .
>
> The second case that has outraged Canadians and has illustrated the deficiencies both in immigration and in the priorities of this government was the very recent case of one Mr. Forbes. He is currently being sought for the senseless shooting of several people in Toronto over the weekend.
>
> Tragically two of those people died at the hands of this individual. Mr. Forbes, who is also from Jamaica, came to Canada on a visitor's visa, as so many illegal entrants do. He overstayed that visa and a deportation order was issued.[75]

Similarly, MP Sharon Hayes noted the necessity of the legislation, citing the death of Todd Baylis and the ongoing threat faced by police officers given the limits of immigration enforcement. MP Hayes tied this threat to Black, Jamaican men in Canada, stating:

> [T]his weekend in a national news report . . . it was reported that Canada returned 227 deportees to Jamaica from January to July of this year, one-quarter of the total from all sources. It also pointed out that wealthy countries such as Canada are viewed by some countries as dumping our problems on them.
>
> . . .
>
> We need to equip those in the trenches not just with a book of rules but with the tools to do the job. We need to assure the

> shopkeepers, the businessmen, the parents and the police, Canadians by birth or by choice that they do not need to fear the system that should protect them.[76]

MP Hayes's statements plainly reflect the link between anti-Black racism, dangerousness, and enforcement.[77] Danger decisions in the immigration context would, as a result, necessarily reproduce the individual and systemic racisms and discrimination that marred the operations and practices of the criminal justice system (as had at that point been clearly determined by Stephen Lewis in his report for the Ontario government).[78]

Drawing on socio-historically racist narratives, these migrants were ultimately described as "undesirable" and "not worthy of being allowed to stay in Canada."[79] Comparatively, in the cases involving Anglo-European appellants, reasons for refusal of appeals were based primarily on the crimes committed by these individuals or on "legal issues" that concerned "why the individual cannot be allowed to stay."[80] While the *IRPA* replaced the "danger opinions" introduced by Bill C-44 with the limits on right of appeal under section 64(2) following determinations of inadmissibility for criminality, the legislation continued to disproportionately affect Black men, given the ongoing social context in Canada that saw these men being overpoliced and overincarcerated by the criminal justice system.[81] It can therefore be seen that anti-Black racism has been foundational to the development of immigration legislation over the past thirty years.[82]

2SLGBTQIA+

The 1952 *Immigration Act* introduced new restrictions to prohibit "homosexuals, drug addicts and drug traffickers" from entering the country.[83] It was not until the 1978 *Immigration Act* that the twenty-six-year ban was removed. But the restrictions persisted. Gay men and lesbians could not sponsor their partners. Only married, heterosexual Canadians could sponsor their spouses as family class immigrants. Lesbians and gay men were able to sponsor parents and siblings and some other members of the family class.[84] In 2002 with the passage of the *IRPA*, twenty-four years later:

> For the first time in Canadian immigration history, gay men and lesbians will be able to formally sponsor their partners. In changing its immigration policy to include same-sex couples, Canada joined several other countries in extending immigration rights to prospective gay and lesbian immigrants.[85]

The recent decision of *AP v Canada (MCI)* in 2020 is an example of the lingering effects of long-standing negative laws and policy toward 2SLGBTQIA+, evidencing there is still more road to travel. Justice Fuhrer held in reviewing a negative decision of the Immigration Appeal Division regarding a family class sponsorship:

> [27] Finally, AP submits, and I agree, the IAD's decision was based on a closed mind or bias resulting in an unreasonable assessment of the evidence regarding the possibility of a mixed-orientation couple meeting the criteria for a conjugal partnership. In AP's view, with which I also agree, the IAD focused exclusively on what appear to be pre-determined conclusions on the ability of mixed-orientation couples to engage in sexual relations and form conjugal relationships, contrary to the evidence provided and to the findings in *M. v. H.* The IAD had a closed mind as to the couple's decision to engage in unprotected sex, despite this factor having no relevance to, or bearing on, their conjugal relationship status. The IAD also had a closed mind as to why AP did not disclose his sexual orientation readily to AM and her parents despite evidence of his prior negative lived experiences in his country of origin from his refugee claim.[86]

Quebec's Ban on Religious Clothing

In Canada, Quebec has taken official positions opposing multiculturalism,[87] and by extension it can be argued has taken significant steps to ensure that it remains culturally homogenous. On 16 June 2019, Quebec became the first jurisdiction in North America to ban religious clothing when Bill 21, officially known as "An Act respecting the laicity of the State," was passed into provincial law using section 33 (the "notwithstanding clause") of the *Canadian Charter of Rights and Freedoms* (the *Charter*).[88] The law now prohibits certain public sector employees, including teachers, judges, police officers, and government lawyers, from wearing religious symbols while on the job. The ban applies to all religious symbols, including hijabs, kippahs, turbans, and crosses. Currently, the law includes provisions that allow for exemptions for certain individuals, such as those who were employed before the law was passed and who wish to continue wearing religious symbols.

However, new hires are not eligible for exemptions. By virtue of Canada's political system, and the authority given to Quebec by the Constitution, the Quebec government asserted that this law is "drafted by democratically elected politicians, passed democratically in the Quebec Legislature and continues to enjoy the support of a majority of Quebecers."[89] The law has faced various challenges on the grounds that it unquestionably violates the *Charter* freedoms of religion and expression. This law was challenged at the Quebec Superior Court in 2020. In their arguments, supporters of the law argued that it promotes state neutrality and prevents public sector employees from displaying religious symbols that could be seen as promoting a particular religion, while opponents argued that it violates religious freedom and targets specific religious groups.

In December 2020, the Quebec Superior Court ruled that the law is constitutional. In his decision, however, Blanchard J noted that, "the evidence *undoubtedly* shows that the effects of Law 21 will be felt negatively above all by Muslim women."[90] In addition to Canadian legal challenges, the law has been criticized by human rights organizations and religious groups, including the United Nations Human Rights Committee, which has called on Quebec to repeal the law, stating that it violates international human rights law.

If immigrants are seeking jobs in the public sector, they may need to adhere to the ban if they want to work for the Quebec government. Specifically, this could have a disproportionate impact on immigrants who come from religious minorities, particularly Muslim women who wear hijabs. It could also make it more difficult for immigrants who practise their religion openly to integrate into Quebec society and feel a sense of belonging.[91]

Moreover, the ban can create a negative perception of Quebec among potential immigrants who view the ban as discriminatory or against their religious beliefs, thus affecting the province's ability to attract and retain skilled workers and professionals, particularly those who value diversity and religious freedom. While the ban on religious clothing does not apply to private sector employees or to individuals in their personal lives, including immigrants, the ban could still create a chilling effect, making immigrants who wear religious symbols feel unwelcome in Quebec or reluctant to express their religious identity publicly. At the time of writing, the decision of the Quebec Superior Court has not been appealed and with the provisions of the notwithstanding clause, it will remain in effect until 19 June 2024.

The Road to Equity, Inclusion, and Diversity Continues

The examples above, to list a few, are part of a complex and tainted history. These stark realities must, however, be balanced with the groundwork laid in the 1970s — both the *Green Paper on Immigration Policy* and a *Report to Parliament (1975) by a Special Joint Committee of the Senate and the House of Commons* coupled with embracing multiculturalism at least in law — that has persevered above all else. Canada's immigration program, law, and policy today are not without issue; however, they are strong and vibrant. That view depending on one's lens may not be fully shared, but we continue to work as a nation to better our immigration delivery. The law and policy are at times tardy in expressing societal values and growth, yet we can take solace in its evolution and rich jurisprudential history to support the progress that distances us from law that was outright racist. The work continues and our history must both guide us and remind us of roads that should never be travelled again.

Present Era in Canadian Immigration History

In the 1990s, a return to expansive ministerial discretion began, following the murders at the Just Desserts café in Toronto and the death of officer Baylis of the Toronto Police at the hands of Clinton Gayle noted above. These two events together propelled changes to the *Immigration Act*, expanding ministerial authority to remove permanent residents' right of appeal following a determination of inadmissibility for criminality where they were deemed to represent risks to the safety and security of Canadian citizens. Here, the minister would investigate, during which permanent residents could submit evidence and legal arguments. Following this investigation, the minister could issue a danger to the public certificate, which would allow for the removal of the migrant without appeal.

The *IRPA* was passed following the events of 11 September 2001, which of course changed our legal and enforcement landscape in myriad ways. As a result of the *IRPA*, there was an increased emphasis on enforcement and national security. In 2014, after multiple attempts to make changes to Canadian immigration policy in a post-9/11 world, the Conservative government passed Bill C-24, the *Strengthening Canadian Citizenship Act* (*SCCA*).[92] The *SCCA* 2014[93] was enacted at the tail end of Prime Minister Stephen Harper's government's time in office.

Canada, like many of its allies, had strongly considered an overhaul of its immigration approach on multiple occasions since 9/11, and it was these efforts that pushed the pendulum, eventually resulting in the passage of the *SCCA* in 2014. The minister of citizenship and immigration was now able to revoke citizenship where individuals had committed criminal offences that were grouped together as national security threats. In practice, the threshold of "reasonable belief" gave the minister broad discretion in deciding such cases.

These enforcement powers continued to expand to date while remedial and appellate options were diminished. Chapters 3 and 4 delve into these intricate developments that continue to redefine the scope and application of Canadian immigration law and policy.

Primary Canadian Immigration Institutions

Immigration, Refugees and Citizenship Canada

Created in 1994, Immigration, Refugees and Citizenship Canada (IRCC) is a federal institution that is responsible for the *Citizenship Act* of 1977, and given the interests of national security, it shares responsibility with the minister of public safety for the administration of the *IRPA* and:[94]

> Screens and approves for admission, immigrants, foreign students, visitors and temporary workers who help Canada's social and economic growth; resettles, protects and provides a safe haven for refugees; helps newcomers adapt to Canadian society and become Canadian citizens; manages access to Canada to protect the security and health of Canadians and the integrity of Canadian laws; and helps Canadians and newcomers to participate fully in the economic, political, social and cultural life of the country.[95]

IRCC commits to supporting applicants as they transition to Canadian citizens. One in every six Canadian residents is now born abroad.[96] It is unsurprising that the immigration and refugee system and network of organizations to help newcomers settle and integrate are among the best in the world.

Canada Border Services Agency (CBSA)

Consistent with this effort toward enforcement and security in the early 2000s, the CBSA was created as a stand-alone enforcement agency in December 2003 through an order in council.[97] The CBSA operates both in Canada and overseas. Within Canada, CBSA officers control the admission of persons by enforcing the various inadmissibility provisions of the *IRPA*. Outside of Canada, CBSA officers support immigration officers in North America and overseas in assessing applications for persons seeking to enter Canada by screening for serious criminality and other inadmissibility. As an added measure, the CBSA has a network of migration integrity officers around the world. As part of their work, they review documents to prevent people from using improper information to board planes destined for Canada.

The CBSA collaborates with several partners in conducting their work, including IRCC, the Royal Canadian Mounted Police (RCMP), the Canadian Security and Intelligence Service (CSIS), provincial and municipal police in Canada, and international police and law enforcement agencies. This assists the CBSA in preventing criminals, people involved in organized crime or in human or international rights abuses, those that have been sanctioned, and people who pose a security threat from taking advantage of Canada's immigration program.

Tribunals and Courts

Tribunals and courts also play a key role within the Canadian immigration system, with some of the key institutions being the four divisions of the Immigration and Refugee Board (IRB) (the Immigration Appeal Division (IAD), the Immigration Division, the Refugee Protection Division, and the Refugee Appeal Division), and the Federal Court (FC), the Federal Court of Appeal (FCA), and occasionally, the Supreme Court of Canada. Citizenship, immigration, and refugee litigation continues to meaningfully shape the progression of immigration law and who will become our future Canadians. Canada remains at the forefront of creative, sophisticated, and important issue identification, debate, and ultimate resolution. I explore these institutions in Chapter 4.

Canadian and American Immigration: Similarities and Differences

Immigration to Canada has historically occurred in a much more limited capacity than has immigration to the United States, our closest neighbour and an important frame of reference. While it is key to understand individual push/pull factors, it is nevertheless possible to conclude that immigration to Canada has been more restrictive than in the United States.

Immigration to Canada, as described above, tended to focus on communities that would most likely adapt to the Canadian cultural identity, as well as providing the greatest economic output. While the United States equally valued economic productivity and relative cultural homogeneity, it differs from that of Canada through its precedent of relatively unencumbered immigration for nearly a century after its independence, at a time when immigration was steadily increasing,[98] suggesting, perhaps, that the existence of immigrant communities served to incentivize those who had remained behind.

FIGURE 1.1. NUMBER OF IMMIGRANTS TO THE UNITED STATES BETWEEN 1850–2021[99]

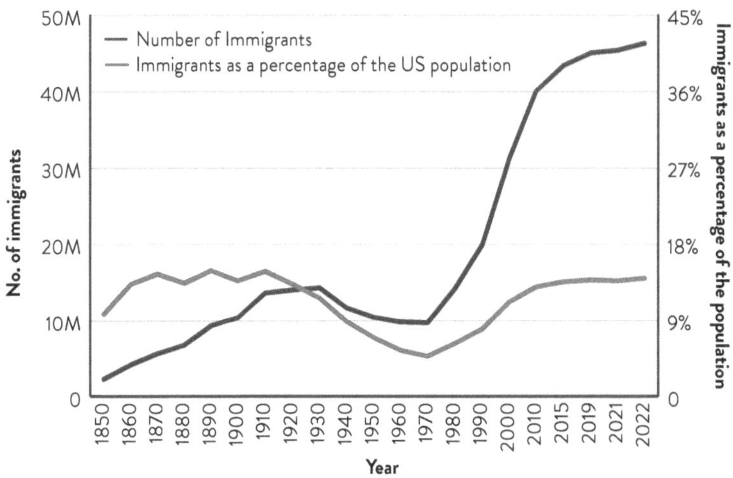

We Boldly Go into the Future

In 2022, the highest number of newcomers in a single year were welcomed to Canada, making it a historic year for Canadian immigration.[100] Many people choose to immigrate to Canada based on its reputation as a politically moderate, economically prosperous, and culturally rich society. At the end of 2022, the Honourable Sean Fraser, Minister of Immigration, Refugees and Citizenship, released Canada's 2023–2025 Immigration Levels Plan, in which it was proudly announced that by 2025, Canada will accept half a million immigrants.[101]

I briefly discussed how immigration regulations introduced in the 1960s were crucial to Canada's development as a multicultural state. First, regulations that had been introduced in 1962 "eliminated overt racial discrimination from Canadian immigration policy, [and promoted skill as] the main criteria for determining admissibility rather than race or national origin."[102] Second, those introduced in 1967 "established new standards for evaluating potential immigrants. To enhance the objectivity of admissions procedures, a system was set up in which independent immigrants were assessed points in specific categories relating to their education, occupational skills, employment prospects, age, proficiency in English and French and personal character."[103] Canada was moving away from the racist standard that had predominated the state's immigration policy since Confederation. As a result of this shift, immigration from non-European countries increased dramatically.

Within a few years, in 1971, multiculturalism became an official policy. In his speech to the House of Commons, Prime Minister P.E. Trudeau stated that no singular culture could define Canada and that the government accepted "the contention of other cultural communities that they, too, are essential elements in Canada."[104]

> A policy of multiculturalism within a bilingual framework commends itself to the government as the most suitable means of assuring the cultural freedom of Canadians. Such a policy should help to break down discriminatory attitudes and cultural

> jealousies. National unity if it is to mean anything in the deeply personal sense, must be founded on confidence in one's own individual identity; out of this can grow respect for that of others and a willingness to share ideas, attitudes and assumptions. A vigorous policy of multiculturalism will help create this initial confidence. It can form the base of a society which is based on fair play for all.[105]

The combination of progressive regulations and policy culminated in the *Immigration Act* of 1976 discussed in this chapter, a major shift in Canada's immigration policy, as "it was the first immigration act to clearly outline the objectives of Canadian immigration policy, define refugees as a distinct class of immigrants and mandate the federal government to consult with other levels of government in immigration planning and management."[106]

The history of Canadian immigration seen thus far suggests that immigration policy is in a constant state of flux. Figure 1.2 provides an overview of immigration from 1871 to today.

In all, no doubt immigration and the subsequent integration of once disparate cultures has proved a dynamic and vital force in the development of Canada's political, economic, and social histories. In the twenty-first century, more than ever before, the human face of Canada is culturally rich and varied. In recent years, multiculturalism has become more than just a catchphrase — it is now established as an enduring facet of Canada's policy and legislation. This explains, in large part, why Canada has become a top choice of residence for both permanent and temporary immigrants.

Now with the emergence of artificial intelligence (AI), immigration processing, delivery, and selection will be transformed in the coming years in a way we have never experienced before (see Chapter 5). It presents new challenges and opportunities and that will be informed in part by our history. More than ever, an earnest call to understand our immigration roots is acute because to understand Canada — immigration the Canadian way — where we can build on our strengths and distance ourselves from our grave mistakes is imperative, so the technology of the future moves forward on a transparent, inclusive, and democratic foundation.

FIGURE 1.2. FOREIGN-BORN POPULATION IN CANADA, HISTORICAL FIGURES AND EXPECTED FIGURES[107]

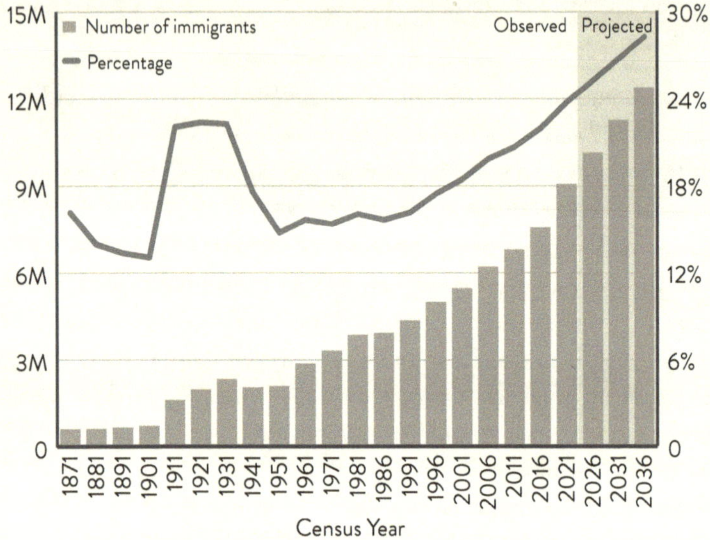

Source: Census of Population, 1971–2006, 2016, and 2021 (3901); National Household Survey, 2011 (5178); *Population projections on immigration and diversity for Canada and its regions*, 2016–2041 (5126). The presented data are based on the reference scenario.

Conclusion

Canada's immigration path has been complicated. The legal and policy development have mirrored that experience. Today, one of Canada's main goals, like many countries, is to increase its global competitiveness surrounding the selection, processing, and delivery of our immigration programs. For all classes of immigrants, integration, inclusion, and equal treatment into and within Canadian communities are vital. It was not enough to process immigrants to Canada — we must retain and integrate them within Canadian society. This goes beyond ensuring that they have employment opportunities. Historically at the front end these applicants were habitually assessed primarily as economic units, some disgracefully so, but on the back end they were people who required support and a fair chance to thrive in a country with a national immigration and integration plan that considered not only their workplace but the country in which they will live. I look next to Canadian immigration pathways in Chapter 2.

CHAPTER TWO

Canadian Immigration Pathways

Introduction

Intending migrants to Canada seek entry primarily through two sets of pathways: permanent and temporary residence. Permanent residence is for those who wish to live in Canada and potentially become naturalized citizens. Permanent residence can be a misnomer in certain cases because that status can be revoked for myriad inadmissibility reasons. Inadmissibility is explored in the next chapter. Temporary residence, in turn, is for those who only wish to stay in Canada for a specified amount of time — for example, to study, work, or visit. Temporary residence does not necessarily preclude a foreign national from eventually applying for permanent residence if they are eligible but, at the time of entering Canada, they must have at minimum a dual intention. Specifically, foreign nationals may still intend to eventually apply for permanent residency, provided a temporary intent exists at the time of applying.[1] This intention must be temporary in nature, and they must be prepared and willing to leave Canada at the time that temporary intention has been fulfilled — for instance, graduating, gaining the work experience that they set out to achieve, and so on. Both streams are provided for in the *Immigration and Refugee Protection Act* (*IRPA*) and the *Immigration and Refugee Protection Regulations* (*IRPR*).

In this chapter, I briefly explore the various pathways by which intending immigrants can enter Canada on a permanent or temporary basis, including the requisite eligibility requirements and key jurisprudence to help understand how Canadian immigration pathways have developed.

Permanent Residence Pathways

Economic/Federal Programs

The main pathway to Canada is economic. It constitutes the largest number of immigrants each year. Canada provides several categories for economic migrants to become permanent residents, including:

1. Federal Skilled Worker Class (FSW) — processed via Express Entry (EE)
2. Federal Skilled Trades Class (FST) — processed via EE
3. Canadian Experience Class (CEC) — processed via EE
4. Provincial Nominee Program (PNP) — processed via EE or independently
5. Business Class Immigration
6. Caregiver Program

EE is an inventory management system by which the various classes can apply for economic immigration and is composed of three stages.[2] First, interested applicants must qualify for one of the programs under the FSW, CEC, FST, or PNP. Immigration, Refugees and Citizenship Canada (IRCC) assesses the applicants to see if they meet certain eligibility criteria. Second, if eligible for one of these three programs, they can create a profile to enter the express entry pool. Third, those candidates whose profiles align with the identified needs of the government and certain Canadian employers will be issued an "invitation to apply" (ITA) based on a point allocation and can proceed to apply for permanent residence within sixty days of receiving the invitation. EE has been in part an inland program, and so those in Canada with experience, work, and/or provincial nominations (see below) have been the bread and butter of the program, especially during the COVID-19 pandemic.

Applicants must meet a minimum point score of a particular draw to receive an ITA. Since its inception in January 2015 there have been nearly 250 draws. Draws can be specific to a certain immigration category and usually occur every two weeks, but during the pandemic draws were infrequent. The program has been a success in terms of allowing IRCC the maximum flexibility in selecting applicants.

FEDERAL SKILLED WORKER CLASS

The FSW program selects permanent residents based on their ability to become economically established in Canada. Federal skilled workers are selected based on six indicators: age, education, work experience, knowledge of English and/or French, arranged employment, and adaptability. These factors are graded on a grid of one hundred points. To be eligible, one must score at least sixty-seven points, then create their EE profile.

Skilled work experience refers to duties reflected in the National Occupational Classification (NOC) list, which is organized in TEERs (Training, Education, Experience, and Responsibilities) reflecting the requirements for the occupations. There are four TEERS: 0, 1, 2, and 3 that would qualify somebody to apply under this program. These include management occupations or occupations that require a college diploma or apprenticeship training.[3] Applicants must use the EE system to first create their profile on the IRCC portal. To qualify as an FSW, candidates must meet the following requirements:

1) One year of continuous full-time (or an equal amount of continuous part-time) qualifying skilled work experience in the last ten years.

2) Achieve the Canadian minimum language threshold on an official language test in all four sections: reading, writing, speaking, and listening.
3) Have a Canadian secondary or post-secondary certificate, diploma, or degree or an Educational Credential Assessment report indicating the Canadian equivalent of their foreign education.
4) Have proof of funds to support themselves and their family for at least six months — funds must be readily available for transfer to Canada and be used. The amounts of the low-income cut-off (LICO) are established by Statistics Canada each year, and the applicants must take into consideration the size of their family.
5) To be admissible medically or criminally to Canada (see Chapter 3).
6) Obtain a passing mark of sixty-seven out of one hundred on the selection grid.[4]

FEDERAL SKILLED TRADES PROGRAM

The FST program is for individuals with qualifications in a skilled trade to enter the Canadian workforce. The IRCC website explains that applicants for the FST program must meet the following requirements:

- meet a basic language requirement in all four sections: speaking, listening, reading, and writing
- have a minimum of two years of full-time (or an equal amount of part-time) work experience as a skilled tradesperson within the five years before applying
- meet the job requirements for that skilled trade as set out in the NOC, except for needing a certificate of qualification
- have a valid job offer of full-time employment for a total period of at least one year *or* a certificate of qualification in that skilled trade issued by a Canadian authority[5]
- proof of funds — may be required, depending on the case

TEER 2 and 3 positions are typically technical jobs and/or skilled trades that usually call for a college diploma or training. Skilled trades under the FST program are organized under the following groups:

- technical trades
- general trades
- supervisors in natural resources, agriculture, and related production
- occupations in natural resources and related production
- processing, manufacturing, and utilities supervisors, and utilities operators and controllers
- central control and process operators
- cooks, butchers, and bakers
- chefs

To improve one's score in the EE pool of applicants, it is advisable to have the foreign educational credentials assessed before creating the profile on the IRCC portal.

CANADIAN EXPERIENCE CLASS

The CEC, unlike the FSW and FST programs, requires candidates to have previous experience within Canada, and the candidate must plan to live outside of Quebec. The required experience is one year of full-time (or part-time equivalent) skilled work experience in Canada in the three years before applying, and it must have been gained with a proper work authorization. Skilled work experience under the NOC system includes managerial occupations, professional occupations, technical occupations, and skilled trades. Applicants must also meet language requirements based on writing, reading, listening, and speaking. As with the FSW and FST programs, CEC applications are processed under the EE system.

PROVINCIAL NOMINEE PROGRAMS

The PNP requires applicants to be nominated by a Canadian province or territory. So, applicants must apply first to a province or territory, which will assess applicants based on its immigration needs and the applicant's genuine intention to settle there. Applicants nominated under the PNP are expected to have the skills and experience needed to make an immediate economic contribution to the province or territory. After nomination, applicants must separately apply to IRCC for permanent residence, either via the PNP stream or EE system.

Each province has different PNP requirements based on its immigration needs. For example, the British Columbia PNPs are divided into three categories: Business Skills, Regional Business, and Strategic Projects. The main programs under the Ontario Immigrant Nominee Program (OINP) are:

Job offer programs:

- Foreign worker stream.
- International student stream.
- In-demand skills stream.
- Master's or PhD degrees who graduated in Ontario.
- Human Capital Priorities stream — Ontario's Express Entry stream — where the province chooses from the pool of applicants who have their EE profile and present interest to Ontario — they might receive a notice of interest (NOI) from the province, which will allow the applicants to apply and receive a provincial nomination. This will add 600 points to the EE profile of the applicant.
- Skilled Trades stream — Ontario's EE stream as well, allowing the province to extend their NOI to the skilled applicants who are of interest to Ontario.
- French-Speaking Skilled Worker stream — is another EE stream for the province, allowing Ontario to extend their NOI to the French-speaking applicants with noticeable skills for the province.
- Entrepreneur program — giving the applicants the opportunity to establish or buy a business in Ontario, which gives the province the opportunity to choose from the applicants who intend to develop significant, efficient business in Ontario.[6]

Entrepreneurs in Ontario can also apply for permanent residence through the Entrepreneur Program.[7] This stream is open to foreign nationals (and a maximum of one foreign national business partner) wishing to implement a new permanent business or buy an existing business in Ontario, *with the purpose* of making a profit from active income through the sale of goods and services. Once their business has been successfully established in Ontario, entrepreneurs can be nominated through the OINP for permanent resident status.

For entrepreneurs starting a new business in Ontario, they must meet the following requirements, with some variations, depending on location and type of business:

- have at least two years of full-time business experience as an owner or senior manager within the previous five years
- have minimum $400,000–$800,000 net worth
- invest a minimum of $200,000–$600,000, and a minimum ownership of one-third
- create at least one-to-two full-time permanent jobs for Canadian citizens or permanent residents (PRs)
- meet a minimum language requirement of Canadian Language Benchmark (CLB) 4 or equivalent in English or French
- be actively involved in managing the business and be physically living in Ontario for three-quarters of the time in which the business is being established

For entrepreneurs purchasing an existing business in Ontario, they must meet all the requirements above and the business must have been in continuous operation by the same owner(s) for the previous five years before purchase. The purchase must completely transfer ownership and must not have been previously owned by OINP stream nominees.

All existing permanent full-time jobs must be preserved, and the applicant must submit a proposed business plan demonstrating that they intend to grow the business in Ontario. They must also make an exploratory visit to Ontario within one year of registering an expression of interest.

BUSINESS CLASS IMMIGRATION

The *IRPR* provides a pathway for self-employed persons and certain entrepreneurs to gain permanent residency in Canada. Since 2014, the investor and general entrepreneur programs have been terminated, although the self-employed class remains. A self-employed person is defined by the *Regulations* as having relevant experience, intention, and ability to be self-employed in Canada and to make a significant contribution to specified economic activities in Canada.[8] Within five years of submitting the application, applicants must demonstrate two years of self-employment in cultural activities or athletics, participation at the world-class level in cultural activities or athletics, or farm management experience.

While the Entrepreneur Program has been terminated, the Federal Start-Up Visa Program has been implemented as an alternative to encourage foreign entrepreneurs to come to Canada, create new jobs, and stimulate economic growth. Foreign nationals applying for a Start-Up Visa must meet the following requirements:

- have a qualifying business;
- obtain a letter of support from a designated organization;
- attain the specified level of language proficiency, currently set at CLB 5; and
- have the appropriate funds available, depending on the family size, as established each year by Statistics Canada under LICO.

CAREGIVER PROGRAM

The Caregiver Program helps Canadians identify qualified workers to care for their children and elders. The Caregiver Program has evolved over the past decade, and under the current legislation it is split into two programs: Home Child Care Providers and Home Support Workers.[9] In both streams, caregivers apply for both permanent residence and work permits from the very beginning. If one does not meet the requirements for permanent residence under this class, then the application is refused.

The job offer process is now more "user-friendly" to employers in dire need of caregivers by not requiring employers to submit a labour market impact assessment (LMIA) application. A LMIA is in place to analyze the Canadian job market to ensure no Indigenous persons, Canadian citizens, or permanent residents are negatively affected by the hiring of a temporary foreign worker. Given the clear gap in the job market, LMIAs were an unnecessary qualifier for caregivers and were eliminated for these categories.

When the work permit as a caregiver is approved, the caregiver's dependent family members can accompany them to Canada with immigration status of their own. IRCC established a cap of 2,750 applicants per year for each of the categories. In both 2022 and 2023, the Home Child Care Provider stream had reached its cap at the beginning of January in each year.

The work permit issued via the caregiver streams is not restricted to working for a specific employer, an attempt by legislators to eliminate abuse and exploitation of the foreign workers. However, it is considered "occupation-restricted," meaning that the caregiver can work for other employers, but not in other occupations — they can only work as caregivers. Potential caregivers must also meet language and education requirements. In February 2023, IRCC announced that the duration of work experience in Canada required for a caregiver to qualify for the permanent residence application will be reduced from twenty-four months to twelve months.[10]

Family Class Sponsorship

A Canadian citizen or permanent resident can sponsor their spouse, common law partner or conjugal partner, or dependent child to immigrate to Canada as a permanent resident. Citizens and permanent residents can also sponsor their parent(s) or grandparent(s).[11] Both the sponsor and sponsored person must meet certain requirements to qualify, and all applicants must undergo medical, criminal, and background screening.

An applicant can also be considered a *de facto* family member. For instance, in *Sioco v Canada (MCI)*,[12] the sponsor had been relinquished into the care of the applicant by her parents at age three. The sponsor's biological father died in 1997 and her biological mother's whereabouts were unknown, leaving the applicant as her only family member. The applicant was considered to be a *de facto* family member and considered a member of the family class.

All family relationships must be genuine to qualify for family class sponsorships. For spouses, common law partners, or conjugal partners (generally, "partners"), they will not be eligible for the family class if the relationship was entered into primarily for the purpose of acquiring status or privilege under the *IRPA*, or if it is not genuine. Similarly, adopted children will not be considered members of the family class if the adoption was entered into primarily for the purpose of acquiring status or privilege, or if it did not create a genuine parent-child relationship. The burden of proof is upon the applicant — however, this is not to say that the presumption is that the relationship was entered into for immigration purposes.[13] The applicant is still entitled to be heard before an impartial decision-maker.[14]

In considering whether a relationship is genuine, the immigration officer looks at a variety of factors, including financial interdependency. However, these factors must be treated on a case-by-case basis — for example, in *Laifatt v Canada (MCI)*, the marriage of a seventy-six-year-old US citizen and a seventy-year-old Canadian citizen was found to not be genuine by an officer because they were not sufficiently interdependent.[15] The Federal Court held that this decision was unreasonable given the life circumstances of both parties being retired and advanced in age, and had led separate lives for many years. The fact that they had a different financial interdependency than might be expected of a younger couple did not disprove the genuineness of their marriage. Relationships have also been held to be genuine despite officers' concerns relating to age differences,[16] arranged marriages,[17] and the relationship not being long-lasting.[18]

A spouse, common law partner, or conjugal partner must also meet certain statutory requirements to qualify for the family class, including that the foreign national must be at least eighteen years of age. In addition, the sponsor must not have an existing sponsorship undertaking for a spouse, common law partner, or conjugal partner. If married, the spouse of a sponsor will not be eligible if either were already married at the time of their marriage, or if the sponsor and foreign national have lived apart for at least one year and either of them have entered a new common law or conjugal relationship. A spouse will also not be eligible if, during the marriage ceremony, one or both spouses were not physically present (unless the sponsor's physical absence was due to membership in the Canadian Forces).

Lastly, a foreign national will be excluded if the sponsor had previously become a permanent resident and, at that time, the foreign national was a non-accompanying family member of the sponsor and was not examined. The exception is if the foreign national was not examined because an officer determined that they were not required to be examined pursuant to the *IRPA*.[19]

Any Canadian citizen or permanent resident can become a sponsor provided they meet various legal pre-conditions. For one, they must be at least eighteen years of age, and two, they must reside in Canada.[20] If they do not reside in Canada, citizens (but not permanent residents) may still sponsor their dependent child or partner if they will reside in Canada upon a successful sponsorship. A person cannot become a sponsor if they are subject to a removal order, if they are detained, or if they have been convicted in or outside of Canada for certain enumerated offences, including any sexual offences or offences that result in bodily harm to a family member.[21] Sponsors are also disqualified if they are in default of a sponsorship undertaking, in default of debt repayment, an undischarged bankruptcy, or in receipt of social assistance for a reason other than disability.

The sponsor must also make an undertaking to the minister of citizenship and immigration or a competent provincial authority. This undertaking obliges the sponsor to reimburse the Crown for any benefits provided as social assistance to the sponsored person and their family members. The undertaking lasts a varied duration: three years for a partner, ten years for a child under the age of twenty-two years or until the age of twenty-five years (whichever comes first), three years for a child over the age of twenty-two years, or twenty years for a parent or grandparent.[22]

Refugee Protection

Following the 1951 *United Nations Convention relating to the Status of Refugees*, an individual may gain refugee status in Canada and become a "Convention refugee." They must have a well-founded fear of persecution in their country of citizenship for reasons of race, religion, nationality, membership in a particular social group, or political opinion.[23] The individual must also demonstrate that their country of citizenship is unable or unwilling to provide them with adequate state protection. Refugee claimants with multiple nationalities must prove that none of these countries would be able and willing to protect them from persecution, and a mere impediment to accessing state protection is not sufficient to exclude that country from the scope of "country of nationality."[24]

A "well-founded" fear of persecution requires the refugee claimant to establish two components: subjectively, that they fear persecution; and objectively, that there is a valid basis for that fear.[25] As the subjective component is essentially the question of whether the board member believes that the claimant fears the persecution, it is an issue of credibility, and claimants must be given an oral hearing.[26] The objective component is based on a balance of probabilities. The applicant does not need to prove that there is a *probability* of persecution, but that persecution would be more likely than not; that there is a "reasonable chance" of persecution.[27]

Another aspect of a refugee claim is whether the claimant has an "Internal Flight Alternative" (IFA); that is, if it is reasonable for the claimant to relocate to another area in their country of nationality where the state could provide protection and they could lead a normal life. As a matter of procedural fairness, the board member or minister must raise the possibility of an IFA to the applicant during the oral hearing so that they have an opportunity to respond and explain why they would be unable to live in a different area of the country.[28]

Refugee status is not limited to individuals who flee persecution but can also arise due to events in their home country after they have arrived in Canada ("*sur place*" refugees). For example, in *Balog v Canada (MCI)*,[29] a Hungarian family of Roma ethnicity had already arrived in Canada and applied for refugee status when one of their sons was killed in a car accident. The accident was reported in the media, including a Toronto newspaper, naming the family and identifying them as Hungarian refugee claimants. This article was picked up by the Hungarian media and widely disseminated among extremist groups, resulting in threatening comments online toward the family.[30] The failure to address this aspect of their claim was successfully appealed.

Refugee claimants can be ineligible for several reasons set out in the *IRPA* and its regulations, namely, if the claimant already has refugee status in another country, if they arrived through a designated country under the Safe Third Country Agreement, or if they are inadmissible for certain criminal convictions.[31] Also, failed claimants in Canada are not allowed to make a second claim. In 2022 and 2023,[32] IRCC has given specific attention to those fleeing Afghanistan and Ukraine. In both situations, Canada adopted emergency measures to accept refugees, but these measures have differed. For example, IRCC's commitment to Afghanistan is to resettle 40,000 Afghan nationals by the end of 2023, while an unlimited number of Ukrainians can enter temporarily for up to three years, and 10,000 can become permanent residents if they are family members of citizens or permanent residents.[33]

IRCC has explained that the different situations have necessitated different responses; in particular, many displaced Ukrainians have left Ukraine, whereas the majority of Afghans remain in-country. However, Ukrainians have been welcomed in third countries in great numbers, while Afghans have been refused by many neighbouring countries.[34] Nonetheless, the difference in numbers is notable. As of November 2022, IRCC and CBSA reported that 420,000 Ukrainian applications have been approved, and about 117,000 have arrived in Canada.[35] In contrast, as of January 2023, IRCC reported that 27,345 Afghans have arrived in Canada, despite the crisis in Afghanistan beginning months before the invasion of Ukraine.[36]

A possible explanation for these different approaches is pressure from within Canada, as the Ukrainian diaspora has been significantly larger than the Afghan one. Per the 2021 census, the Canadian population included more than 1,258,000 people of Ukrainian origin, compared to less than 97,000 of Afghan origin.[37] Another proposed explanation is that the Canadian public has lost sensitivity to the human suffering in Afghanistan, while Russia's invasion "strikes people at the very core of their being."[38] Another explanation is systemic racism against Afghan refugees. For example, Afghans arriving in Calgary were forced to wait for weeks in hotels, struggling to afford rent, while Ukrainians were welcomed into homes by individuals and faith groups.[39]

Once a person has been determined to be a person in need of protection or a Convention refugee or if a person receives a positive decision on their Pre-Removal Risk Assessment (PRRA) from IRCC, they are a Protected Person and may apply for permanent residence within Canada and include their dependants.[40] Foreign nationals may also apply outside Canada if they are a member of the Convention Refugees Abroad, Humanitarian-Protected Persons Abroad, and Protected and Temporary Residents Class. Protected Temporary Residents are individuals admitted to Canada on a temporary resident permit and who have been determined to be in urgent need of protection by a visa office.[41]

Humanitarian and Compassionate Considerations

Humanitarian and compassionate considerations (H&C) are an exception to the rule that permanent residence applications must be submitted from outside of Canada and are created under section

25(1) of the *IRPA*. The purpose of this section is to provide an exemption for foreign nationals who would not otherwise meet the requirements of the Act (for example, due to inadmissibility) to request that the immigration officer examine their circumstances and consider an exemption from the *IRPA*.

This request must be justified by H&C considerations relating to the foreign national, considering the best interests of any children (BIOC) directly affected. It is meant to be an exceptional measure. For many years applicants under this category had to demonstrate that they would experience *unusual and undeserved or disproportionate hardship* if they were required to leave Canada. This posed a high threshold and now these three terms are merely descriptive and should not be used as separate legal thresholds to be strictly construed.[42]

The requirement of hardship has the effect of making H&C applications an exceptional measure indeed, as it can only be used as a last case scenario. If an individual applies for H&C consideration, but they would otherwise be eligible to obtain (or at least apply for) status in another form, they will not have established hardship.[43] In the case of *Kanthasamy v Canada (MCI)*, which reached the Supreme Court of Canada, the officer had assessed a number of factors to determine whether it represented hardship, and as none of the individual factors amounted to "unusual and undeserved or disproportionate hardship," the officer refused the application.[44] This decision was found to be unreasonable because it "had the effect of improperly restricting [the officer's] discretion."[45]

While no single factor can guarantee a successful H&C application, Canadian courts have recognized that, if applicable, the BIOC must be considered. This was absorbed into Canadian law through the 1992 *Convention on the Rights of the Child*,[46] as recognized by the Supreme Court of Canada in *Baker v Canada (MCI)*.[47] The Supreme Court held that decision-makers should consider BIOC, give them substantial weight, and be "alert, alive and sensitive to them."[48]

Additionally, as noted in *Kanthasamy*, the BIOC analysis must be viewed through the lens that children will "rarely, if ever, be deserving of any hardship."[49] This means that the BIOC analysis is properly conducted at a different threshold than the other H&C factors: officers should consider whether staying in Canada is in the child's best interests, *not* whether leaving Canada would cause them undue hardship.[50] These factors also include "establishment in Canada." Foreign nationals who have spent many years in Canada without gaining permanent resident status may have established deep ties in their communities such that it would cause them undue hardship to leave Canada, as well as hardship to the people with whom they have forged relationships. Courts have cautioned that the establishment factor will not always be treated as a positive factor.

For example, an individual may come to Canada without status or remain past the expiration of their status and proceed to develop strong community ties because of their unauthorized overstay. The Federal Court of Appeal decided in *Canada (MCI) v Legault* that in such cases, the minister can consider that the hardship would be the result of the person's own actions.[51] The Federal Court held in *De Vazquez v Canada (MCI)* that "positive factors may not prevail if an applicant has not acted in good faith and in compliance with Canadian laws.... When establishment is a function of having deliberately chosen to evade removal, it should not provide an applicant with an advantage over those who have complied with the law."[52] The establishment factor is reserved for instances where the individual came to Canada and was then unable to return for reasons that were legitimate, such as working with status for several years before becoming out of status. Alternatively, there may be reasons outside of their control, such as changes in the country that could put them in danger if they returned, or if they came to Canada as a child and had no control over their status.[53]

Temporary Public Policies

In recent years, IRCC has experimented with short-lived pathways. These have included the Hong Kong Permanent Residency pathway, the construction worker pathway, and Temporary Resident to

Permanent Resident (TR to PR) Pathway, which are designed to provide alternative routes to applicants who would otherwise be out of status.

1. The **Hong Kong Permanent Residency pathway** is a public policy in effect from 1 June 2021 until 31 August 2026. It provides a route for Hong Kong residents who are currently in Canada to apply for permanent residence two ways: in-Canada graduates ("Stream A") or Canadian work experience ("Stream B"). Under Stream A, Hong Kong residents who have valid temporary resident status in Canada and intend to live in Canada are eligible to apply for permanent residence. They must have graduated from a post-secondary designated learning institution in Canada within the last three years with at least 50 percent of the program completed in Canada (including online). They must have also received a diploma for a program of at least two years, a degree, or a graduate or post-graduate diploma or certificate for a program of at least one year. If the latter, the applicant must have also completed a post-secondary diploma or degree as a prerequisite to this program. The diploma or degree can be from a Canadian institution or from abroad.[54]
2. In January 2023, IRCC announced a pathway for **out-of-status construction workers in the Greater Toronto Area**, designed to help address critical labour shortages.[55] This served as a continuation of a permanent residence program that was initiated by IRCC and the Canadian Labour Congress in 2019, and expanded the program from 500 workers to 1,000 out-of-status construction workers in the GTA. The public policy first took effect on 2 January 2020, and individuals can now continue to apply until 2 January 2024 and may include their spouse, partners, and dependent children in their applications for permanent residence. To be eligible, the workers must have entered Canada with valid temporary residence status and have since become out-of-status.[56]
3. The **Temporary Resident to Permanent Resident Pathway** (TR to PR Pathway) was available to temporary residents and their

families who meet one of three streams: workers in Canada in the health or health services field, workers in Canada in a non-health care but essential occupation, or international graduates.[57] There were also another three streams for francophone health care workers, francophone essential non-health care workers, and francophone international graduates. Essential non-health care occupations include cashiers and other sales-related occupations, contractors and supervisors, electricians, and many others.[58] This pathway was closed as of 5 November 2021.

Immigration Amnesties[59]

Since 1960 in Canada, at least nine programs directed at regularizing the status of undocumented persons, although not always undocumented workers, were launched, including:

- Chinese Adjustment Statement Program: 1960–1972
- Section 34 and the *Immigration Appeal Board Act*: 1968–1973
- Adjustment of Status Program: 1973
- Special Regularization Program for Haitians in Quebec: 1981
- Minister's Review Committee: 1983–1985
- Administrative Review: 1986
- Backlog Clearance Program: 1989
- Deferred Removal Orders Class (DROC): 1994–1998
- Special Regularization Procedure for Algerians in Quebec: 2002

These programs ranged in size and scope from regularizing as few as 900 persons to more than 100,000. Many required in-person applications, good moral character, some form of lengthy residency, and a need for more workers. Response to political or backlog pressure and market adjustment were most often the impetus behind the measures. The 1960 program guaranteed no prosecution or detention, while the 1973 program was well advertised and as such received considerable response but only allowed a sixty-day period in which to apply. As a result of the Backlog Clearance Program from 1986 to the end of 1992, approximately 160,000 applications were accepted.

The 1986 program was efficient and effective but there was a serious flaw in the program, in that there was a significant delay in implementing a new refugee determination system that would allow for an oral hearing for each applicant. During this delay, tens of thousands of new refugee applicants flooded into Canada, believing that Canada was offering a kind of amnesty. The 1973 program also led to a significant backlog. There has not been such a program in almost twenty-five years and there may exist half a million undocumented workers.[60] In his 2021 mandate letter to IRCC Minister Sean Fraser, Prime Minister Trudeau directed the minister to "Build on existing pilot programs to further explore ways of regularizing status for undocumented workers who are contributing to Canadian communities."[61] It may be that 2023 is the year of the next amnesty in Canada.

Temporary Residence Pathways

Visitor Visas

The visitor class of temporary residents is prescribed by sections 191–193 of the *IRPR* for foreign nationals who have been authorized to enter and remain in Canada as visitors. Visitors can be provided a multiple entry or single-entry visa to travel and enter Canada. Individuals applying for a visitor visa must have a valid travel document, be in "good health,"[62] and have sufficient funds for their stay.[63] They must also satisfy an immigration officer that they have ties to their country of origin which compel them to return, and that they will leave Canada at the end of their visit. In certain circumstances, applicants may also need a letter of invitation from someone who lives in Canada (see Super Visas below). Visitors are subject to the same conditions as other temporary residents, namely, that they must leave Canada by the end of their authorized stay and must not work or study unless authorized.[64]

Super Visas

The *IRPA* explicitly states that one of its objectives is to see that families are reunited in Canada.[65] One way by which this is addressed is the Parent and Grandparent Super Visa, which allows parents and grandparents to visit their family in Canada for up to five years,[66] and may be issued a multiple-entry visa valid for up to ten years. The eligibility requirements include having a child or grandchild who is a Canadian citizen or permanent resident, not having any inadmissibility issues, having a written commitment of financial support from their child or grandchild, buying Canadian medical insurance coverage for at least one year, and completing an immigration medical examination.[67] At present, Canadian citizens and permanent residents cannot sponsor their parents as the program is not open. It usually opens once per year.[68]

Intending visitors must be genuine visitors to Canada who will leave by choice at the end of their visit. In assessing this, officers may consider the person's ties to their home country, the purpose of the visit, the person's family and financial situation, the overall economic and political stability of the home country, and an invitation from a Canadian host.

Work Permits

A foreign worker who wishes to enter Canada to work on a temporary basis will generally require a work permit. While work permits are designed to address skill shortages in Canada, foreign workers can generally apply for any occupation subject to certain restrictions provided in the *IRPR*: the employer must not offer stripteases, erotic dances, escort services, or erotic massages on a regular basis.[69]

Many work permit applications require a labour market impact assessment (LMIA) for the application to be approved (more on LMIAs below). If an LMIA is not feasible, the employer must submit an offer of employment to IRCC along with paying an employer compliance fee before the foreign worker applies for a work permit.

These are considered LMIA-exempt work permits. Some LMIA-exempt work permits include Intra-Company Transfers (for example, from a foreign office to a Canadian office under the same parent company, branch, subsidiary, etc.), International Experience Canada (IEC) Work Permits (for young professionals aged eighteen to thirty-five years with citizenship in certain countries who signed agreements with Canada), and the Canada-United States-Mexico Agreement (CUSMA) Work Permits (previously NAFTA, for American and Mexican nationals).[70]

These applications do not require as high a degree of procedural fairness as certain other applications: officers need not engage in dialogue with applicants regarding the strengths and weaknesses of their application, nor do they need to provide extensive reasons. Nevertheless, the reasons provided must include analysis of the evidence, not merely recitation of the evidence.[71]

Work permits may be refused if the officer decides that the foreign worker cannot adequately perform the work. In other words, the officer may decide that the foreign worker does not meet the employer's requirements. To do so, the officer has to verify the foreign worker's credentials and work experience to see if they are apt for the position. However, the officer should not override the employer's decision to set the requirements at a certain level. For example, if the employer decides that no experience is required,[72] or that the applicant does not need to meet the language requirements,[73] the officer should not supersede the employer's decision (at least, not without explaining their reasons).[74]

Another ground for refusal is if the officer decides that the offer of employment was not genuine. This can include if the prospective employer is unable to pay the applicant[75] or if experience requirements are inconsistent with the position.[76] In work permit applications, there is no statutory requirement to grant an interview to respond to the officer's concerns as the duty of fairness is on the lower end of the spectrum. However, the officer cannot, without a reasonable basis, impugn evidence of genuine employment given evidence to the contrary without giving an opportunity, in writing or otherwise, for the applicant or prospective employer to address the concerns — referred to as a procedural fairness letter.[77]

Foreign nationals who are working on an expiring permit and have already applied for permanent residence through EE may also be eligible for a bridging open work permit (BOWP), which bridges the gap between the expiry of the work permit and the final decision of the permanent residence application. Applicants must be residents in Canada (but outside of Quebec), have a work permit expiring within the next four months, and be the main applicant on the permanent residence application.

The Global Talent Stream (GTS) began in 2017 under the Temporary Foreign Worker Program. It is a key part of the Innovation and Skills Plan, the primary objective of which is making Canada a world-leading centre for innovation. It includes a Labour Market Benefits Plan to detail the specific benefits that the worker will bring to the Canadian labour market and the Canadian economy. These benefits must include job creation and investment in skills and training, and can also include transferring knowledge to Canadians and permanent residents and enhancing company performance.[78] The GTS stream is not bound by the advertising requirement, but the employer's commitments in the plan are subject to a mandatory progress review.[79] Work permits are a viable way that may lead to the applicant to qualify for permanent residence and score higher in EE if they decide to apply for permanent residence in the long run.

Labour Market Impact Assessment (LMIA)

Where the employer submits the work permit application, most work permits will require an LMIA, a document issued by Employment and Social Development Canada (ESDC)/Service Canada (SC). LMIA-based work permits can range from one to three years of validity.[80] Prior to applying for the LMIA, the employer must advertise the position on the government Job Bank website and at least two other national advertising boards for at least four calendar consecutive weeks.[81] This is meant to prove that Canadian citizens and permanent residents are not qualified or available to take the position, thus requiring a foreign national to supply their services.

Wages and work conditions must also be consistent with the prevailing rates/standards for that occupation in the same region to ensure that the foreign worker is not being taken advantage of.[82] Due to COVID-19 and post-COVID-19 economics, ESDC has issued variations on the advertising requirements for various industries.[83] For example, from January 2022 to 30 June 2023, the advertising requirements for employers who want to hire temporary foreign workers in primary agriculture are suspended.[84]

Study Permits

Like foreign workers, foreign students who seek to study at Canadian institutions at all levels can apply for study permits. Study permits can be provided to children accompanying their working parents or to prospective students seeking education in Canada, but are dependent on the student first being accepted by a designated learning institution (DLI).[85] Intending students must demonstrate to IRCC that their study plan is consistent with their past education and work history, that they are able to financially support themselves and pay their education fees, and that they have sufficient ties to their home country to return home after completing their studies. Applicants must apply before entering Canada, unless they are a resident of the United States, Greenland, or St Pierre and Miquelon,[86] or if they are already in Canada with valid status as a student or worker.[87]

Again, applicants must propose a study plan that is consistent with their past education and their objectives. That is not to say that the officer can "assume the role of career counsellor"[88] and give their opinion on whether the intended studies will enhance the applicant's work. While applicants are required to leave Canada at the end of their stay, there are venues for them to remain in Canada with status, such as post-graduate work permits, if they meet all the conditions. Thus, even though applicants must establish ties to their home country, they can still want to live in Canada in the future without defeating their application.[89] This can be found in the immigration legislation under the "dual intent" section. Under certain circumstances, individuals can study in Canada without a study permit:

- The program lasts six months or less;
- They are family or a staff member of an accredited foreign representative to Canada;
- They are a member of a foreign armed force on official duties in Canada;
- They have Registered Indian status in Canada; or
- Minor children if they are in kindergarten, are refugees/claimants or the children of refugees/claimants, or their parent has a work or study permit, and they are in secondary school or below.[90]

Canada's International Student Program (ISP) has grown explosively over the past few years. The ISP pre-COVID-19 was valued at $21.6 billion and has produced up to 712,000 jobs,[91] affecting various stakeholders (government, schools, potential migrants, residents, and citizens alike). Demand for study permits has dramatically increased, and particularly for those seeking pathways for permanent residence. Immigration to Canada remains the lifeblood for our country, and that will not change. The ISP no doubt plays an important role in achieving those objectives, but the program has been exploited and is now under heavy scrutiny.[92]

There are several serious issues surrounding the scope of the program and issues relating to educational recruitment, program integrity, and enrolling in learning institutes that are not designated by the government. Also, applicants are experiencing the inherent tension between mass processing, especially with the aid of expanding technologies like AI and the need for officers to undertake individualized assessments to avoid stereotypes and generalizations that would deny entry and bar applicants who otherwise meet the requirements for a study permit. It is likely this program will be revisited and changed.

Temporary Resident Permit (TRP)

Like H&Cs, TRPs present an opportunity under the *IRPA* for foreign nationals who would otherwise be inadmissible to enter or remain in Canada for social, humanitarian, or economic reasons. Anyone seeking to come to Canada is eligible for a TRP if they are inadmissible and an officer is of the opinion that it is justified in the circumstances.[93] Applicants can be subject to reports for violation of the *IRPA* or do not otherwise meet the requirements of the Act. TRPs may be granted for a maximum of three years and may be extended for another two years.[94] Some TRPs are authorized for multiple entries, while others only allow one entry. In these cases, if the permit holder leaves Canada, the TRP will be deemed cancelled.

When considering a TRP, officers *must* consider the factors that make the person's presence in Canada necessary (for example, family ties, job qualifications, economic contribution, temporary attendance at an event) and the intention of the legislation (for example, protecting public health or the health care system). They may also consider the following factors:

- **History** — Is there a pattern of non-compliance with the *IRPA* or *IRPR*? Is the violation inadvertent and accidental or the result of careless or flagrant disregard for the law? A history of non-compliance with immigration laws, including in other countries, will weigh against the applicant.
- **Credibility** — This may be assessed during an interview.
- **Previous removal** — Have the original grounds for removal been overcome or diminished? Are there any statutory bars, other than the removal order, remaining against the person?
- **Controversy** — Are there high-profile, complex, or sensitive elements of the case that warrant referral or consultation?
- **Social assistance** — If there is a possibility that the foreign national intends to become a permanent resident, is there any risk that the person would require social assistance?[95]

The individual's purpose to enter or remain in Canada must be balanced with the objectives of the Act, and the issuance of the TRP must outweigh any risks that might exist. In issuing a refusal, the officer must provide some justification for their decision.[96]

The guidelines published by the Government state that a TRP is issued if the foreign national's need to enter or remain is *compelling* and their presence outweighs any risk to Canadians or Canadian society. This "compelling reasons" test has been largely accepted by the Federal Court.[97] However, it should be noted that the guidelines are merely meant for internal use and are not determinative; every application must be decided on its own unique basis.

In some instances, a strict approach to the guidelines has been found to be unduly restrictive, as the Act itself only states that the foreign national's need to enter or remain must be *justified*, not *compelling*, in the view of the officer.[98] In *Palmero v Canada (MCI)*, the Federal Court concluded that, "Not only are Guidelines not law, but they cannot go beyond the boundaries of the statute itself."[99] TRPs can also act in tandem with other applications. In *Shah v Canada (MCI)*,[100] for example, a permanent residence application on H&C grounds also included a TRP application, which the officer did not consider. This application was returned for reconsideration because when a TRP request is made, it must be considered, and a failure to do so is a reviewable error.[101] In *Abdelrahman v Canada (MCI)*,[102] a TRP was refused for being too similar to a refugee claim. Although an applicant cannot bypass the refugee determination process by applying for a TRP, the visa officer remained under a duty to assess the TRP. Section 151.1 of the *IRPR* specifically prescribes how a protected temporary resident can become a permanent resident.

Quebec

Due to its history as a former French colony, the province of Quebec is unique in Canada in that it has retained its civil code. Even though immigration law is not an exclusive matter of federal jurisdiction,[103] Quebec stands alone as the sole province to enact its own immigration laws, the *Québec Immigration Act* (*QIA*).[104] This was the result of a gradual process between 1971 and 1991, culminating with the 1991 *Gagnon-Tremblay-McDougall Agreement* (also known as the

Canada-Québec Accord), which gave Quebec control over the full selection process of immigrants.[105] The *QIA* separates itself from the *IRPA* as it explicitly states that its purposes also include preserving French language.[106] The *QIA* creates three classes for both permanent and temporary residents to settle in Quebec. The permanent resident classes are economic, family, and humanitarian; the temporary resident classes are temporary foreign workers, international students, and persons on a temporary stay for medical treatment.[107] Additional classes and immigration programs can be determined by the provincial government.[108] The online system where applicants may enroll their expression of interest for Quebec and submit their applications is called "Arrima."[109]

Quebec Permanent Residence Classes

The *economic class* is designed to attract persons who can contribute to Quebec's prosperity by settling in Quebec.[110] It consists of programs for skilled workers, investors, entrepreneurs, and self-employed workers.[111] To apply for the regular skilled worker program, applicants must file an expression of interest to settle in Quebec[112] and meet a cut-off score based on the province's selection criteria.[113]

Individuals can also immigrate to Quebec under the Québec Experience Program (QEP) if they previously stayed in Quebec as a student or as a temporary worker. The QEP requirements include the foreign national to have obtained a university, college, or secondary vocational diploma in Quebec within the past three years, have an intermediate oral knowledge of French, and have full-time employment in Quebec.[114]

To meet the investor class, foreign nationals must have at least two years of experience in management in the past five years, net assets of at least $2 million and must make a five-year term investment of $1.2 million with a subsidiary of Investissement Québec, and meet the cut-off score.[115]

Self-employed workers include foreign workers who practise a profession or commercial activities alone or with others, with or without paid help. They must be free to choose the means of work performance, organize their own work, provide the required tools and equipment, carry out most of the specialized duties, and collect the profits and support the loss risks.[116]

Foreign workers can also participate in Quebec's entrepreneur program. The first component is that the minister selects a foreign national who is at least eighteen years old to settle in Quebec to conduct a business project. The minister will then select the foreign national if their business project meets certain requirements, such as the enterprise being managed by the foreign national themselves and holding at least 51 percent of the equity of the enterprise.[117]

A unique element of the Quebec legislation is the requirement that foreign nationals in the economic class and any accompanying family members over the age of eighteen years must "obtain an attestation of learning about democratic values and the Québec values expressed by the Charter of human rights and freedoms."[118] To do so, applicants must achieve a passing grade of at least 75 percent on the minister's assessment on those values or participate in a prescribed course in Quebec.

The *family class* consists of the following relationships:

- Spouse, de facto spouse, or conjugal partner;
- Dependent child;
- Parent or grandparent;
- Sibling, niece, nephew, grandchild, or an orphan who is under eighteen years of age who is unmarried and not a de facto spouse;
- An unmarried minor whom the Quebec resident sponsor intends to adopt and may adopt under Quebec law; or
- A person related to the foreign national, regardless of age or degree of relationship, if the sponsor does not have any of the relatives listed above.[119]

Humanitarian applications are set for foreign nationals who are in "a special hardship situation."[120] In considering special hardship, the minister takes into account risks to their physical integrity, personal qualities and language proficiency, any relationships with Quebec residents, and their work experience.[121] Foreign nationals can be selected by the minister under three programs: for refugees abroad, for persons selected on the basis of humanitarian considerations, and a special program for asylum seekers during COVID-19.[122] Temporary residents can also file an application to settle permanently under the Regulations.[123]

Quebec Temporary Residence Classes

The *temporary foreign worker* class is eligible for foreign workers who have a written employment contract signed with an employer. The employment offer must receive a positive assessment as to its impact on Quebec's labour market. The employment must also meet conditions listed in the National Occupational Classification and any terms specified in the employment offer.[124] The written employment contract must also contain specific information such as an undertaking from the employer to pay the contributions necessary for the employee to benefit from protections respecting industrial accidents and occupational diseases.[125]

The *international student program* is open to students who have been accepted to an educational institution and have sufficient financial resources to pay for transportation, health and hospital insurance, and their basic needs. For students under the age of seventeen years and unaccompanied by a parent, their parents must delegate the custody, supervision, and education of their child to an adult Quebec resident.[126]

The program for *temporary stay for medical treatment* enables foreign nationals to visit Quebec to receive medical treatment in a public institution. The Quebec minister will consent to their stay if the minister of health and social services certifies that the medical treatment may be given, and if the foreign national has sufficient financial resources to pay all relevant expenses.[127]

Conclusion

In Chapter 1, I looked at, in part, the heavy emphasis on enforcement versus facilitation after 9/11. In the past five years and somewhat in response to the unprecedented disruption of COVID-19, IRCC has become more creative in the types of migrant streams, as highlighted above. In Chapter 5, I examine the modernization of the delivery of immigration processing and what that may mean for individualized versus mass processing in the future. The trend to implement major changes to immigration policy by way of Ministerial Instructions (MI) and policy continues. It is important to recall that the *Federal Conservative Budget Implementation, Bill C-50*, which introduced the power for MIs, passed a final reading in the House of Commons on 9 June 2008, by a 120:90 vote.[128] The government embedded these changes in the budget, which was very unusual at the time and resulted in a confidence vote. Although all the opposition parties opposed the bill, very few Liberals attended the vote for fear of an election being triggered. So, the bill passed, and MIs became a pillar of immigration law and policy making.

Today, no matter the mode of changes to programs, the historic tension between the share of the pie between family class versus economic classes will continue. Canada long did away with the inclusion of siblings in the family class, for example, because selection was based primarily on relation rather than on potential economic benefit. More emphasis on economic categories has benefited Canada, and this could not have been accomplished through family class migration.

TRUE OR FALSE?

Parents and grandparents immigrating to Canada are elderly, will not assume employment in Canada, and present with excessive health and social services costs.

TRUE OR FALSE?

Elderly relatives or children who need to be cared for would benefit from this care coming from a relative as opposed to a social or private service, and this could result in less of a burden on our stretched social resources and services.

TRUE OR FALSE?

In addition, the sponsor's time and anxiety would be freed and they could focus on their employment and social integration, which benefits the Canadian economy, culture, and society.

TRUE OR FALSE?

The answers are not readily apparent and can be a moving target. The issues of which categories should be prioritized and how the programs should be structured is complex. Public perception also plays a role. Often, I hear the familiar refrain questioning someone new to Canada who has difficulty with English — *how did they immigrate to Canada*? The truth is that those individuals, if not sponsored through the family class, are often fleeing for their life and seeking Canada's protection. A different class, different admission requirements.

But it is difficult for many to appreciate the nuances between the refugee stream, the family class stream, and economic streams, to list a few. All are vitally important to Canada, and our international obligations are distinct in law. Plus, all have a role to play, but striking that balance to the satisfaction of many is elusive. This does not mean we stop trying to heighten awareness, one of the main impetuses for me to write this book. Ultimately, "If you change the way you look at things, the things you look at change."[129]

In the next chapter, I look at immigration inadmissibility. The relationship between immigration pathways and inadmissibilities is closer than many consider. It is the latter that defines not only the former, but sometimes the very core values of the country.

CHAPTER THREE

Canadian Immigration Inadmissibility

Introduction

Indeed, an immigration program is defined as much by the applicants it permits entry as to those it denies. When an individual applies to enter or remain in Canada either as a temporary resident or a permanent resident two steps must be satisfied. One, applicants must be eligible and meet specific program criteria. Two, applicants must also be admissible to Canada. Our focus in this chapter is on what is termed in immigration law as "inadmissibility." A finding of inadmissibility can happen at the time of an application, at a port of entry, after arriving in Canada, and in some cases, even after temporary or permanent status is secured. Depending on when and where this occurs, an applicant can be denied a visa or an Electronic Travel Authorization (eTA) to travel to Canada, refused entry to, or removed from Canada.

On an application, in practice admissibility is determined after an eligibility assessment is made under the category under which an applicant applies. Once that is completed an admissibility assessment is triggered and involves conducting medical, criminal, and security examinations. If found inadmissible, an applicant is either not allowed to enter or remain in Canada, even if they meet the requirements of the immigration category. This can be the result of one or more of the grounds set out in sections 34 to 42 of the *Immigration and Refugee Protection Act* (*IRPA*).[1] These grounds include:[2]

- Security (section 34)
- Human or international rights violations (section 35)
- Serious criminality and criminality (section 36)
- Organized criminality (section 37)
- Health grounds (section 38)
- Financial reasons (section 39)
- Misrepresentation (section 40)
- Cessation of refugee protection (section 40.1)
- Non-compliance with *IRPA* (section 41)
- Inadmissible family member (section 42)

Out of the ten identified grounds, the first four (sections 34–37) are the most serious with lasting consequences. To find an individual inadmissible on the grounds of security, human or international rights violations, criminality as well as serious criminality, and organized criminality, an officer must have reasonable grounds to believe that the events have occurred, are occurring, or may occur.[3] Essentially the officer must have a genuine belief in a serious possibility that the allegation is true, that is, based on credible/objective evidence.[4] Certain of the ten grounds are only applicable to foreign nationals, while others are applicable to both foreign nationals and permanent residents. Depending on the ground of inadmissibility and the status of the individual there will be different consequences and remedies. In cases of foreign nationals, the responsibility is on the individual to establish that they are not inadmissible. Where the individual has been authorized to enter Canada and is a permanent resident, the burden to establish inadmissibility is shifted to the minister.[5] I look next to a brief history of how inadmissibility has evolved in Canadian immigration law, and then I will examine each ground of inadmissibility in the current legislation and the procedures followed by immigration officers when assessing inadmissibility pursuant to sections 34 to 42.

The Genesis of Canadian Immigration Inadmissibility

I noted in Chapter 1 that Canada's first *Immigration Act* was adopted in 1896, and its focus was on populating the vast Canadian territory. Therefore, few barriers were placed on migrants crossing the border. This open border policy was short lived, however. By 1910, Frank Oliver, the then-Canadian federal minister, enacted changes to the legislation that barred a broad spectrum of individuals and increased government power in the areas of immigration selection and deportations of individuals. Successive legislation continued to define who were desirable to Canada by establishing expanded definitions of inadmissibility and appellate mechanisms. In 2002, the former *Immigration Act* was replaced by the *IRPA*, which is Canada's current immigration legislation.[6]

This amended Act was an attempt to balance Canada's tradition of continuing to welcome newcomers and protecting refugees, with implementing tougher enforcement measures meant to strengthen national security and the public safety of Canadians. However, in many respects, the new Act marked a return to some legislative principles of previous Acts, with expanded focus on enforcement and inadmissibility.[7] The objectives expressed in the *IRPA* indicate an intent to prioritize security, identifying:

1. Furthering the domestic and international interests of Canada;
2. Protecting the health and safety of Canadians and maintaining the security of Canadian society; and
3. Promoting international justice and security by fostering respect for human rights and by denying access to Canadian territory to persons who are criminals, serious criminals, or security risks.[8]

Inadmissibility Grounds

Security (Section 34)

Pursuant to section 34(1) of the *IRPA*, a permanent resident or a foreign national can be found inadmissible for security reasons, including espionage, subversion by force, subversion, terrorism, or generally being a danger to the public of Canada. It not only includes individuals who an officer has reasonable grounds to believe are engaging, have engaged, or will engage in any of the aforementioned activities in or outside Canada, but also includes individuals who an officer has reasonable grounds to believe are or were members of an organization that engages, has engaged, or will engage in these activities.[9] There are a number of listed entities and organizations drawn from the *Special Economic Measures Act* (*SEMA*),[10] as well as a number of other sources.

The terms "espionage," "subversion," and "terrorism" are not defined in the *IRPA* and its regulations, the *Immigration and Refugee Protection Regulations* (*IRPR*), although caselaw and the IRCC Enforcement Manual *ENF 1: Inadmissibility* provides the following definitions:

- "espionage" is the practice of gathering information by spying; usually seeking out information secretly from a hostile country to benefit one's own country[11]
- "subversion" refers to overturning or overthrowing an organization by illicit means or for an improper purpose[12]
- "terrorism" relates to threats or use of acts of violence against persons or property to achieve some political objective. The purpose of such acts, by its nature or context, is to intimidate a population, or to compel a government, or an international organization to do or to abstain from doing any act.[13]

According to section 34(1)(a), espionage captures activities against Canada and, more broadly, those contrary to Canada's interests, which includes actions against Canada's allies.[14] The two provisions with respect to subversion and subversion by force of any government (section 34(1)(b)) and subversion against a democratic government/institution/process (section 34(1)(b.1)) serves to exclude those who may have engaged in actions to undermine the power and authority of an undomestic government through peaceful means.

The membership provision ensnares a wider range of actors. To be determined as a member of an organization that engages in espionage, subversion by force, subversion, or terrorism, the person does not need to hold any official role in the organization. Simply "belonging to" or "supporting" the organization could establish membership.[15] Further, the timing of the person's membership in the organization is not required to be correspondent with the time when the organization commits the identified acts. However, the individual must be considered (on the referenced reasonable grounds) as a genuine member of the organization, which means that the person intentionally carries out acts to further the organization's goals.[16] If the membership was during a period when the organization was so fundamentally different from the organization that engages the above activities, the person could potentially be deemed admissible.[17]

Individuals may also be found inadmissible under section 34 for being a danger to the security of Canada or engaging in violence that may endanger persons' lives or safety in Canada. To be found as a danger to the security of Canada, the individual must pose a serious threat to national security, whether directly or indirectly, and the threat must be "serious," in the sense that it must be grounded on objectively reasonable suspicion based on evidence and in the sense that the threatened harm must be substantial rather than negligible.[18] This section casts a very wide net and could affect individuals who even have thoughts or beliefs that could be interpreted to cause a danger to the security of Canada. As such, it is one of the most difficult provisions to overcome.

Human or International Rights Violations (Section 35)

A permanent resident or foreign national who has committed human or international rights violations outside Canada would be inadmissible under section 35(1) of the *IRPA*. This provision is often applied in situations where an officer has reasonable grounds to believe that an individual has engaged in war crimes or crimes against humanity due to their involvement in a domestic or international war or with an organization that practises such conduct, for example, a police force in a communist country. The terms "Crimes against humanity" and "war crime" are defined in section 4(3) of the *Crimes Against Humanity and War Crimes Act*,[19] which include the following:

> **Crimes against humanity** means murder, extermination, enslavement, deportation, imprisonment, torture, sexual violence, persecution or any other inhumane act or omission that is committed against any civilian population or any identifiable group and that, at the time and in the place of its commission, constitutes a crime against humanity according to customary international law or conventional international law or by virtue of its being criminal according to the general principles of law recognized by the community of nations, whether or not it constitutes a contravention of the law in force at the time and in the place of its commission.
>
> **War crime** means an act or omission committed during an armed conflict that, at the time and in the place of its commission, constitutes a war crime according to customary international law or conventional international law applicable to armed conflicts, whether or not it constitutes a contravention of the law in force at the time and in the place of its commission.

To determine whether an individual is complicit in war crimes or crimes against humanity under section 35(1)(a), in a landmark case before the Supreme Court of Canada (SCC), *Ezokola v Canada (MCI)* affirmed that mere association or passive acquiescence is not sufficient to establish complicity and provide a contribution-based test for complicity. That is, the individual must have made a *voluntary*, *knowing*, and *significant* contribution to the crimes or criminal purposes of the group.[20] To elaborate, assessing whether a person has voluntarily *made a significant and knowing contribution to a crime or criminal purpose*, the SCC provided six factors to guide the assessment:

1. the size and nature of the organization;
2. the part of the organization with which the individual was most directly concerned;
3. the individual's duties and activities within the organization;
4. the individual's position or rank in the organization;
5. the length of time the individual was in the organization, particularly after acquiring knowledge of the group's crime or criminal purpose; and
6. the method by which the individual was recruited and the refugee claimant's opportunity to leave the organization.[21]

It is worth noting that these factors are not exhaustive and are not always given the same weight in all cases. The focus rather remains on the individual's contribution to the crime or criminal purpose, and the analysis and the weight of each factor will depend on the facts of each case.[22] Moreover, a permanent resident or foreign national can be found inadmissible for violations of human and international rights under section 35(1)(b) for being a senior official in the service of a government that the minister of public safety (the representative who governs the security of Canadians) has designated as a regime that has been involved in terrorism, systematic or gross human rights violations, a war crime, crime against humanity, or genocide.

The two main elements to establish inadmissibility under this provision are (1) "prescribed senior official" and (2) "designated regime." In following the IRCC Enforcement Manual *ENF 18: Human and International Rights Violations*, "senior official" refers to a person who is in the top 50 percent of an organization or, if not holding a formal position, is or was able to exert significant influence on the exercise of government power or is or was able to benefit from their position.[23] With respect to a designated regime, at the time of the writing, there are nine listed:

1. the Bosnian Serb regime between 27 March 1992 and 10 October 1996;
2. the Siad Barré regime in Somalia between 1969 and 1991;

3. the former military governments in Haiti between 1971 and 1986, and between 1991 and 1994, except the period August to December 1993;
4. the former Marxist regimes of Afghanistan between 1978 and 1992;
5. the governments of Ahmed Hassan al-Bakr and Saddam Hussein in power in Iraq between 1968 and 22 May 2003;
6. the government of Rwanda under President Habyarimana between October 1990 and April 1994, as well as the interim government in power between April 1994 and 18 July 1994;
7. the governments of the Federal Republic of Yugoslavia and the Republic of Serbia (Milosevic) between 28 February 1998 and 7 October 2000;
8. the Taliban regime in Afghanistan between 27 September 1996 and 22 December 2001; and
9. the government of Ethiopia under Mengistu Haile Mariam between 12 September 1974 and 21 May 1991.[24]

Therefore, unlike section 35(1)(a), which renders a person inadmissible for their actions of being complicit in certain crimes, section 35(1)(b) renders a person inadmissible for their status if they are a prescribed senior official in a designated regime. All in all, individuals who have committed or been complicit in a war crime, a crime against humanity, genocide, or any other act defined as reprehensible will be found to be inadmissible to Canada under section 35.

As of 22 June 2023, section 35 inadmissibility received royal assent. Bill S-8 is an *Act to amend the Immigration and Refugee Protection Act, to make consequential amendments to other Acts and to amend the Immigration and Refugee Protection Regulations*.[25] Section 35(1)(c) to (e) of the *IRPA* currently captures three separate grounds of inadmissibility for foreign nationals relevant to the proposed amendments. Inadmissibility may result from international sanctions, sanctions relating to the *Special Economic Measures Act (SEMA)*,[26] based upon section 4(1.1)(c) or (d) of that Act, and an order or regulation made under section 4 of the *Justice for Victims of Corrupt Foreign Officials Act*

(Sergei Magnitsky Law).[27] These three grounds result in inadmissibility for foreign nationals tied to grounds of "violating human or international rights." Section 35(1)(c) related to international sanctions was enacted in 2002 upon the *IRPA* receiving royal assent, and section 35(1)(d) and (e) have been in force since 2017. The *IRPA* has thus had the authority to render individuals inadmissible on grounds of international sanctions for twenty years, as well as based on parts of the *SEMA* and the *Sergei Magnitsky Law* for the past five years.

The current law additionally restricts access for persons deemed inadmissible under section 35(1)(c) to (e) and their family members to temporary and permanent residency, humanitarian and compassionate relief, and appeals at the Immigration Appeal Division (IAD). Referral to the Immigration Division (ID), eligibility for ministerial relief, and/or a refugee claim are also presently prohibited (except for foreign nationals described in section 35(1)(c)).[28] For one, Bill S-8 separates the word "sanctions" as tied to "grounds of violating human or international rights." It further expands the grounds for inadmissibility for migrants pursuant to all of section 4 of the *SEMA*, including section 4(1.1)(a) and (b),[29] which read:

> (a) an international organization of states or association of states, of which Canada is a member, has made a decision or a recommendation or adopted a resolution calling on its members to take economic measures against a foreign state;
> (b) a grave breach of international peace and security has occurred that has resulted in or is likely to result in a serious international crisis.

This amendment places the brunt of economic sanctions and the "potential for serious international crisis" squarely on individual applicants for the actions of foreign states. Bill S-8 also eliminates access to the Immigration Division and/or ministerial relief, even for those currently captured by section 35(1)(c), which would be replaced by the proposed section 35.1(1)(a).[30] At the same time, Bill S-8 permits full eligibility for all three grounds of inadmissible foreign nationals to make a refugee claim and ceases inadmissibility in all three groups if sanctions, orders, resolutions, and so on are rescinded.[31]

What is not clear is if foreign nationals will be treated in law as violators of human or international rights regardless of whether the sanction involves personal wrongdoing or it is economic, geographic, or involves an entity or foreign state. Will proof of an individual, entity, or state as having engaged in "grounds of violating human or international rights" be required? The word "sanction" is not defined in the *IRPA* or the *IRPR*, nor is the term "entity." A definition of "entity" can be found in the *SEMA* as "a corporation, trust, partnership, fund, an unincorporated association or organization or a foreign state." This is a sweeping definition. These proposed amendments significantly enhance the scope and resulting magnitude of sanctions in the *IRPA*'s inadmissibility regime.

Serious Criminality and Criminality (Section 36)

An individual may be found inadmissible under section 36 if they have been convicted of an offence in Canada or have been convicted of an offence or committed an act outside Canada that is equivalent to and considered an offence under an Act of Parliament in Canada. This includes several federal Acts:

- the *Criminal Code*;
- the *Immigration and Refugee Protection Act*;
- the *Firearms Act*;
- the *Customs Act*;
- the *Controlled Drugs and Substances Act*; and
- the *Cannabis Act*.[32]

For foreign offences, an officer will need to conduct what is referred to as an "equivalency assessment" to determine whether the offence convicted/committed in the foreign country is a criminal or federal offence if convicted/committed in Canada.[33] To determine equivalence, "essential elements" must be considered. There are three leading cases that have developed the legal test to be followed.

These include *Brannson v Minister of Employment and Immigration*, *Hill v Canada*, and *Li v Canada*. *Brannson* instructed to expect differences in the wording of statutory offences in different countries.[34] *Hill* determined that equivalency can be determined in three ways:

- First, by a comparison of the precise wording in each statute;
- Second, by examining the essential ingredients or elements of the offence in Canada as is found in the foreign proceedings; and/or
- Third, by a combination of one and two.[35]

Li found that a comparison of the "essential elements" of the respective offences requires a comparison of the definitions of those offences, including defences particular to those offences.[36] These cases establish that "essential elements" can be compared, or an examination of the evidence to establish the essential elements of the offence in Canada have been proven in the foreign proceedings is conducted, or a combination of each. So, even if the laws are similar in nature, they must still be equivalent. This involves an examination of the essential elements of both laws, including a comparison of the intent, definitions, and defences of offences. It is important to know that it is not necessary to compare all the general principles of criminal responsibility in the two systems — what is being examined is the comparability of offences, not the comparability of possible convictions in the two countries. So, although it may seem straightforward, it is rather complicated.

Whether an offence is considered "serious criminality" depends on the length of the possible sentence (if a foreign offence) or actual imprisonment (if in Canada), rather than the nature of the crime. If the offence is punishable by a maximum term of imprisonment of at least ten years, it is serious criminality under section 36(1). This would include provisions that call for imprisonment for a term of not more than ten years.

For a conviction inside Canada, if a term of imprisonment of more than six months has been imposed, it is serious criminality. Here "term of imprisonment" means jail, not including a conditional sentence.[37] As well, the maximum punishment is based on the time of the commission of the offence, not the time of a finding of inadmissibility, except when the person received a sentence of more than six months' imprisonment.[38]

In Canadian criminal law, there are really three types of offences: summary, indictable, or hybrid. Most criminal offences are hybrid offences. Summary offences are less serious than indictable offences and the punishments reflect the lesser seriousness of the offence. There are also hybrid offences where the Crown uses the specific facts of each case to decide whether to prosecute the case as a summary offence or as an indictable offence.[39] However, under the *IRPA*, an important consideration for both individuals in Canada and outside Canada is that if it is a hybrid offence, even if prosecuted summarily, they are deemed to be indictable offences for immigration purposes.[40]

Serious criminality renders both foreign nationals and permanent residents inadmissible, while criminality only applies to foreign nationals. Also, for permanent residents who have committed an act outside Canada,[41] the standard of proof is higher, that is, on a balance of probabilities.[42] It means that the officer believes the allegations are more probably true than not true. There are few exemptions to inadmissibility on the ground of serious criminality and criminality. For instance, when the offence is designated as a contravention under the *Contraventions Act*, or when the person is found guilty under the *Young Offenders Act*, chapter Y-1 of the Revised Statutes of Canada, 1985, or received a youth sentence under the *Youth Criminal Justice Act*, the person concerned may not be inadmissible.[43]

Organized Criminality (Section 37)

The activities of organized crime present a major threat to the security of all nations, and as such are treated seriously, and the provision is designed specifically to bar entry. Under section 37 of the *IRPA*, a permanent resident or a foreign national may be found inadmissible if the individual is a member of an organization that is believed — on reasonable grounds — to be or have been engaged in activity that is part of a pattern of criminal activity, or if the person is believed to be engaged in any transnational crime activity, such as people smuggling, trafficking in persons, or money laundering.[44]

According to *ENF 2, Evaluating Inadmissibility*, officers generally await the court disposition with respect to the charges before assessing this ground of inadmissibility. A conviction related to organized crime in Canada will result in a finding of inadmissibility under section 37. However, in the scenario where no charges are laid or there is no formal proceeding, officers may investigate and apply the inadmissibility if they believe on reasonable grounds that the person has engaged in organized crimes.[45]

Apart from the low standard of proof, the threshold for the rules of evidence for a finding of inadmissibility on the ground of organized criminality is also low. No conviction is required; mere membership in an organization is sufficient. The definition of "membership" is broad. But it does not include a person who has no knowledge of the criminal purpose or acts of the organization. Instead, membership refers to anyone who is knowingly linked to an organized crime group and benefits from this association, such as:

- persons who devote themselves full time or almost full time to the organization;
- persons who are associated with members of the organization, especially over the course of a lengthy period;
- persons who do not personally commit acts, if they are connected to the criminal organization;
- persons who are directly, indirectly, or peripherally involved with the organization;
- persons who are not involved in the management of the organization but derive an economic benefit from their association with the organization;
- persons working for a legitimate company while knowing it is controlled by organized crime; and
- persons who do not have formal membership if they belong (or belonged) to a criminal organization. Belonging to an

> organization is assumed where persons join voluntarily and remain in the group for the common purpose of actively adding their personal efforts to the group's cause.[46]

There is one exemption, however. If a person whose only involvement with the organized crime was to travel to Canada with the assistance of the organization to make a refugee claim, the person can be exempted from inadmissibility.[47] The rationale behind the exemption is because such a person is doing so only for survival and is unlikely to be a future danger to Canada.

Health and Social Services Grounds (Section 38)

In general, temporary resident applicants must undergo a medical examination if they intend to stay in Canada for more than six months, if they plan to work in certain occupations, or if they have lived or travelled for at least six consecutive months in the past year in one or more designated countries or territories.[48] All permanent residents must undergo a medical examination. The medical examination must be conducted by a "panel physician" designated by IRCC. After the examination, the results are sent to IRCC and assessed by IRCC medical officers. Medical officers will then make a report to IRCC officers on whether the person is admissible, inadmissible, or requires medical surveillance (not bar from admission). If there are concerns that may lead to medical inadmissibility, IRCC may request additional examinations/tests from specialists and/or send a letter to the individual to give them an opportunity for explanation. An individual may be found medically inadmissible if their health condition is or could be:

- a danger to public health, such as a communicable disease;[49]
- a danger to public safety, such as a mental health issue that leads to sudden incapacity or unpredictable or violent behaviour;[50] or
- likely to cause excessive demand on publicly funded health or social services, such as a health condition that needs long-term expensive treatment or related social services.[51]

Most medical inadmissibility cases are about excessive demand on health or social services, rather than danger to public health or safety. The consideration of an excessive demand centres on the cost that an individual would impose measured against a threshold and/or services that would tax Canada's resources. It can also be based on adding to waiting times. Ultimately, section 38(1)(c) of the *IRPA* was established to protect Canadians from people who might reasonably be expected to cause excessive demand on health or social services. The legislative scheme aims to protect public safety and a finite resource base.

The Supreme Court of Canada decision in *Hilewitz v Canada (MCI)*[52] mandated individualized assessments of applicants with medical conditions that could lead to a finding of medical inadmissibility. The Supreme Court highlighted the need for fair, diligent, and proactive assessments by visa officers and medical officers, and a move away from a cookie cutter methodology that focused on the medical condition rather than the person. Following the decisions in *Hilewitz* it was clear an individualized assessment, considering both medical and non-medical factors, was required to determine excessive demand. Following *Hilewitz*, decision-makers were obliged to consider applicants' ability to offset the excessive cost.

Despite *Hilewitz*, the law concerning medical admissibility had remained unchanged for many years and had not caught up with the advances and developments in medical conditions and treatments. Seeking to address these concerns, beginning in 2018,[53] positive progress was made in this area, first with a governmental temporary policy, which was later enacted into law in 2022.[54] The permanent amendments were the result of a meaningful consultation process.

The major changes included an increase to the excessive demand cost threshold for foreign nationals to three times the Canadian average cost per person (now more than $24,000 per year), considered in a five-year period. Another change included redefining "health services" and "social services" to, respectively, provide clarity and remove the previous consideration of certain social services like special education, occupational therapy, behavioural and speech language therapy, and so on into the equation. The new law also eliminated a ten-year forward-looking period of consideration and standardized it to a five-year period, which served to further streamline and simplify the process. One important consideration that remained intact was maintaining the individualized assessments requirement established in *Hilewetz* and further developed through Federal Court of Appeal decisions in *Canada (MCI) v Colaco*,[55] *Sapru v Canada (MCI)*,[56] and *Canada (MCI) v Lawrence*.[57]

All these changes served to allow for a more facilitative and inclusive means to allow entry to individuals who are still able to make socio-economic contributions to Canada, who would likely have been inadmissible otherwise. In the result, pursuant to the *IRPR*, excessive demand *now* refers to a demand on health or social services:

1) where the anticipated costs exceed triple the average Canadian per capita health services and social services costs over a period of five consecutive years following the most recent medical examination required; or
2) that would add to existing waiting lists to these services and thus may cause a delay for Canadians and would increase morbidity or the mortality rate in Canada.[58]

> **Health services** means any health services — including the provision of devices related to the services, laboratory services, and the supply of pharmaceuticals — for which more than half of the funds are contributed by governments, either directly or through publicly funded agencies.[59]
>
> **Social services** means residential or institutional care, including the provision of devices related to the care that is recommended by a health professional and for which more than half of the funds are contributed by governments, either directly or through publicly funded agencies.[60]

Finally, certain applicants are exempted from medical inadmissibility when considering excessive demand, including refugees and protected persons and their families, and certain members in the family sponsorship class, such as spouses, common law partners, and their dependent children.[61]

Financial Inadmissibility (Section 39)

Foreign nationals may be found inadmissible for financial reasons if an officer believes that they cannot or will not support themselves and any dependants in Canada without social assistance. This applies to economic immigrants who must demonstrate self-sufficiency and are required to provide proof of settlement funds.[62] This applies to sponsors in the family class category as well, although in a different way. By signing an undertaking, all sponsors promise to give financial support for the basic needs of the people being sponsored. An officer will assess the sponsor's income that is equal to or greater than the "minimum necessary income" that sponsors and a co-signer (where applicable) must meet to satisfy IRCC that they are able to provide the basic requirements like food, clothing, and shelter for themselves, the person(s) being sponsored, and any other persons for whom they are responsible, for instance, their children. The minimum necessary income is based on Statistics Canada's low-income cut-off (LICO) level, which establishes the annual income level to be met.[63]

A sponsor is exempted from having to meet the minimum necessary income if they are sponsoring their spouse, common law partner, conjugal partner, dependent child, or a person under the age of eighteen years whom the sponsor intends to adopt in Canada.[64] However, if an officer is of the opinion that the sponsor will be unable to provide adequate support and that the sponsored person will be unable or unwilling to support themselves and may have to rely on social assistance, the applicant may be found to be inadmissible for financial reasons.[65] Although, if the person can satisfy the officer that adequate arrangements for care and support (not involving social assistance) are in place, the individual will not fall within this inadmissibility provision. This would involve an officer assessing an individual's financial resources, such as tax documents, bank statements, pay slips, and the person's arrangements in place, such as job offers.[66] Refugees and protected persons who apply for permanent residence in Canada are exempted from being found inadmissible on financial grounds.

Misrepresentation (Section 40)

Misrepresentation is a common and growing ground of inadmissibility, often resulting from innocent mistakes that are often interpreted to mean false pretenses, including lies and omissions. An individual can be found inadmissible for misrepresentation if they directly or indirectly misstate or withhold material facts that affect or could potentially affect the overall application process.[67] Some examples include failing to disclose a previous visa refusal from Canada or any other countries, submitting a false education certificate in order to meet the requirements of an immigration program that they would not otherwise meet, or having an agent submit false information on behalf of the entrepreneur regarding the establishment of the business. Since misrepresentation applies regardless of whether it is directly or indirectly made through a representative, the law is strict, and it often does not matter if it was intentional or unintentional.

The legal test is, if a misrepresentation was made, and it could affect the application process, this will rise to meet the definition. As such, it is always important to be honest and answer each question carefully because a finding of misrepresentation is difficult to challenge. If found to have been misrepresented, it is not just a refusal of an application but essentially a bar from entering Canada temporarily or applying for any status for a period of five years.[68]

Misrepresentation also applies when a person is sponsored by an individual who is determined to be inadmissible for misrepresentation.[69] In addition, if a refugee or naturalized citizen is found to have misrepresented to obtain their status, the refugee status could be vacated, or citizenship could be revoked.[70] The intent of the misrepresentation provision is to ensure that applicants provide complete, honest, and truthful information in every manner when applying for entry into Canada.[71] It covers a wide range of people, from foreign nationals to naturalized citizens and protected persons, with few exemptions, such as persons with pending refugee claims and their family members abroad. There is a narrow exception that IRCC *may* recognize when a person makes honest errors in completing application forms and responding to questions; however, this is an entirely discretionary consideration on the part of an officer and difficult to obtain because it has a very high threshold to meet. It is generally only applied in extraordinary circumstances, but the law has become more forgiving recently, acknowledging technical or innocent errors do arise.[72]

Cessation of Refugee Protection (Section 40.1)

An individual becomes inadmissible when their refugee status ceases. This generally begins with an investigation if a protected person returns to their country of nationality permanently or even temporarily for a visit years later with the passport of their country of origin. The cessation application is generally made by the minister to the Refugee Protection Division (RPD) of the Immigration and Refugee Board (IRB). A member of RPD will hear the case from both sides and make the final decision. Each case is assessed based on the individual facts when considering the potential loss of protected person status. The leading case in this area is *Canada (MCI) v Galindo Camayo*.[73]

Non-compliance with the IRPA (Section 41)

An individual is inadmissible if they fail to comply with the *IRPA*. This includes contraventions of the *IRPR* made under the *IRPA*. For foreign nationals, the most common examples of non-compliance include "overstay," when an individual remains in Canada beyond the end of the authorized period granted or engages in work without being authorized. For permanent residents, this provision usually refers to not meeting the residency obligation (for instance, being physically present in Canada for a minimum of 730 days in a five-year period) and not meeting any conditions imposed. Thus, a non-compliance allegation is usually not a stand-alone allegation; it is often coupled with a violation of a specific requirement of either the *IRPA* or the *IRPR*. Inadmissibility for non-compliance can result in six months, one year, or permanent bars from the country.

Inadmissible Family Member (Section 42)

For temporary and permanent residence applications, an individual must declare all dependants, even if they are not accompanying the applicant, as dependants must also be examined for admissibility (medical, criminal, security). A foreign national, on a balance of probabilities, may be inadmissible for having inadmissible family members, either because their accompanying family members, or sometimes their non-accompanying family members, are inadmissible, or because they are accompanying an inadmissible person. The rationale behind this provision is that a non-accompanying family member today may become a sponsored person in the future, so it is a protective measure. This provision does not apply to permanent residents and protected persons[74] or temporary applicants (such as a visitor visa) if their family members are not inadmissible on the most serious grounds of security, violations of human or international rights, or organized criminality (sections 34, 35, 37).[75]

Inadmissibility Process

A finding of inadmissibility means an individual is not allowed to enter/remain in Canada. If the person is making visa/Electronic Travel Authorization (eTA) applications abroad as one example, the application may be refused. As well, if the person arrives at the port of entry, they may be denied entry to Canada. Further, if the individual is inside Canada, they may be removed. Depending on the status of the applicant and where the decisions may be made, there are certain legal steps to be undertaken before a finding is made, and avenues of recourse to challenge or overcome an officer's decision.

Inadmissibility Report (Section 44 report)

When an officer is of the opinion that a foreign national or a permanent resident who is in Canada or seeking entry to Canada is inadmissible, the officer may prepare a report called an "inadmissibility report" setting out the ground(s) of inadmissibility and the relevant facts following section 44(1) of the *IRPA* (also called a "Section 44 report" or "A44 report"). The scope of discretion whether to write the inadmissibility report varies depending on the nature of inadmissibility and the status of the individual.[76]

Generally, the reports are written by IRCC officers, although when the grounds of inadmissibility involve security, violations of human or international rights, or organized criminality (sections 34, 35, and 37), it is Canada Border Services Agency (CBSA) officers who handle the reports. Once the section 44 report is written, the officer then submits the report to the minister's delegate for review. The onus is on the applicant to demonstrate that the allegation is not true, and they are admissible.

An officer has discretionary power to decide whether to write an A44(1) report, although it does not mean that the officer can disregard the fact that someone is, or may be, inadmissible, so that discretion is extremely limited. The minimal flexibility does allow for some remedies, which can involve (1) an officer allowing the voluntary withdrawal of an application to enter Canada ("Allowed to leave") option at a port of entry, (2) an officer can decide to issue a temporary resident permit (TRP) to a foreign national who is seeking entry to work in Canada and who was convicted of a non-violent offence many years ago, taking into account the relevant assessment risk factors, or (3) an officer restores status to a foreign national who has remained in Canada beyond the period authorized.[77]

For permanent residents and protected persons, before the section 44 report is referred, the individual is usually given an opportunity to request that the report not be referred to the Immigration Division (ID) of the Immigration and Refugee Board (IRB). In this circumstance, the CBSA would invite the individual to make submissions and consider the individual's mitigating factors. The officer routinely considers:

- age at the time permanent residence in Canada was acquired;
- what courses or programs the individual has taken as well as the steps taken toward rehabilitation;
- the length of time spent, and the degree to which the individual is established in Canada;
- the individual's family in Canada and the impact on the family that removal would cause;
- the family and community support available; and
- the degree of hardship that would be caused if removed from Canada.

The CBSA officer assesses the submissions and decides if the individual will be allowed to remain in Canada or to seek to have a removal order issued. Where fortunate, a permanent resident will be permitted to remain outright or receive a "warning letter" instead of being referred for a removal order.[78] If the submissions do not satisfy the officer, a report is prepared, the delegate may issue a removal order if it is within their authority, or refer the matter to the ID of the IRB, depending on the type of case.[79]

Removal Orders

When all the avenues of recourse available to an individual are exhausted, the removal order will take effect. A removal order is a document that orders an individual to leave Canada. A removal order can be issued by IRCC, the CBSA, or the IRB.[80] There are three types of removal orders: departure orders, exclusion orders, and deportation orders,[81] all with different consequences as follow:[82]

- With a **departure order**, the individual must leave Canada within thirty days after the order takes effect and must confirm their departure with the CBSA at the port of exit. If the individual leaves Canada after thirty days or does not confirm their departure with the CBSA, the departure order will automatically become a deportation order, which will require an approved Authorization to Return to Canada (ARC) by the minister of IRCC to enter Canada in the future. This involves a separate application process that is discussed further in Chapter 4.

- With an **exclusion order**, the individual is generally not permitted to return to Canada for a period of one year. If, however, an exclusion order has been issued for misrepresentation, the individual cannot return to Canada for a period of five years. If the individual wants to return within the one- or five-year ban, they must apply for the aforementioned ARC. The exclusion period starts when the individual leaves Canada and obtains a certificate of departure from the CBSA.
- With a **deportation order**, the individual is permanently barred from returning to Canada and is not permitted to return unless approved for an ARC. As well, if the CBSA paid for the individual's removal from Canada, they must also repay that cost before re-entry. If the removal is based on criminality, an individual where and when eligible must seek redress by way of a record suspension (inside Canada convictions) or a certificate of rehabilitation (outside of Canada convictions, commissions).[83]

If an individual fails to appear for removal at the set time or location, the CBSA will issue a Canada-wide immigration arrest warrant. Once arrested, the CBSA may detain the individual in a holding facility before removal for an undetermined period of time.

Detention Reviews

According to section 55(2) of the *IRPA*, a foreign national or permanent resident may be arrested or detained by the CBSA if the officer has reasonable grounds to believe that the individual is unlikely to appear for an examination, hearing, or removal (also called "flight risk"); is a danger to the public; or has not established their identity (this only applies to a foreign national).

When the CBSA detains an individual, they may be released from detention by a CBSA officer before the first detention review (within forty-eight hours) if the officer finds that the reasons for detention no longer exist. The CBSA officer may impose conditions for release, including the payment of a deposit (cash bond) or the posting of a guarantee (performance bond) for compliance with the conditions.[84] The amount of the deposit or guarantee is based on factors such as the financial resources of the person, the obligations that result from the conditions imposed, and the likely cost to locate/arrest the individual.[85] The detainee and guarantor must notify IRCC or CBSA of any change of address and must appear at the time and place as directed.[86] If any imposed condition is broken, the cash bond is forfeited, and in the case of a guarantee, the guarantor must forfeit/pay the set amount of money.

If a CBSA officer decides not to release an individual, the decision must be reviewed by another officer.[87] CBSA then refers the case to the ID of the IRB and provides the ID with a "request for detention review," which generally contains the grounds for detention and the basic information about the individual concerned. Within forty-eight hours (or as soon as possible), a member of the ID will conduct the first detention review to decide whether there is reason under the *IRPA* to continue detention.[88] If the ID member orders continued detention, another detention review will be held within seven days, and then at least once every thirty days thereafter until release.[89] The individual concerned may ask for an early review of detention at any time, although must present new facts to justify the request.

Generally, a detention review is attended by one ID member, a hearings officer on behalf of the minister, the individual concerned, their counsel where retained, and an interpreter and witness (if any). After hearing arguments from both sides, the ID member usually gives the decision and reasons for the decision orally at the end of the hearing and the decision takes effect immediately. However, if the case is more complicated, the decision and its reasons may be rendered in writing post-hearing, in which case it takes effect on the date the ID member signs and dates the decision.

Like an admissibility hearing, a detention review before the ID is quasi-judicial and adversarial. The ID is not bound by any legal or technical rules of evidence and may receive and base their decision on evidence adduced in the proceedings that it considers credible or trustworthy in the circumstances.[90] It also follows its own set of rules[91] with respect to the roles and responsibilities of each party, as well as the procedures and practices to be followed in proceedings before the ID. The hearing is a two-step process. First, the ID member must be satisfied that there are grounds for detention under section 58 of the *IRPA*. Second, depending on the grounds for detention, the ID member must consider several factors set out in sections 245–249 of the *IRPR* to decide whether to continue to detain or to release the person concerned.[92]

It is important to note that the default of each detention review is release, and the onus of proof for continued detention is always on the minister. Each detention review is a *de novo* hearing, which means that at each detention review, the hearings officer as the minister's representative must satisfy the ID member as to the grounds for continued detention. The Federal Court of Appeal (FCA) in *Brown v Canada (MCI)* has confirmed that the onus always remains on the minister and never shifts during a detention review or any successive detention reviews. The FCA also held that the burden of proof on the minister increases with the passage of time and each successive detention review.[93]

Although there is no statutory maximum length of detention, there must be a nexus between detention and an immigration purpose.[94] If an ID member finds that there are no longer grounds under the *IRPA* for continued detention, the member must order the person released. The ID may also order a release with certain conditions, such as the payment of a deposit or the posting of a guarantee,[95] after balancing the grounds for detention and factors to be considered under the *IRPR*. According to the *IRB Chairperson Guideline 2: Detention*, the ID may also consider imposing other conditions, including reporting to the CBSA periodically (in person or by phone), remaining within (or outside) a particular location or geographic area, enrolling in a community case management and supervision program, and so on.[96] However, caselaw has affirmed that the conditions imposed must be proportional, realistic, and attainable with respect to the person's situation.[97]

Although there is no limit as to the length of detention in the legislation, according to *ENF 20, Detention*, the CBSA considers detentions that have lasted more than ninety-nine days to be long-term detentions and the officers should actively determine if alternatives to detentions (ATDs) could be available or suitable to mitigate the risk.[98]

Habeas Corpus Application — A Potential Remedy to Immigration Detainees

Detention engages the *Canadian Charter of Rights and Freedoms* (the *Charter*), including section 7 (right to life, liberty, and security), section 9 (right not to be arbitrarily detained or imprisoned), and section 10(c) (right to *habeas corpus*).[99] Section 10(c) of the *Charter* reads that "Everyone has the right on arrest or detention to *habeas corpus*." However, it was only after the 2015 Ontario Court of Appeal decision in *Chaudhary v Canada (PSEP)* [100] that *habeas corpus* application[101] was considered an available remedy for immigration detainees, which was later re-affirmed by the Supreme Court of Canada in *Canada (MPSEP) v Chhina*.[102] Justice Rouleau stated in *Chaudhary*:

> [81] On their *habeas corpus* applications, the appellants would have to show that reasonable and probable grounds exist for their complaints. The grounds will be the exceptional length of their detentions and their uncertain continued duration.... Where there is no reasonable prospect that the detention's immigration-related purposes will be achieved within a reasonable time (with what is

> reasonable depending on the circumstances), a continued detention will violate the detainee's ss. 7 and 9 Charter rights and no longer be legal.[103]
>
> [106] As outlined earlier, in *habeas corpus* applications, once a legitimate ground is raised by the detainee, the onus is placed on the Minister to justify the lawfulness of the continued detention.[104]

Habeas corpus application has become an important potential remedy, especially for long-term detainees. However, one should know that, if a *habeas corpus* is granted, the detainee is released although their immigration status is unchanged.

Conclusion

Since 1869, Canada has enacted laws and regulations governing the admission of immigrants. I set out in Chapter 1 how the initial open-door policy gradually gave way to more restrictive and discriminatory measures. Eventually skills and education became the main criteria for determining entry into Canada, still leaving elements of discrimination in place. Once Canada adopted a multiculturalism policy, cultural diversity has been promoted as a key component of our identity but not without some still being left behind. The twentieth century codified greater discretionary authority concerning the admissibility and deportation of immigrants. This was originally shaped as being unsuited to the climate or requirements of Canada and these individuals were prohibited.[105]

With the many amendments to the Acts over the years, discretionary powers over admissibility and deportation became more inclusive, with the migration controls introduced in the 1978 *Immigration Act* distancing immigration law and policy from overt racism and discrimination. Today, this has served to establish Canada's primary objectives: to protect the health and safety of Canadians, maintain the security of Canadian society, promote international justice and security, and deny access to Canadian territory to persons who are criminals or security risks. Tools to do so have expanded with the government having modernized and improved information sharing with other countries and identification practices.

Commencing in 2013, biometrics were introduced, using fingerprint data to confirm a person's identity and identify individuals who may have a criminal record. Several information sharing agreements have been in place for several years, and over the last decade many more have been added domestically as well as internationally to support administration and enforcement. This includes a stockpile of admissibility concerns: travel to Canada and authorization to enter Canada, the investigation of matters relating to program abuse, criminality, public safety and health, the coordination and streamlining of enforcement cases, detention, as well as combatting international terrorism, war crimes, crimes against humanity, and organized crime.

In addition, the federal government has taken a very hard line to stem immigration fraud and abuse of the system. I have seen a significant increase in misrepresentation cases as one example. In part due to the aforementioned information sharing, IRCC has access to substantial information on an individual. Beyond security, misrepresentation has become a critically important facet of Canadian immigration practices. Unfortunately, all misrepresentations, whether or not intentional, are treated the same. I hope that the government will in time recognize there are differences that should be treated differently.

Immigration legislation can be a snapshot of our society's beliefs and attitudes, but also reveals Canada's history of inclusion and exclusion. With the imposition of and emphasis on security measures and preventing abuse of the system using immigration policy, it remains to be seen how the legislation will continue to develop, and if it will sustain a balance between fostering immigration and maintaining security. We surely have a responsibility to protect our resources and our citizenry, but that must be tempered by the ability to address deficiencies within our own immigration programs and meet international obligations while building a country that always assesses persons and not simply regulations.

We must also be on guard to not slip backwards. We cannot shroud discriminatory animus in inadmissibility policy and bypass critical input, consensus building, measured scrutiny, and worse yet, the rule of law. Inadmissibility law should always see its full expression in legislation in the full light of day. The opposite has happened before, and it can happen again.

CHAPTER FOUR

Challenging Canadian Immigration Inadmissibility

Introduction

Chapter 3 set out many of the ways foreign nationals and permanent residents may be found inadmissible to Canada. This chapter focuses upon remedial measures. The importance of these remedies cannot be underestimated beyond the obvious that decision-makers can make mistakes. These remedies often infuse life and humanity into an increasingly technical and sterile compilation of rules, regulations, and guidelines that often foreshadow the need for legislative change down the road. The provisions are not simply the exception to the rule, it is the relief where the law does not speak to sometimes competing objectives; where there is a disconnect between an individual's circumstances and the application of laws. After all, the product is human.

The provisions can also address imbalances in different immigrant categories. So, if found inadmissible, foreign nationals do have options to challenge the finding or alternative pathways to obtain lawful immigration status. This chapter discusses the statutory grounds by which inadmissibility can be challenged, namely humanitarian and compassionate consideration, temporary resident permits, and ministerial relief, among others. I also survey the administrative mechanisms by which decisions relating to inadmissibility can be appealed and judicially reviewed.

Humanitarian and Compassionate Application and Exemption Requests

Section 25(1) of the *IRPA* allows individuals who are inadmissible (excepting subsections 34, 35, 37) or who are ineligible to apply in an immigration program to apply for permanent residence, or for an exemption from a requirement of the *Immigration and Refugee Protection Act* (*IRPA*).[1] Section 25 is based on humanitarian and compassionate considerations (H&C). H&C requests may be a stand-alone application or can also be part of an application where the applicant qualified for an immigration program but has specific eligibility or admissibility issues. H&C stand-alone applications can only be made from within Canada.[2] There are no legal definitions of "humanitarian" and "compassionate" in the *IRPA* and the *Immigration and Refugee Protection Regulations* (*IRPR*).[3] Jurisprudence has defined and clarified the interpretation of this provision in *Kanthasamy v Canada*.[4] Prior to this the definition and legal test for H&C in the Immigration, Refugees and Citizenship Canada (IRCC) guidelines was whether there would be unusual and underserved or disproportionate hardship to an applicant if the application was refused, which was a stricter definition.

In *Kanthasamy*, the Supreme Court of Canada held that the words "unusual and undeserved or disproportionate hardship" should be treated as instructive but not determinative.[5] The Court also affirmed the legal test for assessing H&C applications in *Chirwa v Canada (Minister of Citizenship and Immigration)*[6] — that is, to offer equitable relief in circumstances that "would excite in a reasonable [person] in a civilized community a desire to relieve the misfortunes of another."[7] Following *Kanthasamy*, IRCC revised its guidelines with respect to H&Cs:

> What warrants relief will vary depending on the facts and context of the case, but officers making humanitarian and compassionate

> determinations must substantively consider and weigh all the relevant facts and factors before them (*Kanthasamy v. Canada (Citizenship and Immigration)*, 2015 SCC 61; *Baker v. Canada (Minister of Citizenship and Immigration)*, [1999] 2 S.C.R. 817). Furthermore, individual H&C factors should not be considered in isolation; there must be a global assessment of all the relevant factors.[8]
>
> As of December 10, 2015, there is no hardship "test" for applicants under subsection 25(1); however, the determination of whether there are sufficient grounds to justify granting an H&C request will generally include an assessment of hardship. Therefore, hardship continues to be an important consideration in determining whether sufficient humanitarian and compassionate considerations exist to justify granting an exemption and/or permanent resident status.[9]

IRCC has also provided a non-exhaustive list of factors that are routinely considered:

- establishment in Canada for in-Canada applications
- ties to Canada
- the best interests of any children directly affected by the H&C decision
- factors in their country of origin including adverse country conditions
- health considerations including inability of a country to provide medical treatment
- family violence considerations
- consequences of the separation of relatives
- inability to leave Canada has led to establishment (in the case of applicants in Canada)
- ability to establish in Canada for overseas applications
- any unique or exceptional circumstances that might merit relief

Officers have broad discretion in assessing H&C applications. They can even reconsider a negative decision in certain circumstances.[10] The onus to demonstrate that the H&C relief is warranted is entirely placed upon the applicant. The application process can be lengthy, and the result is unpredictable. An H&C application under consideration does not prevent the execution of enforcement of any removal orders. The section reads:

> 25.1 (1) The Minister may, on the Minister's own initiative, examine the circumstances concerning a foreign national who is inadmissible — other than section 34, 35, or 37[11] — or who does not meet the requirements of this *Act* and may grant the foreign national *permanent resident status or an exemption from any applicable criteria or obligations* of this *Act* if the Minister is of the opinion that it is justified by humanitarian and compassionate considerations relating to the foreign national, taking into account the best interests of a child directly affected.[12]

Noted above, while H&C considerations can be submitted for permanent residence applications, the use of H&C considerations to fight inadmissibility refers to including an H&C request and can be used in various application types, including before the finding of inadmissibility has even been made.[13] For example, if a person applying for permanent resident status through a spousal sponsorship has previous convictions for serious criminality and is aware that they are likely to be found inadmissible, they can request an H&C exemption as part of the sponsorship application. In evaluating H&C applications, officers can rely on the seriousness of the inadmissibility, but should not use it to discount every H&C factor such that it becomes impossible to overcome.[14] While an applicant's inadmissibility is a relevant factor, it "should not be the only or the primary factor, as this would defeat the purpose of section 25 of the *Act*."[15]

In considering an inadmissibility exemption on H&C grounds, the officer must also not consider factors considered during refugee determination (sections 96 and 97 of the *IRPA*),[16] such as a well-founded fear of persecution, risk to life, and risk of cruel and unusual treatment or punishment. The simple fact of having made a previous refugee claim should not create a negative inference — it is only the factors relevant to a refugee determination that should not be considered.

In *Mulla v Canada (MCI)*, for example, the applicant made a refugee claim based on what amounted to a blood feud with another family in Albania, and also made an H&C application based on remaining with his family and his spouse's mental state.[17] The Federal Court ruled that the officer should not have made a negative finding based on the existence of a previous refugee claim. In addition, while the factors under sections 96 and 97 may not be considered, the facts underlying those factors may still be relevant in determining whether the applicant is directly and personally experiencing hardship.[18] A refugee fleeing Colombia, for instance, after being targeted by the Revolutionary Armed Forces of Colombia (FARC), would not be able to argue in their H&C that they would be persecuted by the FARC, but they could still submit country conditions indicating that the country is not safe due to the presence of these FARC, and that it would amount to hardship to return there.

I highlighted in Chapter 2 and above that the test for H&C applications was clarified in *Kanthasamy* and revolves around hardship. However, the analysis should not be based solely around hardship.[19] In *Ali v Canada (MCI)*, positive factors were incorrectly filtered through a hardship lens:

> [17] . . . In *Marshall*, the Court noted that *Kanthasamy* changed the legal tests used to assess H&C factors. Hardship is not the "determinative or sole factor" to be considered in an H&C analysis . . .
>
> [18] . . . in considering the medical evidence, the Officer seems to accept the medical evidence that Mr. Ali requires medical treatment, however he then discounts the diagnosis because Mr. Ali failed to demonstrate follow-up. This sort of line of analysis was explicitly rejected in *Kanthasamy*.
>
> [19] Further the Officer went on to discount medical evidence because the Applicant could receive treatment in Trinidad. In *Marshall*, at para 39 the Court rejected this sort of analysis, calling it a "hardship-centric" analysis."[20]

This more flexible approach has also been applied in cases such as *Yang v Canada (MCI)*, in which the emotional ties between a mother and her adult daughter were discounted for not amounting to hardship. The Federal Court clarified:

> [61] Rather than considering whether humanitarian and compassionate reasons exist in the relationship between these two adults, who are biologically mother and daughter, the Officer applied a test of hardship and focused on the fact that the informal adoption eradicated the parent/child relationship. While this approach may be technically correct in determining whether someone is a member of the family class, it may well be a textbook example of the reason that humanitarian and compassionate grounds were introduced to the legislation: to provide a means by which to ameliorate the rigid application of the legislation.[21]

In *Shah v Canada (MCI)*, the court held that the officer's decision was unreasonable regarding the availability of counselling and isolation:

> [58] I find that in these circumstances where the Officer was faced with evidence of a risk of suicide resulting from the removal itself, it was not sufficient for the Officer to simply examine the availability of medical services in the destination country. The Officer was also required to determine whether putting the Applicant through removal and its potential for possibly leading to suicide amounted to undue, undeserved or disproportionate hardship. I adopt the Court's reasoning in P.M.D. and find that the Officer's failure to do so renders the decision unreasonable.[22]

The officer must also assess the personal circumstances and beliefs of the applicants prior to making an H&C decision. For example, in *Hinzman v Canada (MCI)*, the applicant, an American citizen, was against all participation in war, and thus came to Canada after learning that he would be deployed to Iraq. The Federal Court of Appeal held:

> [39] My conclusion should not be seen as altering the discretion of officers making decisions on section 25 applications, nor as giving the appellants a "right to a particular outcome or to the application of a particular legal test".
>
> [40] However, the H&C Officer had the duty to look at all of the appellants' personal circumstances, including Mr. Hinzman's beliefs and motivations, before determining if there were sufficient reasons to make a positive H&C decision. She did not. Had the Applications Judge addressed the appellants' ground of complaint, as stated at paragraph 57 of his Reasons, I am convinced that he would have concluded as I do and found that the H&C decision was significantly flawed and therefore unreasonable.[23]

When raising hardships, applicants may advance hardship factors that are specific to their circumstances but may also proffer hardship grounds that others in their country face provided they establish a link to their personal circumstances. For example, female applicants are not barred from raising violence against women as a hardship in their country of citizenship simply because most women in that country will face the same hardship. In *Gonzalez v Canada (MCI)*, Mosley J stated:

> [55] An H&C applicant may raise hardship that is also faced by others in the country of removal. She need not prove that the hardship she will face differs from that faced by anyone else. Yet the applicant must prove that there is a link between her personal circumstances and the hardship she alleges.[24]

Advancing that same example of violence against women, an applicant would therefore need to prove that they will be directly affected if they return to their country of citizenship, for example, they came to Canada to escape an abusive ex-partner. Additionally, I highlighted in Chapter 2 one of the key factors that a decision-maker must consider, if relevant, is the best interests of the child (BIOC). While this factor is not determinative, it must be weighed heavily whenever there is a child directly affected by the decision.

Weighing the BIOC requires more than just stating the facts, and the officer's decision must demonstrate that they engaged with these interests. For example, in a separate *Gonzalez* case, the applicants were citizens of Mexico, but all three of their children had been born in Canada. The officer decided that they would be able to assimilate into a Mexican school and society because they had some facility in Spanish and the support of their parents. The Honourable Madam Justice Elliott granted the judicial review:

> [24] The Officer fails to explain how the evidence was weighed and does not justify the conclusion that the socio-economic environment advantage in Canada was not determinative. The Officer's analysis on the children's best interests is neither intelligible nor transparent; it is unclear how the various factors that were reviewed and accepted as indicating that Canada was a better place for the children than Mexico were weighed in arriving at the Officer's conclusion. The Officer fails to identify a best interest either in staying in Canada or being removed to Mexico — the analysis is simply missing.
>
> [25] To arrive at a finding that the children's best interests do not lie in remaining in Canada, there ought to have been factors expressed along the way which, when added together, outweigh the clear finding by the Officer that Canada is a more desirable place for the children to live. The Officer fails to explain why removal to Mexico would not be contrary to their best interests. I am unable to identify any factor mentioned by the Officer indicating that Mexico is a better place for the children, particularly when viewed from the perspective of these young, English-speaking, Canadian children who have never been to Mexico.[25]

Also, simply stating that the BIOC favours non-removal has been described as "artificial," as it can be presumed that the child's best interests, absent exceptional circumstances, will almost always weigh in favour of non-removal of the parent.[26] Also, BIOC must be examined through a different lens than other H&C factors as children will "rarely, if ever, be deserving of any hardship."[27] The case of *Akyol v Canada (MCI)* is an example of unreasonably applying a hardship test:

> [24] Finally, the Officer stated that she was "not satisfied that leaving Canada to return to Turkey in the company of their parents would have a significant negative impact on the best interests of these three children". Requiring evidence of severe harm or hardship to a child is incorrect in the analysis. The question is not: "is the child suffering enough that his 'best interests' are not being met?" Rather, the question is "what is in the child's best interests?" . . . It is the child that must, first and foremost, be considered when conducting a BIOC analysis, rather than whether the child could adapt to another country, or accompany parents.[28]

In considering the BIOC, even the interests of unborn children must be considered. In *Kaur v Canada (MCI)*, the Federal Court decided that the likely birth of a child is directly relevant to H&C concerns, and refusing relief also impacts family separation, family support, and the general well-being of the child. The court wrote:

> [5] This Court has made it very clear . . . that a pregnancy is a relevant consideration in the exercise of humanitarian and compassionate discretion. These decisions significantly curtail the range of the decision-maker's discretion and they certainly cannot be rejected out-of-hand. Although a child has not been born, the decision-maker is required to apply some common sense to the situation and to carefully reflect on the circumstances that are most likely to be present at the end of the pregnancy. Contrary to the apparent view of the visa officer, the pending birth of a child in this context has nothing whatsoever to do with an assertion of fetal rights.[29]

The BIOC must therefore be assessed during pregnancy and can extend to adulthood. "Dependent child," as defined by the *IRPR*, includes children under the age of twenty-two years or twenty-two years of age and over in certain circumstances, namely depending substantially on the financial support of their parents and being a student or being unable to support themselves financially due to a physical or mental condition.[30] However, the best interests of children can only be considered up to the age of eighteen.[31] In *Naredo v Canada (MCI)*, although one of the sons of the applicants was eighteen years old at the time the application was submitted, Gibson J reasoned that both sons

> could reasonably be expected to be dramatically affected by the removal from Canada of their parents.... It goes without saying that the having of the children in Canada while their parents' immigration status was undetermined was not a "decision" that the children had any part in making.[32]

This was further explained in *Ramsawak v Canada (MCI)*:

> [19] That being said, the assessment of the best interests of the children must take into account the relevant facts of each case. The best interests of a two-year-old infant, for example, will most certainly differ from those of a grown up young adult of 21. For example, it is clear from a reading of Mme Justice L'Heureux-Dubé's decision in *Baker* that what she had in mind were the interests of minor children ...
>
> [20] Similarly, if one is to look at the hardship that a negative decision would impose upon the children of an H&C claimant, the autonomy of these children or, conversely, their state of dependency upon their children, must be a relevant factor. In that respect, it is interesting to note that Justice MacKay came to the conclusion that the 19-year-old child of the applicant was still a "child" for the purposes of the *Baker* analysis because he was still a dependent and was not authorized to work or to continue his studies in Canada. Similarly, Justice Mandamin considered that the adult sons of the applicant were deserving of a best interest of the child analysis because they were financially dependent on their father as they were pursuing their education.[33]

The IRCC operational instructions and guidelines outline specific procedures for when an H&C exemption should be granted according to some of the various inadmissibilities (described in detail in Chapter 3, above). H&C exemptions, highlighted above, cannot be granted based on sections 34, 35, or 37 — they can only be granted to applicants who are inadmissible for criminality, health grounds, financial reasons, misrepresentation, non-compliance with the Act, or because of an inadmissible family member.[34] Thus, not all H&C requests must be considered. Certain restrictions include the following:

- The person already has an outstanding H&C request and the H&C application *should not* be examined, and the fee returned.[35]
- As above, the person is inadmissible under sections 34, 35, or 37 of the *IRPA* (security, human or international rights violations, or organized criminality) and the H&C application *should not* be examined, and the fee returned.
- The person is *suspected* to be inadmissible under sections 34, 35, or 37 of the *IRPA* and the application should be sent to the Centre of Expertise in Security Cases for assessment of the suspected inadmissibility, and the fees kept. If found to be inadmissible, the application is *refused*.
- The person becomes a permanent resident or Canadian citizen after processing of the application has begun and the application *should not* be examined, and the fee should be kept.
- The person is a former permanent resident or Canadian citizen and the application *should* be examined.
- The person has a pending refugee claim and the application *should not* be examined and the fee returned.
- The person has received a negative decision on a refugee claim, has not appealed to the Refugee Appeal Division (RAD), and has not applied for leave and judicial review of the decision and the application *should not* be examined until twelve months after the Refugee Protection Division (RPD) decision, and the fee returned. An exception is if there is a risk to life caused by the inability of their home country to provide adequate medical or health care, or if there would be an adverse effect on the best interests of a child directly affected by the removal.

- The person has received a negative decision on a refugee claim and has either made an appeal to the RAD or an application for leave and judicial review and the application *should not* be examined until twelve months after the last rejection, and the fee returned. The same exceptions as above apply.
- The person has abandoned a refugee claim and the application *should not* be examined until twelve months after the claim was abandoned (as determined by the IRB), and the fee returned. The same exceptions as above apply.
- The person has withdrawn a refugee claim after substantive evidence has been heard (for instance, the RPD or RAD has started to examine the merits of the claim) and the application *should not* be examined until twelve months after the claim was withdrawn, fee returned.
- The person had a refugee claim that was determined to be ineligible to be returned to the RPD and has a PRRA (Pre-Removal Risk Assessment) application that is pending and the application *should not* be examined, fee returned.
- The person has withdrawn a refugee claim before substantive evidence has been heard at their RPD hearing and the application *should be* examined.[36]

If the individual is inadmissible for serious criminality or criminality (*IRPA* section 36(1) and (2)), officers are instructed to consider whether the inadmissibility, such as a criminal conviction, outweighs the H&C factors. Officers may consider factors such as the applicant's actions, the type of criminal conviction, the sentence imposed, the length of time since the conviction,[37] whether the conviction was an isolated incident or a pattern of criminality, and any other pertinent information about the circumstances.[38] Jurisprudence also indicates other factors that should be considered, including expressions of remorse[39] and whether the offence has been pardoned.[40] In *Chieu v Canada (MCI)*, the Federal Court of Appeal endorsed the finding in *Ribic v Canada (MEI)* that the following six factors should be considered:

1. The seriousness of the offence leading to the deportation order;
2. The possibility of rehabilitation and risk of reoffending;
3. The length of time spent in Canada and the degree to which the applicant is established;
4. The family in Canada and the dislocation to family that would be caused by deportation;
5. The support available to the applicant within the family and the community; and
6. The degree of hardship that would be caused to the applicant by his return to the country of nationality.[41]

However, these factors do not guarantee a positive finding — see *Katwaru v Canada (MCI)*, in which four of the six factors weighed in the applicant's favour, but the seriousness of the offences (manslaughter of his infant son and assault of his wife) outweighed any positive factors.[42] Often criminal offences will have been committed outside of Canada. In those cases, the criminal law of the country that the offence was committed in must be equated with the Canadian *Criminal Code* to determine whether the offence(s) would be inadmissible for criminality or for serious criminality. The officer can also be assisted by the Danger to the Public —Rehabilitation Division in Case Management Branch to help equate the criminal conviction from outside of Canada.

In *Jones v Canada (MCI)*, an applicant with previous convictions for assault with a weapon and manslaughter was the subject of a refused H&C application, despite the best interests of his eleven-year-old daughter. The Federal Court found that the officer did not err in the BIOC analysis, but did err in drawing a negative inference from the applicant's criminal history:

> [43] All of the evidence before the Officer indicated the highly positive rehabilitative steps the Applicant had taken since his incarceration and his remorse for his actions. Nothing in the record could support a negative endorsement of his character since his incarceration. Further, the whole purpose of the Applicant's H&C application was to try to overcome his inadmissibility due to serious

> criminality. Thus, how this negative inference as to the Applicant's character fits into the H&C analysis required of the Officer, is entirely unclear to me. This is unintelligible and again suggests that the Officer misunderstood his role or misapplied the evidence.[43]

Inadmissibility for criminality can also extend to pending charges, but the case of *Avila v Canada (MCI)* underscores the boundaries of procedural fairness, namely that the officer must consider more than the existence of pending charges and provide the applicant(s) with an opportunity to respond. Justice Lagacé, as he then was, wrote:

> [17] In brief, Justice here does not appear to have been done, as a result of this statement combined to the failure of the Officer to wait for the outcome of the criminal proceedings or at the very least to attempt to ascertain the underlying facts and circumstances of the charges and/or to give the applicants an opportunity to respond. It appears therefore from the Officer's decision and her failure to ascertain or wait for the result of the criminal charges that the Officer was influenced negatively and acted under the prism of pending criminal charges through which she viewed the entire file.[44]

If the individual is inadmissible on health grounds (*IRPA* section 38), the officer should request that the applicant complete a medical examination. At stage one of the application, the officer may make this request if the applicant specifically seeks an exemption from medical inadmissibility and the officer believes that the H&C considerations might outweigh the inadmissibility, or if the officer suspects that the case involves medical inadmissibility and there appears to be compelling H&C considerations. The officer should assess the following factors to decide whether the health concern would cause an excessive demand on health or social services:

- What is the cost of the treatment or care, if available?
- When the health inadmissibility is one that affects health or social services, are there arrangements to cover treatment, care, and other costs?

- Is the applicant likely to become self-supporting?
- Is there a risk the person will require public assistance?
- The extent of the applicant's anticipated need for health or social services in relation to the average demand for these services by Canadian residents.[45]

The officer may then consult with provincial health authorities and the migration health branch, and refer the application to a designated decision-maker or determine that the exemption is not warranted and refuse the application. If medical inadmissibility is discovered at stage two of the decision process, then the officer may either make a referral to a delegated decision-maker or refuse the application. Ultimately, decisions under section 25(1) are highly discretionary. Reviewing courts can review whether the officer's decision was reasonable, but they cannot, for example, reweigh the evidence.[46]

In certain cases, where the applicant has lied or is otherwise guilty of misconduct, the reviewing court may dismiss the H&C application with the finding that the applicant does not have "clean hands."[47] This can include, as seen in *Wong v Canada (MCI)*, an applicant failing to attend meetings with immigration authorities.[48] In *Kandhai v Canada (MCI)*, the H&C application was dismissed for misrepresentation, but the reviewing court overturned the decision, finding that the facts underlying the misrepresentation supported the applicant:

> [24] That said, there are other considerations that favour the exercise of the Court's discretion in Mr. Kandhai's favour. While Mr. Kandhai's pattern of misconduct is serious, it does not appear that he sought to gain any advantage through the misrepresentation made in connection with his 2007 H&C application. As his counsel has pointed out, Mr. Kandhai's H&C application may well have been strengthened had he acknowledged that he had a wife in Canada. In these circumstances, it is difficult to see how Mr. Kandhai's misrepresentation regarding his marital status would have undermined the integrity of the immigration process insofar as this H&C application is concerned.

> [25] Moreover, Mr. Kandhai appears to have come forward voluntarily with his admission of misrepresentation. There has been no suggestion that he only admitted the misrepresentation in his most recent H&C application when he was caught in a lie, or when he otherwise became aware that "the jig was up".
>
> [26] Insofar as the apparent strength of Mr. Kandhai's case is concerned, for the purposes of this "clean hands" analysis, suffice it to say that he has a very strong case.[49]

Interestingly, even where the applicant does not directly request an exemption but the facts of their application suggest that they are requesting an exemption for inadmissibility, officers are directed to treat the application as if the exemption has been requested.[50] For example, if the applicant makes a case in their application for why they should be exempted from their inadmissibility, but does not explicitly ask for an H&C exemption, the officer should assess the matter as if the H&C relief had been requested. The onus remains on the applicant to make their case and prove any claim upon which they rely.[51] To be fair, though, the applicant should be notified that H&C is being considered and afforded an opportunity to present their own reasons. Alternatively, if the applicant provides updated or additional submissions and requests an H&C exemption from *new or newly discovered* inadmissibility, the request must be considered.[52]

Temporary Resident Permits

Section 24(1) of the *IRPA* provides for the use of temporary resident permits (TRPs) to overcome inadmissibility:

> 24(1) A foreign national who, in the opinion of an officer, is inadmissible or does not meet the requirements of this *Act* becomes a temporary resident if an officer is of the opinion that it is justified in the circumstances and issues a temporary resident permit, which may be cancelled at any time.[53]

The Act further provides certain restrictions beginning at subsection (4): foreign nationals may not request a TRP within twelve months of a rejected, withdrawn, or abandoned refugee protection. TRPs can also be refused if the foreign national has failed to comply with any imposed conditions, per subsection (7). If a foreign national is found inadmissible yet has a valid reason to travel to Canada that is justified in the circumstances, an individual can apply for a temporary resident permit (TRP) following section 24(1) of the *IRPA*. If granted, a TRP does not remove the individual's inadmissibility, but instead grants an exemption for the period of a TRP. It may be issued at visa offices outside Canada, at a port of entry, and/or from inside Canada. The TRP may be issued for up to a period of three years and can be cancelled at any time.

To obtain a TRP, a complete application is required, including application forms, processing fees, and providing compelling supporting evidence. In the TRP application, an individual must convince an officer that their reason to enter or remain in Canada is sufficiently compelling to outweigh the health or safety risks to Canadian society.[54] Some examples would include a family member's terminal illness, employment that will serve to provide significant benefits to Canada, and a performer attending an event that involves significant revenue to Canada and would affect a number of other individuals if not permitted. The degree of need is measured relative to the type of case. If granted, the duration of the TRP is determined based on the needs of the individual and the circumstances of the case. Officers have broad discretion when assessing a TRP application. One of the reasons is that unlike a temporary resident visa, there are more benefits for TRP holders.

An individual who has been issued a TRP with a validity of six months or longer can apply for a work permit from within Canada[55] or a study permit.[56] As well, TRP holders may be eligible for permanent residence as a member of "permit holder class" if they have continuously resided in Canada as a permit holder for at least three years and have not become inadmissible on any ground since the permit was issued.[57] Specifically, foreign nationals who have been granted a TRP can become members of the permit holder class in the following circumstances:

65 (a) they have been issued a temporary resident permit under subsection 24(1) of the *Act*;

(b) they have continuously resided in Canada as a permit holder for a period of

(i) at least three years, if they

(A) are inadmissible on health grounds under subsection 38(1) of the *Act*,

(B) are inadmissible under paragraph 42(1)(a) of the *Act* on grounds of an accompanying family member who is inadmissible under subsection 38(1) of the *Act*, or

(C) are inadmissible under paragraph 42(1)(b) of the *Act* on grounds of an accompanying family member of a foreign national who is inadmissible

(I) under subsection 38(1) of the *Act*, or

(II) under paragraph 42(1)(a) of the *Act* on grounds of an accompanying family member who is inadmissible under subsection 38(1) of the *Act*,

(ii) at least five years, if they are inadmissible on any other grounds under the Act, except sections 34 and 35 and subsections 36(1) and 37(1) of the Act;

(c) they have not become inadmissible on any ground since the permit was issued; and

(d) in the case of a foreign national who intends to reside in the province of Quebec and is not a member of the family class or a person whom the board has determined to be a Convention refugee, the competent authority of that Province is of the opinion that the foreign national meets the selection criteria of the Province.[58]

The continuity of a TRP will be rendered invalid if the permit holder leaves Canada unless re-entry has specifically been authorized on the TRP. If the holder leaves Canada and wants to re-enter after the expiry date, they must apply for a new TRP. Finally, an individual cannot apply for an extension of a TRP, rather it is a subsequent TRP that is available,[59] so it is important to apply well in advance of the expiry date to ensure an individual remains in valid TRP status.

The officer and the minister are given broad discretion to allow a person who would otherwise be inadmissible to enter or remain in Canada.[60] TRPs can also be requested in the context of an H&C application. In *White (Litigation Guardian of) v Canada (MCI)*, the applicant had suffered a permanent brain injury when he was eighteen years old following which he had reduced mental capacity, behavioural changes, and delusions and depression, resulting in several crimes, including kidnapping and aggravated sexual assault. The Federal Court regarding the director's decision to refuse held:

> [49] Finally, the Director considered Mr. White's request for a TRP as an alternative to an exemption on H&C grounds. She concluded that a TRP was inappropriate in this case. She characterized it as a "wait and see" approach, in which the parties could wait to see if Mr. White re-offended or not. She found this would be at the expense of others. The Director concluded that, even if Mr. White were to remain crime-free for five years (the lifespan of a TRP), given that his problems are permanent with no significant potential for rehabilitation, a relapse was likely to occur beyond the five-year mark.
>
> ...
>
> [67] Third, the fact that Mr. White's subsequent criminality was caused entirely by the accident he was involved in, through no fault of his own and at a young age, was recognized by the Director as a tragedy, and his blameworthiness for his subsequent criminality was low. The Director concluded that "the fact that Mr. White's criminality is due to an accident and not because he has a bad character is a factor in his favour; it is the element of his case which makes the balancing of factors very difficult."[61]

The guidelines supporting TRP were discussed in length in the case of *Lee v Canada (MCI)*, a TRP based on medical inadmissibility:

> [4] Justice Shore of this Court, a judge very experienced in matters dealing with [the *IRPA*] gave careful consideration to the issue of temporary resident permits (TRP) in his recent discussion in *Farhat*.... He concluded in that respect that:
>
> - in addition to being exceptional, the issuance of TRPs is highly discretionary ...
> - a highly discretionary decision of this type is to be reviewed on the standard of patent unreasonableness ...
> - the objective of the relevant provisions of *IRPA* is to soften the sometimes harsh consequences of the strict application of *IRPA* which surfaces in cases where there may be compelling reasons to allow a foreign national to enter or remain in Canada despite inadmissibility or non-compliance with *IRPA*, it allows officers to respond to exceptional circumstances while meeting Canada's social commitments ...
> - Before a TRP is issued, consideration must be given to the fact that TRP's grant their bearer more privileges than do visitor, student or work permits. A TRP bearer becomes a temporary resident after being examined upon entry to Canada, but may also be eligible for health or social services and can apply for a work or student permit from Canada. TRP's thus should be recommended and issued cautiously.[62]

The manual instructs officers to investigate whether the applicant's need to enter or remain in Canada is compelling and sufficient to overcome the health or safety risks to Canadian society. The evaluation should include the following factors: history of non-compliance, credibility, previous removal(s), controversy, and social assistance. IRCC must perform in-depth examinations of all relevant factors presented by applicants to address the relevant needs and risk factors, including best interests of the child.[63] For example, in *Zlydnev v Canada (MCI)*, the Federal Court held that the officer had not addressed relevant factors, which included:

- The applicant's daughter's pending appeal of a sponsorship application;

- The applicant's recognition and explanations for his initial non-compliance;
- Attempts to rectify the non-compliance;
- The applicant's need for support from his family in Canada;
- Establishment in Canada;
- Hardship that the applicant would face in Ukraine; and
- Best interests of his grandchildren and great-grandchildren.[64]

The jurisprudence, however, is divided as the *IRPA* does not make any specific references to BIOC in the TRP analysis, but does when defining H&C applications. Thus, in *Stordock v Canada (MCI)*, the court held:

> [11] In any event, as to this issue, there is simply no requirement in IRPA that an Officer, in considering a Temporary Resident Permit, is required to consider the best interests of a child [....] Even if best interests of a child could somehow come into play in considering "compelling reasons" to grant or extend a Temporary Resident Permit, there simply is little or nothing in the present record that would permit an Officer to do so. As in *Farhat, supra*, it was not unreasonable for the Officer not to consider the best interests of the child.[65]

The language of section 24(1) highlighted above calls for TRPs to be granted if the officer "is of the opinion that it is justified in the circumstance." Caselaw remains divided as to what threshold to use for applications to be justified, with the "compelling reasons" terminology frequently used. *Krasniqi v Canada (MCI)* is an example where this language can result in unreasonable decisions:

> [27] Moreover, the decision-maker's analysis of Ms. Hashani's situation was wholly insufficient and demonstrated a complete lack of appreciation for her circumstances. Although framed in the language of "compelling reasons" (which I have already described as problematic above), Justice Shore wrote in the oft cited decision of *Farhat v. Canada* ... "[b]asically, the TRPs allow officers to respond to exceptional circumstances while meeting Canada's

> *social, humanitarian, and economic commitments* [emphasis added]." In my view, the case at bar potentially engages all three of those criteria, and I believe that a fulsome analysis of those interests may have yielded a different result.[66]

In *Alabi v Canada (MCI)*, the applicant had a previous conviction in the United States for conspiracy to distribute heroin. He entered Canada and applied for status, and requested a TRP so that he could attend his daughter's convocation in the United States. His application was refused, as no evidence of his daughter's convocation was provided, and the officer was not satisfied that his business or the community would suffer if he was removed (the need to enter or remain in Canada). The reviewing court held that even though the applicant did not provide evidence relating to his daughter or his wife of sixteen years, the decision-maker still ought to have been aware of these key factors and considered the same in the assessment:

> [24] Some of the fault for this administrative breakdown belongs to Mr. Alabi as his submissions and evidence are sparse. However, the totality of his application was not sparse given his lengthy background with CIC which was all before what he saw as the decision maker. This is an exceptional circumstance and these findings will be distinguishable because of the distinctiveness of the situation.[67]

The minister must annually report to Parliament the number of TRPs granted, categorized by the grounds of inadmissibility.[68] Consequently, decisions are highly discretionary and often upheld — see *Vaguedano Alvarez v Canada (MCI)*, in which the officer's decision was brief but adequate because it had a "chain of reasoning."[69]

Authorization to Return to Canada (ARC)

Unlike a TRP which is used to overcome inadmissibility for a temporary period, an authorization to return to Canada (ARC) is a remedy available to overcome a removal order permanently. When an individual who has left Canada because of a deportation order (a lifetime ban) or an exclusion order (a one-year or five-year ban) seeks to enter Canada within the period of the ban, they must obtain an ARC.[70] An ARC can be granted for return to Canada as a permanent resident, for a one-time visit, or for occasional entries for a specified purpose (for example, medical treatments, work-related activities) over a prescribed period.

It is important to note that even if an individual receives a pardon for a particular conviction that may have led to a removal order and is therefore no longer inadmissible, they still require an ARC to enter Canada because the removal order has already been enforced and was actionable at the time of issuance. However, individuals who have been issued any removal order on the basis that they are an accompanying family member under section 42(b) of the *IRPA* do not require an ARC. Merely meeting eligibility requirements for the issuance of a visa is not sufficient to grant an ARC.[71] Instead, an individual who applies for an ARC must demonstrate that there are compelling reasons to return to Canada, weighed against the circumstances of the issuance of the removal order. The individual must also demonstrate that they will pose a minimal risk to Canadian society. With reference to the IRCC Manual, *OP 1, Procedures*, when assessing an ARC application, officers routinely consider the following factors:

- the severity of the *IRPA* violation that led to the removal;
- the applicant's history of cooperation with IRCC; and
- the reasons for the applicant's request to return to Canada.

Bona fide marriage, attendance at the funeral of a family member, or acceptance under a provincial nominee program are some examples of "compelling reasons" for returning to Canada. However, no one factor alone would automatically override concerns related to the safety and security of Canada; decisions are made on an individual basis.[72]

Record Suspension — For Convictions Inside Canada

Individuals who were convicted of a criminal offence in Canada and have completed their sentence in full may apply for a record suspension (previously called a "pardon") if eligible.[73] If granted, it does not erase a conviction but sets it aside. Even though not removed, an individual who is granted a record suspension will be admissible to Canada. For an individual who receives a foreign pardon this is not accepted at face value; rather, officers will examine whether the foreign pardon is equivalent to a record suspension in Canada to determine whether the person is admissible. This involves a separate legal test.

When an individual is eligible to apply for a record suspension depends on when they were convicted and the type of offence. If an individual was convicted before 29 June 2010 and up to 12 March 2012 and convicted of a summary offence, they are eligible to apply in three years, and if convicted of an indictable offence, in five years from the completion of the sentence. This is also true for offences committed between 29 June 2010 and 12 March 2012 that involved serious personal injury (for instance, manslaughter), for which the applicant was sentenced to a prison term of two years or more, or an offence referred to in Schedule 1 of the *Criminal Code* of Canada (sexual offences).

Finally, anyone convicted on or after 13 March 2012 must wait ten years for an indictable conviction and five years for a summary conviction. An individual is never eligible if they have been convicted of more than three offences prosecuted by indictment, each with a sentence of two years or more, or an offence referred to in Schedule 1 of the *Criminal Code* of Canada (sexual offences).[74]

Rehabilitation/Deemed Rehabilitation — For Offences and Convictions Outside Canada

Rehabilitation, although not defined in immigration law, looks to whether a person is unlikely to commit new crimes in the future.

Whether a person needs to apply for rehabilitation or is deemed rehabilitated depends on the crime, how long ago it happened, and how the person has behaved since. For convictions/commission of an offence outside Canada that have a maximum prison term of less than ten years (if committed in Canada), a person can apply for rehabilitation five years from the completion of all sentences (payment of all fees, jail time completed, restitution paid, etc.). An individual is deemed rehabilitated if at least ten years have passed from an indictable conviction, again, from the completion of all sentences, which also includes periods of probation.[75]

If convicted for two or more offences outside Canada that, if committed in Canada, would constitute summary convictions, the individual is deemed rehabilitated five years from the day after the completion of the imposed sentence and if there are no other convictions during the five-year period. There are, however, limitations: if the foreign convictions are equivalent to an offence in Canada punishable by a maximum of imprisonment of ten years or more, deemed rehabilitation is not an option.

The Federal Court has repeatedly held the focus of the review of an application for a certificate of criminal rehabilitation is forward-looking and concerns whether someone is unlikely to be involved in any further criminal activity, consistent with the common meaning of "rehabilitation." This requires officers at minimum to "expressly weigh whether the foreign national will likely reoffend." While this has been recognized to be discretionary, "it is insufficient for the delegate simply to balance mitigating and aggravating factors [. . . .] On a rehabilitation application, the delegate must go on to assess what those factors reveal about the person's tendency to commit additional offences." Where this has not been done, such as in *Ramirez Velasco*, a decision is unreasonable.[76]

In *De Campos Gregorio v Canada (MCI)*, the court found it was unreasonable for the officer to simply list a few factors and state a conclusion without any intervening analysis, as the applicant "was entitled to an explanation for the Officer's conclusion that her circumstances did not warrant a finding of criminal rehabilitation [citation omitted]." The jurisprudence firmly establishes, "[r]ehabilitation does not mean that there is no risk of further criminal activity only that the risk is assessed as 'highly unlikely.'"[77]

Procedural Fairness Letter — Defences and Mitigation Plans

If an officer believes an individual may be inadmissible for misrepresentation or excessive demand (medical), the officer is required to send a procedural fairness letter to provide the individual an opportunity to respond and/or provide further documents within a set period, before a final decision is made on the application.[78] In the case of an allegation for having misrepresented, this would involve an explanation for the perceived misrepresentation and a request for the innocent mistake exemption discussed above if applicable.[79]

In the case of medical admissibility, discussed in Chapter 3, the Supreme Court of Canada has ruled that to establish inadmissibility on the ground of causing excessive demand, an individualized assessment is required. The applicant can challenge the medical officer's assessment (for instance, diagnosis, cost estimation) and/or provide a plan to mitigate the costs where possible. In this circumstance, this would involve presenting a response and plan to try to mitigate the anticipated demand for treatment and care in Canada, identifying the likely demands on health and social services, and not mere eligibility for them.

They can also advance both medical and non-medical factors, such as the availability, scarcity, or cost of the identified publicly funded services, along with the willingness and ability of the applicant or their family to pay for the services — where possible.[80] The individual must submit a declaration of ability and intent together with supporting documents demonstrating the plan is reasonable.[81]

Ministerial Relief

Individuals who are inadmissible on the most serious grounds (sections 34, 35, and 37) are excluded and not permitted to make H&C applications or request an H&C exemption. For some, ministerial relief (MR) (also called "a declaration of relief") may be the only option to stay in or enter Canada. Pursuant to section 42.1(1) of the *IRPA*, a foreign national can apply for MR if they have been found to be inadmissible to Canada under section 34 (security), section 35(1)(b) or (c) (human and international rights violations), as well as section 37(1) (organized criminality).[82] However, foreign nationals who are inadmissible to Canada under the *IRPA*, section 35(1)(a) for commission of, or complicity in, genocide, war crimes, or crimes against humanity are precluded from applying for MR. They effectively have no remedy and will be indefinitely banned from Canada. It is important to know that MR is not an alternative form of an H&C review.

The legal test is hugely different. Pursuant to section 42.1(3) of the *IRPA*, the minister may only consider security and public safety as well as Canada's interests over that of the individual. The Supreme Court of Canada explored what is to be considered in *Agraira v Canada (PSEP)*, confirming that it is reasonable for the minister to focus on matters related to national security and public safety, but also examine the other important considerations outlined in the guidelines and any analogous considerations.[83]

MR applications are processed by the ministerial relief unit (MRU) of the Canada Border Services Agency (CBSA). When receiving such applications, CBSA officers review and draft recommendations to the minister of public safety on whether relief should be granted or denied. CBSA's recommendation will be disclosed to the applicant for response prior to it being forwarded to the minister for decision. The final decision is then at the sole discretion of the minister of public safety, and it cannot be delegated to government officials. If the minister is satisfied that the presence of the applicant in Canada would not be detrimental to the national interest, the minister may grant MR, which will eliminate the person's inadmissibility as a barrier to any future immigration applications to IRCC. If granted, the individual must then still meet the requirements of any other immigrant category. An approved MR does not facilitate access, it only removes the inadmissibility.

Given the complexity of the process and the non-delegable decision, the waiting time is very lengthy and unpredictable. In addition, like H&C, the burden of proof to demonstrate that relief is warranted rests entirely with the applicant, and an application for MR does not impact the enforcement of removal orders. Section 42.1 of the Act provides:

> 42.1 (1) The Minister may, on application by a foreign national, declare that the matters referred to in section 34, paragraphs 35(1)(b) and (c) and subsection 37(1) do not constitute inadmissibility in respect of the foreign national if they can satisfy the Minister that it is not contrary to the national interest.
>
> (2) The Minister may, on the Minister's own initiative, declare that the matters referred to in section 34, paragraphs 35(1)(b) and (c) and subsection 37(1) do not constitute inadmissibility in respect of the foreign national if the Minister is satisfied that it is not contrary to the national interest.
>
> (3) In determining whether to make a declaration, the Minister may only take into account national security and public safety considerations, but, in his or her analysis, is not limited to considering the danger that the foreign national presents to the public or the security of Canada.

The sections referred to exclude committing or being complicit in genocide, crimes against humanity, and war crimes (section 35(1)(a)). The *IRPR* further provide that an application for ministerial relief may only be made if a permanent or temporary residence application has been refused or a removal order has been issued because of one of the specified inadmissibilities.[84] Such applications cannot be made until all rights of judicial review against the refusal or removal order have expired or been exhausted.[85]

The burden of proof rests on the applicant to prove that relief is not contrary to the national interest. The CBSA's website recommends addressing the following considerations if applicable:

- Describe circumstances where you used, planned or advocated the use of armed struggle, violence, and/or criminal acts to reach political, religious, social, organizational or personal objectives. Be specific (dates, locations, impact of activities);
- Explain your current perspective toward relying on violent, terrorist, subversive, criminal, and other methods, or tactics to achieve organizational, political, or personal goals;
- Address any circumstances where you were arrested and/or detained and/or jailed, and include dates;
- Address any circumstances where you have been charged with, convicted of, on trial for, or party to a crime or offence, or the subject of any criminal proceedings, in any country;
- You may wish to bring to the Minister's attention any personal factors, or mitigating or extenuating circumstances, related to the national interest that you believe may help to satisfy the Minister that relief is warranted.[86]

The CBSA also advises that due to the complexity of this process, they cannot predict an exact timeline as to when a decision will be rendered. This has led to some issues of its own — for example, in *Thomas v Canada (MPSEP)*, a foreign national convicted of extortion was found inadmissible for organized criminality. He requested ministerial relief, and after not receiving any result in five years, applied for *mandamus* to enforce a timeline. The court allowed the application and issued a writ of *mandamus*, requiring the MRU disclose a decision within 180 days.[87] The applicant also cited several other decisions in which three, four, and five years had been held to be unreasonable delays for ministerial relief.[88]

In cases regarding organized crime, visa officers can consider the degree and willingness of the foreign national's participation. In *Canada (MPSEP) v Gaytan*, a young man who had been pressured to work for the Mexican cartel argued the criminal defence of duress. The Federal Court of Appeal stated:

> [103] [I]n membership claims brought under sections 34 or 37 of the *Act*, where the term "member" is not defined by regulation and where the determination of membership is not governed by presumptions. As a result, for those who can establish that they were unable to exert significant influence on their government despite holding an enumerated position, ministerial relief becomes their only recourse against a finding of inadmissibility....
>
> [111] For all these reasons, I conclude that in determining admissibility under paragraph 37(1)(a) of the *Act*, the Board is entitled to consider whether membership was the result of duress or coercion. I am satisfied that this interpretation of the Board's jurisdiction in such matters not only falls within a range of possible, acceptable outcomes, but is correct.[89]

Immigration and Refugee Board

The Immigration and Refugee Board (IRB), as set out in the definitions section of the *IRPA,* consists of four divisions: the Refugee Protection Division (RPD), Refugee Appeal Division (RAD), Immigration Division (ID), and Immigration Appeal Division (IAD). The RPD hears and decides claims for refugee protection made in Canada, a procedure which requires that a hearing be held and that the person who is the subject of the proceeding and the minister are notified of the hearing.[90] Appeals of these decisions must be filed within fifteen days of receiving the reasons for the decision, and are held by the RAD.

Admissibility Hearing at the Immigration Division

If the minister's delegate decides a section 44 inadmissibility report canvassed in the last chapter is well-founded, but has no authority to issue a removal order, the report will be referred to the ID. A hearing before an ID member is quasi-judicial.[91] The purpose of such a hearing is to determine whether the individual concerned is inadmissible under the law and relevant facts. The burden of proof depends on the status of the individual concerned. For foreign nationals, the onus is on them to prove that they are admissible. For permanent residents, the onus is on the minister to establish they are inadmissible.[92]

The standard of proof again depends on the alleged type of inadmissibility. The default standard of proof is balance of probabilities, meaning the member must believe that it is more likely than not that the person is inadmissible. For the most serious types of inadmissibility (sections 34–37), the standard of proof is lower — reasonable grounds to believe. Further, the ID is not bound by any legal or technical rules of evidence and may receive and base their decision on evidence adduced in the proceedings that it considers credible or trustworthy in the circumstances.[93] The ID also has its own set of rules called the *Immigration Division Rules*,[94] which set out the roles and responsibilities of each party, as well as the procedures and practices to be followed in proceedings before the ID. The *IRPA* mandates that the ID must hold hearings (where practicable) and give notice of the proceeding to the minister and the person who is the subject of the proceeding and hear the matter without delay.

For the proceeding, a hearings officer from the CBSA will attend as the minister's counsel representing the applicant, and the individual concerned can represent themselves or hire counsel as the respondent. The individual may also request an interpreter. During the hearing, one ID member will conduct the hearing, listen to both sides (including witnesses if any), and render a decision. The ID member can deliver their decision and reasons orally at the end of the hearing, and the decision takes effect at the time it is delivered.[95] Although there are times when the decision is made post-hearing. If the decision is in favour of the individual concerned, the ID member dates and signs a notice of decision and provides a copy to both parties.[96] If the decision is not in favour of the individual concerned, apart from dating and signing a notice of decision the member will issue a removal order, providing a copy to both parties. The member must also notify the individual concerned of any right to appeal to the IAD or the right to challenge the decision to the Federal Court by way of filing an application for leave and for judicial review.

Appeal to the Immigration Appeal Division

A permanent resident, a foreign national who holds a permanent resident visa, and protected persons have the right to appeal a removal order issued by the ID, unless they are found inadmissible for the most serious grounds — security, human and international rights violations, serious criminality,[97] and organized criminality. In addition, an individual has no right to appeal if they are inadmissible for misrepresentation, unless the person is the sponsor's spouse, common law partner, or child.[98] Similar to the ID, the IAD has its own set of rules called the *Immigration Appeal Division Rules*[99] that outline each party's roles and responsibilities and govern the practices and procedures of the appeals before the division. They are similarly not bound by any legal or technical rules of evidence and may receive and base a decision on evidence adduced in the proceedings that it considers credible or trustworthy in the circumstances.

New rules were introduced in January 2023, replacing the rules introduced in 2002. The changes were made to modernize the appeal process and help to ensure the IAD resolves appeals effectively and in a timely manner. Unlike the ID, appeals to the IAD often begin through paper-based early resolution avenues and end with a hearing. The onus is on the individual concerned to establish why they should be allowed to remain in or resettle in Canada.

The appeal can be based in law or the IAD can allow an appeal on humanitarian and compassionate (H&C) grounds or in the best interests of a child directly affected even if the underlying decision is valid in law.[100] The appeal is *de novo*, meaning like new and never heard before, so the decision-maker can consider everything afresh. The IAD member conducts an independent analysis and determines whether all the circumstances warrant a grant of special relief. The member will assess the nature of the inadmissibility and the mitigating factors.

To provide an example, when the appeal involves criminal inadmissibility of a permanent resident, the factors in *Ribic-Chieu v Canada (Minister of Employment and Immigration)* are usually considered:

- the seriousness of the offence or offences leading to the removal order;
- the possibility of rehabilitation;
- the degree to which the person is established in Canada;
- the family in Canada and the dislocation to that family that removal would cause;
- the family and community support available for the person; and
- the degree of hardship that would be caused to the person by his return to his country of nationality.[101]

The IAD member will assess each factor independently and give each weight. These factors are non-exhaustive, and the weight to be applied to each factor may vary from case to case.[102]

Appeals of removal orders can be submitted by permanent residents, citizens, foreign nationals with a permanent resident visa, and protected persons to the IAD within thirty days of receipt of the removal order. The minister of the ID must then provide the record within thirty days of a request by the IAD. When a hearing is scheduled at the IAD, a decision will be made to either allow the appeal (removal order will be cancelled and the person will be allowed to remain in Canada) or dismiss the appeal (the person will be removable from Canada at any time). The appeal may also be stayed, in which case the removal is temporarily put on hold and the person will be permitted to remain in Canada under specified conditions until the appeal is reconsidered by the IAD. Removal orders *cannot* be appealed if they were found inadmissible on grounds of serious criminality, organized criminality, security grounds, violations of human or international rights, or claimants whose refugee claim has been rejected.[103]

Family class appeals can be made by Canadian citizens or permanent residents who applied to sponsor their family member. These appeals usually involve sending a completed notice of appeal form and a copy of the refusal letter to the IAD within thirty days of receipt of the refusal letter. One such appeal is *Sivasuntharam v Canada (MCI)*,[104] in which the appellant came to Canada from Sri Lanka and made a successful refugee claim, and later attempted to sponsor his mother as a permanent resident. The sponsorship application was refused due to non-compliance (the appellant was requested to but never sent his personal information form (PIF)), but the refusal letter made mention of both the missing PIF letter and missing police clearance certificates, which had in fact been provided. The panel member for the IAD found that the refusal for non-compliance was valid but allowed the appeal on H&C grounds. The member noted that although family reunification is usually not sufficient by itself to allow an appeal, the positive considerations combined with the minister's submissions supported that family reunification was a strongly positive factor, while the only negative factor was the non-compliance, and the appellant had tried to comply in time.[105]

Residency appeals are appeals of decisions made under section 28 of the *IRPA*, which establishes certain residency obligations on permanent residents. Over any given five-year period and subject to the *IRPR*, permanent residents must spend 730 days physically present in Canada; outside Canada accompanying their Canadian spouse, common law partner, or parent; outside Canada employed full-time by a Canadian business; or outside Canada accompanying a permanent resident who is their spouse, common law partner, or parent and who is employed full-time by a Canadian business. Permanent residents who are found to have breached this obligation risk losing their permanent resident status but can appeal such a decision to the IAD.

The use of the word "accompanying" was considered in *Smith v Canada (MCI)*,[106] in which the appellant, a German-born foreign national who had lived in the United States since she was a young child, was in a common law relationship with a Canadian citizen, and for most of the five-year period had lived together in the appellant's home in the United States. The panel member found that "accompanying" means "to go with," and consequently she was not accompanying her partner in the United States — rather, he was accompanying her. The panel nonetheless set the decision aside considering H&C grounds, seeing "no legitimate reason to visit hardship on the appellant and her husband by forcing the couple to go back to the beginning and pursue a sponsorship application."[107] Similarly in *Juarez v Canada (MCI)*,[108] the applicants — a brother and sister who had been sponsored by their father, returned to El Salvador with their mother and were unable to return due to their mother losing their records of landing — were found to be in breach of their residency obligation, but their circumstances warranted special H&C relief.

Judicial Reviews

Federal Court

Section 96 of the *Constitution Act, 1867* provides the courts with supervisory jurisdiction over administrative decision-makers, which includes the bodies referred to in section 4.5, above. If the removal order is upheld by the IAD, for example, the inadmissible person still has three potential routes of appeal: the Federal Court, the Federal Court of Appeal, and the Supreme Court of Canada. The latter two are rare. Courts may review the decision and intervene where the decision was based on a reviewable error or breached principles of fundamental justice. As judicial reviews are highly discretionary, there is no right of appeal or mandate that the courts must hear the review. Inadmissible applicants must apply for leave to judicial review, but there is no guarantee that they will be granted the leave.

The Federal Court has authority over all cases in which relief is claimed against the Crown, including the minister of citizenship and immigration.[109] It can hear and determine matters including questions of law, fact, or mixed law and fact.[110] When a case has been refused at the IRB, anyone who has been directly affected by the matter can bring an application for judicial review to the Federal Court.[111] Many of the cases referred to throughout this chapter were taken to the Federal Court, with the result that the visa officer's or IAD member's decision was upheld or overturned. If overturned, the Federal Court typically returns the matter to a new officer for redetermination and may require that the new decision be rendered within a certain time.

An individual with any immigration matter who receives a decision, determination or order made, a measure taken, or a question raised can seek a judicial review before the Federal Court, provided that the individual has exhausted any right of appeal under the *IRPA*.[112] For example, a foreign national who has applied for a visitor visa outside Canada can challenge the refusal directly to the Federal Court by applying for leave for judicial review as there is no other avenue in which to challenge a temporary application decision. If an individual has a right of appeal to the IAD this must first be exercised, although an individual whose appeal to the IAD was refused can then challenge the IAD's decision through judicial review. It is a two-stage process: first, the application for leave, and second, if leave is granted, the judicial review.[113]

It is important to mention that there are limits with respect to judicial review. First, unlike the IAD, it is not a hearing *de novo*. This means that the court is generally limited to review the case as it was before the decision-maker and can rarely consider new evidence. Further, in a judicial review, the court is only empowered to assess whether there was a breach of procedural fairness by the decision-maker and if the decision is reasonable. If the court decides that there was a breach of procedural fairness and/or the decision was unreasonable, this, however, does not lead to an approval of the application itself, rather, the refusal will usually be set aside and then sent back to the same office, although to a different decision-maker/officer for redetermination. Justice Grammond in the recent decision of *Villanueva v Canada (MCI)* addressed the scope of judicial review:

> [15] The role of the reviewing Court is not to step into the shoes of the decision-maker, to reweigh the evidence or to exercise the discretionary power entrusted to the decision-maker. Rather, the Court's role is to ensure that the decision is justified, transparent and intelligible and that it complies with the factual and legal constraints bearing on the decisionmaker: *Canada (Minister of Citizenship and Immigration) v Vavilov,* 2019 SCC 65 at paragraph 99, [2019] 4 SCR 653 [Vavilov]. It is also to ensure that the decision was made pursuant to a fair process.[114]

Federal Court of Appeal

Immigration decisions by the Federal Court can be further challenged by appealing to the Federal Court of Appeal. This court's basic role is to ensure that federal law is interpreted and applied consistently throughout Canada by the federal government, to supervise the legality of the decisions of federal decision-makers, and to provide a national appellate forum over the Federal Court as well as certain other courts and decision-makers.[115] It acts as a reviewing or appellate court over all administrative decision-makers exercising powers granted pursuant to a federal law, and ensures that the federal government and its agents act within the bounds of the law.

There is no direct right of appeal except in extremely limited circumstances. Certified questions are required by the *IRPA*, which states that appeals may be made to the Federal Court of Appeal only if, in rendering the judgment, the Federal Court judge certifies that a serious question of general importance is involved and states the question.[116] The exception to this rule is that the minister may, if a decision made in a judicial review requires the disclosure of information or other evidence, appeal if in the minister's opinion the disclosure would be injurious to national security or endanger the safety of any person.[117] The test for certifying a question was stated in *Torre v Canada (MCI)*:

> [3] Under subsection 74(d) of *IRPA* only a serious question of general importance may be certified and thus open the possibility of an appeal from a judgment following an application for judicial review. This requirement has been interpreted by the Court several times, and the law is now well settled: to be certified, a question must be dispositive of the appeal and transcend the interests of the immediate parties to the litigation due to its broad significance. In other words, a certified question is not to be a reference of a question to this Court, and a certified question must have been raised and decided by the court below and have an impact on the result of the litigation.[118]

In the context of inadmissibility, some questions that have been certified as being of general importance include: does an inadmissibility hearing engage section 7 of the *Canadian Charter of Rights and Freedoms* (*Charter*) right to liberty and security of the person by the certain uprooting of the applicant from Canada? (no: *Revell v Canada (MCI)*[119]); where a foreign national has been determined inadmissible pursuant to section 34, 35, or 37, and there has been subsequent changes to the interpretation of that ground of inadmissibility, is the foreign national still barred from making an H&C application? (yes: *Subramaniam v Canada (MCI)*[120]); and where the officer believes an applicant is inadmissible pursuant to section 35(1)(a) for crimes against humanity, must the officer specify the offence that they have reasonable grounds to believe the applicant has committed (certified in *Andeel v Canada (MCI)*[121] but not appealed)?

In cases of appeals from the Federal Court, the Court of Appeal has the power to dismiss the appeal or give the judgment that the Federal Court should have made, order a new trial, or make a declaration as to the conclusions that the Federal Court should have reached on the issues and refer the matter back for a continuance of the trial on the issues that remain to be decided.[122] Several challenges to inadmissibility which have been decided by the Federal Court of Appeal have been referred to above, including *Hawthorne*,[123] which stated there is a presumption that the child's best interests, absent exceptional circumstances, will play in favour of non-removal of the parent. Some prominent decisions by the Federal Court of Appeal in other areas of immigration law include *Singh v Canada (MCI)*,[124] which found that the RAD's interpretation of an *IRPA* subsection should be properly reviewed on a standard of reasonableness; *Canada (MCI) v Galindo Camayo*,[125] which found that it is reasonable for the RPD to rely upon evidence that a refugee took measures to protect themselves against their agent of persecution to rebut the presumption that a refugee who acquires a passport issued by their country of origin has intended to avail themselves of that state's protection; and *Brown v Canada (MCI)*,[126] which found that the *Charter* does not impose a requirement on the period of time for detention for immigration purposes.

Supreme Court of Canada

The Supreme Court of Canada is the highest court in Canada, and as the final court of appeal is the last judicial resort. Due to the high legal costs related to challenging decisions to this highest level, immigration decisions by the Supreme Court are rare. In addition, the Supreme Court decides legal issues of public importance, and leave to appeal is usually only given if the case involves a question of public importance or raises an important issue of law (or law and fact).

Consequently, the rare immigration case that does make it all the way to the Supreme Court will also include some other issue of public importance — for example in *Baker v Canada (MCI)*,[127] the Court decided that failure to provide reasons was a violation of procedural fairness, and in *Canada (MCI) v Vavilov*,[128] the Court framed the standard of review, affecting all administrative law. *Kanthasamy* is an example of the rare immigration case that was challenged to the Supreme Court without an accompanying administrative issue.[129]

Supreme Court cases involving inadmissibility are few and far between, but include cases such as *B010 v Canada (MCI)*, in which the applicant and his family challenged the finding of inadmissibility for serious criminality due to organized criminal human smuggling.[130] The Supreme Court allowed the appeal, finding that the IRB had erred in concluding that a migrant aiding in the illegal entry of other refugees or asylum-seekers qualified as "people smuggling" under section 37(1)(b) of the *IRPA*, and that such a finding ran contrary to the intentions of Parliament.[131]

Conclusion

Inadmissibility can therefore be exempted or challenged in many ways with measures of last resort in our courts. The World Justice Program, which ranks judicial systems based on publicized laws and government data, right to information, civic participation, and complaint mechanisms, ranks Canada as having the seventh best judicial system in the world, and the best in North America.[132] It also ranked as the second best among common law countries, behind only New Zealand (ranked second globally). It cannot be understated the critical role these remedies play in the effective delivery of the Canadian immigration program.

In particular, despite the deference to most immigration decisions, the IRB and the courts have been critical in shaping the law and identifying deficiencies in the decision making. Tribunals and courts continue to investigate the possibilities of further streamlining the process, making it easier for self-represented applicants, modernizing and continuing a long-standing tradition of world-class adjudication.

CHAPTER FIVE

The Future of Canadian Immigration Delivery

If you change the way you look at things, the things you look at change.[1]

Introduction

The hope in developing a national immigration program for the future is to avoid falling into reactive, disjointed tinkering. The opportunities arising with emerging technologies like artificial intelligence (AI), and by understanding our lived experiences of the past and by expanding broad based consultation, we can proactively build our immigration program economically and culturally. We can do away with any lingering remnants of tired myopic compartmentalization of "preferred" immigrant applicants and categories. It is a time, in my view, to be bold.

In 2015, following the election of a new majority Liberal government, the Right Honourable Prime Minister Justin Trudeau's mandate letter to then minister of immigration, the Honourable John McCallum, directed several serious changes to immigration delivery.[2] Call it rebranded, repositioned, and renamed, we welcomed Immigration, Refugees and Citizenship Canada, and said goodbye publicly to Citizenship and Immigration Canada.

Minister McCallum spoke to the new government's first Annual Report to Parliament on Immigration, saying, "It outlines a significant shift in immigration policy toward reuniting more families, building our economy and upholding Canada's humanitarian tradition to resettle refugees and offer protection to those in need."[3] The numbers of accepted immigrants would significantly increase.[4] Prior to this, in the mid-2000s, Canada's immigration system was ostensibly broken and stifled by lengthy processing queues, inflexible core programs, and overly bureaucratic measures that led to backlogs of nearly a million people.[5] The aging population, expected to double to 9.3 million by 2030, posed real challenges to Canada's long-term stability as the Old Age Security system was predicted at the time to increase from $36.5 billion in 2010 to more than double at $108 billion by 2030.[6] That was then.

Fast forward to 2023: Immigration, Refugees and Citizenship Canada (IRCC) processing backlog totals to more than two million applications.[7] This backlog reflects many factors, including underfunding, uneven modernization, the practice of establishing annual quotas, the recent COVID-19 pandemic, and the underlying policy choices that drive those quotas. So if the program was broken before it must be shattered now. Imagery aside, the challenges are acute.

IRCC announced that "immigration accounts for almost 100% of Canada's labour force growth, and, by 2032, it's projected to account for 100% of Canada's population growth,"[8] emphasizing just how dependent Canada's economic recovery is on immigration, and by extension, arguably the future of Canada as well.[9] Yet the problems of nearly twenty years ago have seemingly doubled. Given the enormity and complexity of the challenge, meaningful change to the Canadian immigration system will require years of multi-stakeholder consultation and coordination. There will also need to be technological, cultural, and philosophical transformation in immigration policy and delivery.

In the 2022 federal budget, the federal government allocated $2.1 billion over five years and $317.6 million in ongoing funding to assist IRCC in the processing of permanent resident applications to

Canada.[10] They have also committed $385.7 million over five years and $86.5 million in ongoing funding to assist IRCC and other stakeholders in processing temporary migrant applications.[11] While substantial funding is an important step, the challenge is building a new system on a tenuous foundation, with visa offices overwhelmed due to massive numbers of applications. Absent transformative change, the backlog numbers will continue to soar. Holistic measures will be required to support the effort to reform and reimagine an exciting and innovative new Canadian immigration program delivery model for the future.

How do we get there?

I begin by looking at recent trends.

Canadian Demographics

According to the 2021 census, 52.3 percent of respondents identified having European origins, and 52.3 percent identified with a sect of Christianity.[12] Beyond these two demographic elements, Canada offers extensive cultural and religious diversity. To begin, Canada is home to more than 450 different ethnic groups and cultural origins, according to the 2021 census evidenced in Figure 5.1, on the next page.[13]

Aside from the cultural diversity noted above, 2.2 million people reported as having Indigenous ancestry, accounting for 6.1 percent of the population:[14]

> Of these, 1.4 million people reported at least one of 104 First Nations (North American Indian) ancestries, more than half a million (560,000) reported "Métis" ancestry, and 82,000 people reported "Inuit" ancestry. The most common First Nations ancestries reported were "Cree" (250,000 people), "Mi'kmaq" (122,000), "Ojibway" (92,000) and "Algonquin" (56,000). In addition, about 632,000 people reported "First Nations (North American Indian)" ancestry without any additional clarification."[15]

In terms of religious and spiritual identification, a significant portion of the population, about 19.3 million people, reported as

FIGURE 5.1. MOST COMMON ETHNIC OR CULTURAL ORIGINS REPORTED BY THE POPULATION, CANADA, 2021

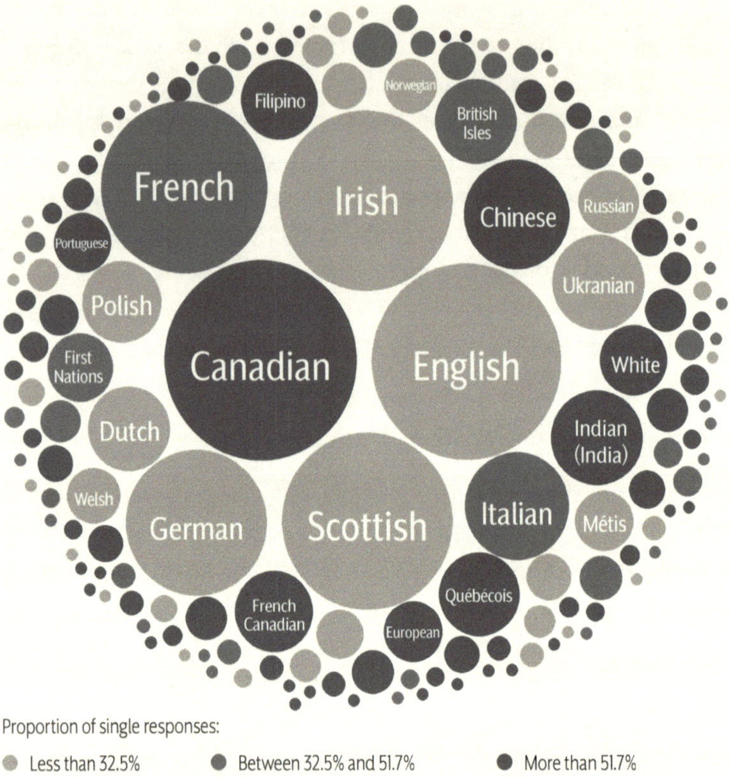

Note(s): The size of the bubble is in proportion to the number of total responses for a given ethnic or cultural origin. The colour of the bubble represents the proportion of single responses for a given ethnic or cultural origin group.
Source(s): Census of Population, 2021 (3901)

belonging to a sect of Christianity.[16] However, this percentage is down from 67.3 percent in 2011 and 77.1 percent in 2001,[17] partly due to the increase in the number of people who do not claim to be a member of any religious group "rising from 16.5 percent in 2001 to 23.9 percent in 2011 and to 34.6 percent in 2021."[18] In addition, the number of adherents to Islam, Hinduism, and Sikhism are increasing. Over the last twenty years the Muslim population has more than doubled, increasing from 2.0 percent in 2001 to 4.9 percent in 2021. Meanwhile, the portion of the population that identifies with Hinduism has grown to 830,000 people, or 2.3 percent of the total population, from the 1.0 percent that claimed this affiliation in 2001. Lastly, the presence of Sikhism has also steadily increased over the last twenty years, so that this community represented 2.1 percent of the total population in 2021. These data are reflected in Figure 5.2, below, drawn from the 2021 Canadian census.[19]

FIGURE 5.2. THE CANADIAN CENSUS

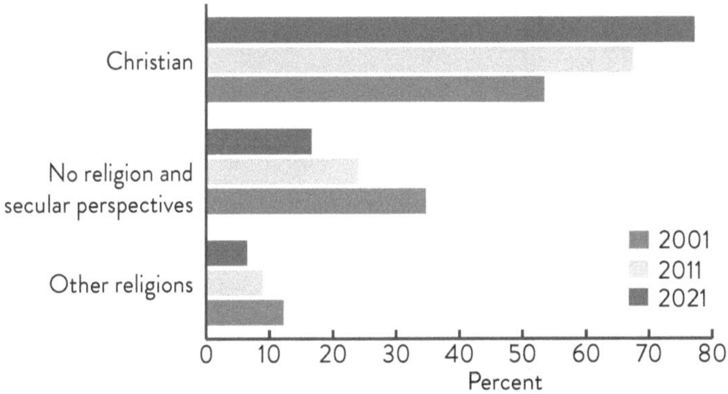

In terms of Canada's ethnic and cultural composition, a similarity is apparent. According to the 2021 census, a quarter of Canadians belong to a racialized group; that is, membership in the South Asian, Chinese, Black, Filipino, Arab, Latin American, Southeast Asian, West Asian, Korean, and/or Japanese communities.[20] Of these, the "South [Asian] (2.6 million people; 7.1 percent), Chinese (1.7 million; 4.7 percent) and Black [communities] (1.5 million; 4.3 percent)," represent 13.6 percent of Canada's total population.[21]

In all, immigrants represent a significant portion of the Canadian population. Between 2016 and 2021, for example, 1.3 million newcomers had settled in Canada, so that in 2021, a quarter of the population represented in the census were either landed immigrants or permanent residents — more than any other G7 state.[22] See Appendix 2 regarding population growth rates.[23]

Over the past fifty years,[24] the diversity across immigrants has increased as a response to Canadian needs and global conditions.

According to a recent Statistics Canada census, immigration continues to focus on three main objectives, that is, "to enhance and promote economic development, to reunite families, and to fulfill the country's international obligations and uphold its humanitarian tradition."[25] In 2022, Canada accepted more than 50 percent of immigrants to enhance and promote economic development through federal and provincial economic immigration streams.[26] Similarly, in contrast to Canada's immigration demographics a century ago, Asia is now the top source of immigrants coming to Canada, with Africa following closely behind. Approximately every one in five recent immigrants to Canada is from India.

"As a sociological fact, multiculturalism refers to the presence of people from diverse racial and ethnic backgrounds."[27] Importantly, the Council on Foreign Relations explains that Canadian multiculturalism is the result of "legislation in the 1960s and 1970s [that] laid the groundwork for Canada's current immigration regime"[28] canvassed in Chapter 1. According to the 2021 census, labour force participation — the proportion of people aged fifteen years of age and older who are employed or unemployed — has decreased from 65.2 percent to 63.7 percent between 2016 and 2021, as the baby boomer generation enters retirement.[29] Statistics Canada highlights that

> the overall labour force participation rate has fallen at each census since 2006, driven by the aging of the baby boom generation. This trend continued from 2016 to 2021, with more than 1.4 million (+13.7 percent) Canadians [turning] 55 [or] older. Although the participation rates of each five-year age group from 55 to 74 increased from 2016 to 2021, they remained substantially lower than the rates of those aged 25 to 54 and were not sufficient to offset the downward pressure on labour supply resulting from population aging.[30]

Statistics Canada goes on to explain that

> a record number of working-age Canadians (21.8 percent) are close to retirement, aged 55 to 64. This means proportionally

> fewer people working, and this can have broader implications for Canadian living standards. Given the importance of demographic [variations] to economic growth, there will be continued focus on the extent to which immigration can mitigate the effects of population aging.[31]

Indeed, current demographic projections predict that by 2043, 23.1 percent of the population will be sixty-five years of age and older, and 25.6 percent in 2068.[32] Statistics Canada warns that "the aging of the population very much remains a reality, and thus seems to be unavoidable over the next 50 years."[33] If Canada's population increases, "it will be mainly because of immigration, which is expected to remain quite significant in the coming decades."[34]

Future Immigration Levels Plans

The Immigration Levels Plan is the means through which Canada aims to respond in part to its demographic vulnerabilities. The plan's promise of long-term benefits rests on its "support [for] short-term economic growth and addressing labour market needs, [as well as ensuring] a well-managed system that maintains public confidence within a well-managed immigration system."[35] The 2023–2025 Immigration Levels Plan will play an important role; see Figure 5.3, below.[36]

FIGURE 5.3. 2023–2025 IMMIGRATION LEVELS PLAN

Projected admissions	2023		2024		2025	
Targets	465,000		485,000		500,000	
Ranges	Low	High	Low	High	Low	High
Economic immigration*	233,000	277,250	250,000	305,000	265,000	326,000
Family reunification	100,000	118,000	105,000	130,000	107,000	135,000
Refugees, protected persons, H&C, and other	77,000	109,750	75,000	107,500	70,500	89,000
TOTAL**	**410,000**	**505,000**	**430,000**	**542,500**	**442,500**	**550,000**

* Under the Canada-Quebec Accord, Quebec has full responsibility for the selection of immigrants destined to Quebec, with the exception of the family class and protected persons.

** For a detailed program breakdown, please see the 2023–25 supplementary table on the Department's website.

The Honourable Sean Fraser, the minister of immigration, refugees and citizenship in 2023, explained that the "immigration levels plan will help businesses find the workers they need, set Canada on a path that will contribute to our long-term success, and allow us to make good on key commitments to vulnerable people fleeing violence, war and persecution."[37] Statistics Canada predicts that, if the intentions of Immigration Levels Plans are realized, by 2041 "half of the population will be comprised of recent immigrants and their Canadian-born children."[38]

Statistics Canada estimates that

> the Canadian population would reach 47.7 million in 2041, and 25.0 million of them would be immigrants or children of immigrants born in Canada, accounting for 52.4% of the total population. In 2016, this population was 14.4 million and accounted for 40.0% of the total Canadian population.[39]

What's more, Statistics Canada expects that by 2041, one in four Canadians will have been born in either Asia or Africa, accounting for "9.9 million to 13.9 million . . . , depending on the projection scenario. [This group] alone could account for 23.1% to 26.9% of the total Canadian population in 2041, up from 13.5% in 2016."[40]

Statistics Canada also expects that by 2041 two in five Canadians will belong to a visible minority group:

> In 2016, it consisted of 8.0 million people. By 2041, the racialized population could reach 16.4 million to 22.3 million people depending on the projection scenario. The racialized population could therefore account for 38.2% to 43.0% of the Canadian population. In 2016, this proportion was 22.2%.[41]

Source Countries and International Competition for Immigrants

While previous years have been marked by discussions of the importance of globalization and the growing movement of people,

2020 saw the most dramatic restriction to cross-border travel in most of our lifetimes because of the COVID-19 pandemic. Families were separated, students moved online, and economic migrants were unable to enter the country to begin contributing to the economy. However, by the end of 2022, Canada had not only broken its previously held immigration records two years in a row, but it also announced plans to accept 1.45 million permanent residents over the next three years, with over 60 percent of new permanent residents belonging to the economic stream.[42] Indeed, the coronavirus pandemic highlighted the need for immigrant labour and skill, which will only increase as more countries, and Canada is no exception, manufacture, create, innovate, and supply within its borders.

The various types of immigrants that have entered Canada and will continue to make Canada their home has a strong correlation to IRCC's organizational goals. In support of implementing these goals, at the end of 2022 IRCC announced that over the next few years there will be "increases in regional programs to address targeted local labour market needs, through the Provincial Nominee Program, the Atlantic Immigration Program, and the Rural and Northern Immigration Pilot."[43] Given that 100 percent of Canada's labour force growth is due to immigration,[44] economic recovery is a priority, and the aging population is a big concern for Canadian policymakers, so at least 60 percent of those immigrating here in the next couple of years will need to meet strict criterion. To remain consistent in the application of this criterion, IRCC has been using a comprehensive ranking system (CRS) to evaluate the eligibility of immigrants in the economic streams for almost a decade, which has proven to be an uneven tool for federal and provincial economic immigration programs. The focus on points and direct needs in the economy are often disconnected. The CRS needs to be better aligned with employer needs.

Over the past few years, candidates from Asia had the highest percentage of permanent residency admissions and took a lead in the economic permanent residency stream admissions as well. Currently, just under 50 percent of the immigrant population in Canada was born in Asia.[45] "India and China have [already] surpassed the

United Kingdom as the country of birth most frequently reported by foreign-born people,"[46] becoming the first two countries to do so since Confederation. In 2021, India became the top source country in Canadian immigration as it took "the top spot as the primary place of birth of new immigrants to Canada (18.6% of recent immigrants from 2016 to 2021)."[47] In 2022, the top source countries[48] for permanent residency streams were:

- India — 27 percent
- China — 7.2 percent
- Afghanistan — 5.4 percent
- Nigeria —5.05 percent
- Philippines — 5.04 percent
- France — 3.2 percent
- Pakistan — 2.6 percent
- Iran — 2.5 percent
- United States of America — 2.3 percent
- Syria —1.9 percent

In November 2022, Global Affairs Canada announced that it will be launching a new Indo-Pacific strategy. Part of that strategy is providing "$74.6 million to enhance Canada's visa processing capacity within Canada's centralized network as well as in New Delhi, Chandigarh, Islamabad, and Manila to support stronger peoples-to-people ties."[49] It is expected that India will continue to be the top source country for Canada in the years to come. Statistics Canada projections show that by 2036, Asian-born immigrants could represent between 55.7 percent and 57.9 percent of all immigrants. While initial sourcing of immigrants may not be an issue, a recent study found that almost 30 percent of newcomers below the age of thirty-five years and 23 percent of university educated new immigrants will likely relocate within the next two years[50] to regions outside of Canada due to the cost of living and recognition of credentials/job opportunities. Given the extremely low fertility rates and an aging population, attracting immigrants to Canada to replenish our population will remain a top priority. Again, more transformative change is required in approach and implementation.

Attracting Immigrants to Canada

Immigration is generally encouraged by the hope of achieving something better. In Canada, for example, recent immigrants have cited the possibility of obtaining a better quality of life as the primary incentive for their settlement in Canada, followed by the possibility of improving their family's prospects.[51] Not an uncommon want.[52] Canada's international allure, therefore, stems from the quality of life offered within its borders. Though a fairly broad sociological term, *quality of life* refers to "the wealth and comfort of individuals based on both material and non-material factors that are important to people's lives, such as health, social connections and material comfort."[53] For example, immediately following the COVID-19 pandemic, the Department of Finance released a report in which it explained that

> [which] matters most to Canadians is not always easily measured or described in economic or financial terms. In addition to the health and safety of Canadians, the crisis has drawn attention to a range of quality of life issues such as mental health, family violence, access to green space, social connections, job security, access to childcare and the quality of long-term care. The pandemic has also highlighted longstanding inequalities, low-paid essential work, gender imbalances in caregiving responsibilities, and gaps in Canada's social safety net.[54]

The *quality of life index* is a much stronger measure beyond standard economic statistics that have seemingly failed "to provide a full picture of societal progress."[55] This has prompted governments around the world to pay increased attention to other metrics that matter to peoples' quality of life, including greater equality and environmental protection, alongside traditional measures of economic performance. Monitoring and reporting on a broader set of measurements aims to better ensure that government actions are coordinated and that decisions are evidence-based, with investments focused on areas that have the greatest impact on Canadians' quality of life. It would also improve policy coherence, transparency, and accountability with respect to government priorities, objectives, and results.[56]

FIGURE 5.4 OECD BETTER LIFE INDEX[57]

	Total	Economic	Family	Refugees
			%	
All reasons cited				
Quality of life better in Canada	55.4	58.4	48.6	54.7
Improve future for family	38.5	42.7	27.3	43.3
Be close to family & friends	31.0	19.1	58.5	30.4
Peace/absence of war	29.6	31.1	20.8	53.5
Access to education	23.4	26.9	13.6	31.6
Canada's social system	17.7	18.5	15.6	18.7
Political or religious freedom	15.8	16.7	11.1	28.5
Job opportunities	15.7	16.4	12.6	20.7
Cultural aspects	15.2	17.1	11.2	13.6
Working conditions	9.9	10.4	8.1	12.6
Salary/pay	7.7	7.7	6.7	10.7
Business climate/free market	3.7	4.4	2.3	3.2e
Other	4.9	6.0	2.6	3.5e
Main reason cited, figures rounded				
Quality of life better in Canada	31.8	35.8	25.3	20.2
Be close to family & friends	20.2	9.8	46.3	12.9
Improve future for family	17.5	20.5	10.2	17.7
Peace/absence of war	8.7	8.1	5.3	29.8
Access to education	5.9	7.1	2.7	6.6
Job opportunities	3.1	3.5	2.4	2.2e
Cultural aspects	2.7	3.3	1.5e	1.9e
Canada's social system	2.7	2.8	2.6	1.3e
Political or religious freedom	1.8	2.1	0.6e	3.9e
Working conditions	0.5e	0.7e	x	x
Business climate/free market	0.3e	0.5e	x	x
Salary/pay	0.3e	0.3e	x	x
Other	4.6	5.6	2.6	3.4e
Total	**100**	**100**	**100**	**100**

According to the Organisation for Economic Co-operation and Development's (OECD) Better Life Index, "Canada performs well in many dimensions of well-being relative to other countries in the Better Life Index. Canada outperforms the average in income, jobs, education, health, environmental quality, social connections and life satisfaction."[58] Undoubtedly, Canada has plenty to offer. Indeed, a recent sociological study on life satisfaction among recent immigrants to Canada revealed just how much. The study aimed at understanding the extent to which those who had immigrated to states with better economic and social conditions, specifically for the purpose of improving one's quality of life, experienced "higher levels of life satisfaction than people in their source country, and levels similar to those of the native-born population in the host country."[59]

Remarkably, the study found that "most immigrant groups in Canada reported higher levels of life satisfaction than people in their country of origin, with the magnitude of this difference largest among those who came from countries with lower levels of economic and social development."[60] This finding persists when the sample is extended to include immigrants residing in Canada for up to twenty years. The results also indicate that immigrants who emigrated from countries with low levels of economic development show larger differences in life satisfaction relative to their source country counterparts than immigrants from nations with higher levels of economic development. That is, the higher life satisfaction of immigrants who come to Canada from poorer nations is explained by their source country's low average life satisfaction, which is, in part, determined by its level of economic development.[61]

The results of this study signal that improvements in national conditions are important to immigrants' life satisfaction. "Immigrant groups largely exhibit higher life satisfaction scores than their source-country populations and the majority of immigrant groups do not differ significantly from the Canadian-born in average life satisfaction."[62] Therefore, the means to attracting more immigrants moving forward is through Canada's high quality of life, enabled through the maintenance of the current economic standard. Yet given the sheer number of migrants Canada needs moving forward and the expanding and persistent backlog, how does Canada — and more specifically, how does our immigration law and policy — evolve to meet these novel and exigent necessities? In short, how do we get there and what is the future of Canadian processing?

The Future of Canadian Immigration Processing

Development of New Organizational Culture and Behavioural Training

Amongst the greatest challenges facing IRCC, despite many laudable efforts to modernize immigration delivery that must be acknowledged, are the lack of transparency and accessibility. The inability for individuals to communicate in a timely manner with IRCC results in many delays, litigation, and repeat or incorrectly filed applications, to list a few, that overwhelms the system. The immigration call centre has limited utility, and uneven processing times plague the process. IRCC's on-the-ground working relationship with authorized representatives, which should expedite the process, is often distant at best. A philosophical shift is sorely needed and begins with training. The necessity for additional training was confirmed in a study by Deloitte, where it was determined that there is an opportunity within government departments to increase efficiency by improving organizational culture and behaviour.[63] Deloitte suggests that IRCC should shift to an outcome-driven approach with an emphasis on training, high-level decision-making, and motivation. Leveraging technology (see below) and a seismic shift to facilitation, transparency, and communication would be ground-breaking and support this transition in culture and practice.

Other countries have deemed it necessary to reformulate training of immigration officers. One successful example comes from Australia many years ago with the 2006 introduction of the College of Immigration.[64] The college focused on standardized training for their immigration officers and allowed for specialized training.[65]

Through these methods, the college attempted to increase efficiency in application processing and reduce the number of processing errors made. The development of the college was based on a review of training models established by other government agencies in partnership with educational institutions and employers.[66] Training for IRCC officers should draw on the Australian example, if not necessarily a college but the implementation of comprehensive and wide-ranging training. The opening of the college highlighted a new approach to training with improved quality standards and a renewed focus on facilitation, diversity, inclusion, and transparency. IRCC must follow, as the gains would be dramatic.

Leveraging New Technology

Substantial time and resources are wasted by applicants, IRCC, and even Members of Parliament seeking simple updates on applicant files. In our brief on the *Canadian International Student Program*[67] before the House of Commons Standing Committee on Citizenship and Immigration, I spoke to the need for real-time access to notes on file. This would include information on the stage of processing, place of processing, and/or reasons for refusal. Access would also allow for concerns to be identified earlier, help preserve the individualization of the process, and act as a second set of eyes for IRCC by those equally interested in the process and the outcome — the applicants IRCC serves. This will in turn support faster processing in certain cases, as any issues can be quickly identified and addressed in real time.

A focus should additionally be placed on establishing online informational sessions and/or interviews rather than solely relying on one-way electronic-based communication. This would offer a quick and efficient way to resolve issues for multiple routine processing matters or areas of confusion that otherwise bottleneck the progress of a file. It would also reintroduce desperately needed two-way touch points on files that humanize the process, deescalate conflicts, and improve transparency and accessibility. The technology allows us expansive possibilities.

Finally, and in support of an effort to leverage technology, it should be highlighted that IRCC has access to enormous volumes of data on processing streams, including processing times per type of stream, number of applicants, efficiency of various visa offices, and so on. This presents IRCC with an opportunity to gain insight into how visa offices process applications from when they are received until a decision is made and standardize global processing. This information can be leveraged to determine how best to approach processing moving forward in a universal manner.[68]

Responsible Implementation of Artificial Intelligence (AI) and Other Technology

With the proper safeguards in place, AI and other technology could be revolutionary. IRCC is currently using AI to pre-screen applications at a far faster rate. While the algorithm pre-screens, officers work on processing screened applications. The use of AI can be expanded to support data collection, the management of multiple application categories, and the production and enforcement of caps and queues (see below). The possibilities are indeed exciting, though we have witnessed AI exacerbate the racial, socio-economic, and political divides and discrimination so entrenched in our society. Damaging though these outcomes may be, "they are not inevitable."[69]

Automated systems are responsible for incredible advancements in several different sectors, from agriculture to zoology. "These tools hold the potential to redefine every part of our society and make life better for everyone."[70] It is important that these developments do not enable a deterioration of democratic values or civil liberties. Thus, the law must keep pace, and it is key that any legislation of AI encompass both the government and private sphere.

One can hardly fathom what the jurisprudential evolution and its critically devalued impact on every sector of society would have been had the *Canadian Bill of Rights* and then the *Canadian Charter of Rights and Freedoms* applied only to private entities. So, it is laudable the Ministry of Innovation, Science and Economic Development

Canada (ISED) is taking an important first step in attempting to legislate the digitization of delivery, information collection, data storage, document management, and the expanding use of "artificial intelligence solutions" with Bill C-27: *An Act to enact the Consumer Privacy Protection Act, the Personal Information and Data Protection Tribunal Act and the Artificial Intelligence and Data Act and to make consequential and related amendments to other Acts*,[71] but it is nowhere near enough; we need a Canadian AI Charter of Digital Rights and Freedoms.

EXPANDING AI POSSIBILITIES

The use of AI globally explodes each year. This has not abated during the COVID-19 pandemic; in fact, AI has reportedly been crucial in addressing the pandemic[72] in many ways, including the development of the vaccines,[73] biomedical research, and AI-driven diagnostic X-rays.[74] Montreal is now a major global hub for AI research, and its AI ecosystem is thriving.[75] In Estonia, "robot judges" are used in small claims court where disputes are for values of less than €7,000.[76] Digital courts with non-human judges have been implemented in China.[77] In an article entitled "Towards Standardization of Data Licenses: The Montreal Data License," data was referenced as the new oil.[78] The emergence of ChatGPT and Dall-E has dramatically raised the profile for AI uses seemingly overnight. Universities, as one example, are beginning to revamp how they teach.[79]

LEGISLATING AI INTERNATIONALLY

Nations have begun implementing transparency and ethical guidelines of their own to eliminate any lack of trust by citizens of the state. A prime example of this is the New Zealand Algorithm Charter that was implemented to provide guidelines on the use of AI by institutions.[80] One of its primary goals is to provide transparency on the implementation of AI and to ensure that citizens' rights and freedoms are upheld despite the use of automation technologies in important decision-making processes.[81] Other governing organizations and bodies such as the European Commission have established core rights and freedoms that include respect for human dignity; freedom of the individual; respect for democracy, justice and the rule of law, equality, non-discrimination, and solidarity; and finally citizens' rights (for instance, human autonomy, prevention of harm, fairness, and explicability).[82] New Zealand, Australia,[83] and the European Union[84] have become pioneers in the newly emerging field of AI use in government institutions.

The United States recently released the *Blueprint for an AI Bill of Rights* (USBofR) intended to serve as a response to the unrestrained potential of automated systems and has also established five fundamental rights.[85] These five principles cover the following:

1. **Safe and Effective Systems** to safeguard the public from the dangers of automated systems, independent evaluation, and reporting on the system's safety and efficacy should be performed regularly;[86]
2. **Algorithmic Discrimination Protections** as the Office of Science and Technology Policy (OSTP) maintains that individuals should be free from digital discrimination, and that data should be deployed in an equitable manner;[87]
3. **Data Privacy**[88] — the OSTP highlights that the public "should be protected from abusive data practices through built-in protections,"[89] just as it should be informed as to how personal data is being used;[90]
4. **Notice and Explanation**, the widespread deployment of automated systems is too often coupled with the individual being denied the knowledge necessary "to address the impact of automated systems on their lives";[91] and
5. **Human Alternatives, Considerations and Fallback** — "the public deserves the assurance that, when rights, opportunities, or access are meaningfully at stake and there is a reasonable expectation of an alternative to an automated system . . . and will not be disadvantaged for that choice."[92] IRCC must follow suit.

PERPETUATING HISTORICAL DISADVANTAGE

AI can turbocharge discrimination.[93] In the AI brief before the Standing Committee on Citizenship and Immigration, which studies matters related to immigration and citizenship, we set out several striking examples of Canadian and international examples of bias in AI-driven data and its application in the immigration processing and enforcement context. A few examples here: the AI powered iBorderCTRL — a lie detector used by the European Union at borders — was demonstrated to discriminate against "people of colour, women, children, and people with disabilities."[94] In New Zealand, technology to identify potential immigrant overstayers was modelled using information such as age, country of origin, gender, usage of public health services, law enforcement encounters, and immigration status.[95] Immigration New Zealand was criticized for the use of ethnicity data in its risk modelling as it had the potential to further marginalize racialized groups.[96] This resulted in the passing of the Algorithm Charter.

UNIVERSAL CANADIAN CHARTER OF FUNDAMENTAL DIGITAL RIGHTS AND FREEDOMS IN THE USE OF AI

Before AI is implemented, it must be ensured that the algorithm and basis upon which the AI is programmed to make recommendations complies with law and policy to ensure that the rights of those affected by the outcomes are not infringed. As noted above, New Zealand became the first nation to develop an Algorithm Charter that states what governments can and cannot do in their use of AI measures.[97] This charter emphasizes and commits to directing government agencies on how to carefully utilize algorithms while striking a balance between privacy and transparency.[98] Moreover, this charter aims to minimize and eliminate unintended bias in the use of algorithms that can result from training by humans whose actions may ultimately have implicit biases or errors, including through the development of a risk matrix.[99] Key features of an innovative AI charter in the Canadian context will similarly include a commitment toward transparency, intelligibility, and equality. All essential given the breadth and scope of immigration law.

LEGISLATIVE RIGHT TO EQUAL TREATMENT IN THE USE OF AI

To avoid discrimination between individuals and groups, efforts should be made to clearly legislate what information is being collected, stored, shared, and used.[100] The collection of data should be limited to the purposes of the collection. Valid consent must be obtained prior to collection.[101] Measures should be established that would mitigate risks of harm or biased outputs that would reduce bias and risks resulting from AI use.[102] Section 2 of the *Artificial Intelligence Data Act* provides a robust definition of AI systems. This is reflected in the algorithmic discrimination protection in both the USBofR and the European Commission's guidelines. Therefore, the rights to equal treatment, freedom from algorithmic discrimination, fairness, and prevention from harm must be clearly delineated and become a recognized right of all persons and supported by other law inclusive of the *Canadian Charter of Rights and Freedoms* and the *Canadian Bill of Rights*.

LEGISLATIVE RIGHTS TO DATA SECURITY AND TRANSPARENCY IN THE USE OF AI

Legislation should set out minimum operating requirements for safe use, storage, and dissemination to ensure the data used and its sources cannot be altered, with models that are multidisciplinary in design and secure technologically.[103] The host organization should be responsible for the data collected and should ensure sufficient protection to data collections.[104] Any legislation and/or policy adopted must provide a clear and explicit definition of AI use to ensure future accountability and oversight. The legislation recognizes the need to prevent harm to individuals or their interests that may result in the use of AI.[105] Data should be consolidated and compiled through a safe and secure process to protect privacy and ensure reliability of information. As a protection to decision-making, we must aspire to more than responsible AI governance but instead to innovative AI governance. There is an opportunity for Canada to become a world leader and codify in law these protections.[106]

I highlighted above that without a proper level of human oversight that is both internal and external to the organization, systemic problems can go undetected and unchallenged, resulting in long-term negative impacts that will certainly be devastating to immigration applicants.[107] Transparent triaging and decision trees are integral to understanding the application, scope, and impact of AI use.[108] Again, the use of AI should enable individual freedoms rather than put them at a disadvantage.[109]

LEGAL TRAINING REQUIREMENT SHOULD BE ENACTED

Training must be undertaken that is reflective and responsive to vulnerable persons and groups such as racialized workers, 2SLGBTQIA+, women, persons with disabilities, ethnic minorities, and children.[110] Many of the recommendations highlighted in the anti-racism report should be legislated in support of achieving this goal, including introducing an anti-racism secretariat, new qualification requirements for executives, and mandatory review of policies, practices, and procedures to identify systemic biases/racisms.

Any new training must additionally extend to those individuals making decisions on applications, including through education on the universality of implicit bias. Finally, legislated personnel allocations should be instilled to ensure diversity and inclusion balances are maintained for those that train and drive the technology. It is essential that a host organization like IRCC implement and maintain a privacy management program that details the policies and procedures that the organization must do to fulfill its obligation. The policies must consider the protection of personal information, training of organization staff, and materials that explain the organization's policies and procedures. All of this is subject to the volume and sensitivity of the data.[111]

New Temporary and Permanent Residence Streams

Armed with new technology, an introduction of more nuanced streams that better target the wide variety of immigration purposes will increase efficiency and control intake within program areas. Targeted streams would not only clarify (not complicate) requirements for potential applicants but also increase economic benefit and diversity. Varied streams could be more responsive to the diverse reasons permanent and temporary migrants seek entry to Canada. It would also allow the flexibility to assign targets and prioritize certain streams over others and pause as required. Chapter 2 highlighted this is already happening in Canadian immigration law and will only intensify to meet the demands of unprecedented immigration processing.

As an example, there could be some combination of the family and economic categories. The family class need not be thought of as a non-economic category, and economic migration need not be thought of as a category that does not affect our nation building. Notably, countries like Australia have for a time successfully embarked upon this approach with a sundry of categories, including sponsored family visitor, temporary business stays (short- and long-term), sponsored business visas, retirement investor visas, and professional development visas.[112] Critically, a variability in streams would support improved specificity of IRCC's priorities and targets.

Consistency and clarity in messaging across all streams (new and old) would also significantly reduce intake and backlog, as applicants would be better able to determine the stream that best suits their goals. For example, parsing student streams into those seeking permanent residence and those simply hoping to study in Canada would significantly reduce subsequent backlogs in permanent resident applications from former students who are ineligible to land in Canada. Students would not only declare their intentions to land at the outset but would also clearly understand their likelihood of obtaining permanent residence in the future. Where one sub-category is prioritized for a time, such as in response to the humanitarian crisis in Ukraine, other streams could be paused. It is an applicant-centric approach that will lead to real change.

New Caps and Queues

Immigration delivery of the future must be nimble, interactive, and transparent. To this end, all temporary and permanent resident streams should have clearly established and well communicated eligibility, targets, processing times, and caps. Applicants should be advised that applications will not be accepted and/or processed once the targets are met. If applications are submitted after these targets and caps are met, then they should be automatically returned. Caps and queues are required in particular for temporary resident streams. Research shows that more than half of the backlog comprises applications for temporary residence.[113] Out of those applications, half are for temporary resident visas (TRV).[114] This is unsustainable.[115]

With the aid of technology, caps and queues processing will be uniform. The introduction of caps and queues for TRVs is particularly appropriate given that many visitors to Canada hope to travel during specified timelines. Any delay in processing ultimately renders their applications moot. Yet these applications remain in the queue despite no longer serving a purpose, increasing the delay and inventory. A cap that reflects available resources can help address this problem and effectively reduce the number of applications that need to be processed.

A similar cap and queue approach should be adopted for study permit applications in an expression of interest AI-driven platform. Not only would the diversification of streams help to reduce the backlog in permanent resident applications, but adding in caps for study permits from diverse types of institutions (for instance, university versus college) would additionally allow for the better identification and direction of resources and protect the vulnerable.[116] This is the future.

All Forms and Messaging Should Be in Plain Language

Transparency and responsiveness equal timely immigration processing. Vital to this goal is the importance of plain language.[117] IRCC should reorient their messaging to focus on customer experience on its website and forms. The introduction of plain language would address the incredible expenditure of resources on the issue of misrepresenting one of the leading grounds for immigration inadmissibility that often results from innocent misunderstandings of questions.

Ultimately, many of these cases do not capture persons seeking to game the system or pose a threat to the integrity of our Canadian immigration programs. An emphasis on clear language would greatly reduce the number of people who make these mistakes and end up in other parts of the immigration system to overcome what could have been avoided. Effective chatbots may also assist with basic informational support and demystifying the application process.

Application of Services Fees Act to IRCC processing

In June 2017, Parliament implemented the *Service Fees Act* (*SFA*).[118] The *SFA* created a requirement for detailed annual reporting from government departments regarding their fee structure.[119] These fees are tied to performance standards.[120] When performance standards are not met, fees should be refunded to the individual who protracted the government service.[121] By April 2021, IRCC had implemented their policy under the *SFA*. It was indicated that the Act would only apply to passport program fees, right of citizenship fees, and international experience Canada participation fees.[122] This was disappointing as all other streams (permanent residence, work permit, temporary residence, study permit, sponsorship, etc.) are not covered. If the *SFA* applied to all (or even most) of IRCC's programs, it would demonstrate IRCC's genuine intention to reduce the backlog and meet processing times. It would also act as an important legal and principled incentive for IRCC to make meaningful strides in service standards and reduce processing times. This will need to be revisited in the future.

Public Portrayal of Authorized Representatives Must Change

Representatives transcend all layers of society, aiding in access to justice, which is all the more important in a technocentric world.[123] The overwhelming focus of IRCC messaging, however, is on the harm in using representatives; communications on IRCC's website refer to representatives as unlawful and/or unscrupulous practitioners.[124] Although the aim to protect the public through this messaging is important and appropriate, the result is a severely distorted image with little mention of the critical role authorized representatives play. This fuels a perception that accessing representation is always a perilous decision.

This messaging is essential to solutions regarding application backlogs in the future. The use of counsel can mean that submitted applications are complete, requirements are met, and any issues are sufficiently addressed. This can save time as officers will receive fewer incomplete applications. IRCC's position on counsel should be informative. In other words, the message from IRCC should be that counsel *can* help applicants better understand the requirements and interpret the law, however, applicants should ensure their representation is licensed and legitimate.

Also, the need for multi-stakeholder consultation and collaboration is acute. It starts with more timely and meaningful consultation, which can result in an enriched, fluid, transparent, responsive, and effective immigration program.

Limited Use of Ministerial Instructions for Pilot Projects

Ministerial instructions (MI) should be utilized for pilot projects only. No doubt, MIs have led to major changes in the Canadian immigration regime. In 2008, the *IRPA* was amended, and section 87.3 was created. This provision granted the then minister of citizenship and immigration broad authority to set processing quotas and priorities for different classes of applications in a given year by way of MIs and to summarily dispose of those that did not meet these criteria.[125]

Although an attractive and nimble tool, MIs must be used sparingly. The concern is that the considerable power granted to the minister to decide how, when, and to what degree applications are to be processed (if at all) without the requirement for consensus building, consideration of the regulatory process, and extensive stakeholder involvement would be a regression to what we saw following Confederation. Practically, this can result in unilateral, reactive, and disjointed tinkering, which can add delay and uncertainty to immigration program delivery. We also saw this when in 2008 an MI was adopted that unilaterally terminated applications in the federal skilled worker backlog, some of which had people waiting for eight years. This MI represents a blight in our immigration history that should not be repeated.[126]

Conclusion

We asked our thousands of followers on social media to answer several questions, two of which are relevant to the discussion here:[127]

FIGURE 5.5. SHOULD CANADA BE INCREASING THE NUMBER OF IMMIGRANTS ADMITTED EACH YEAR?

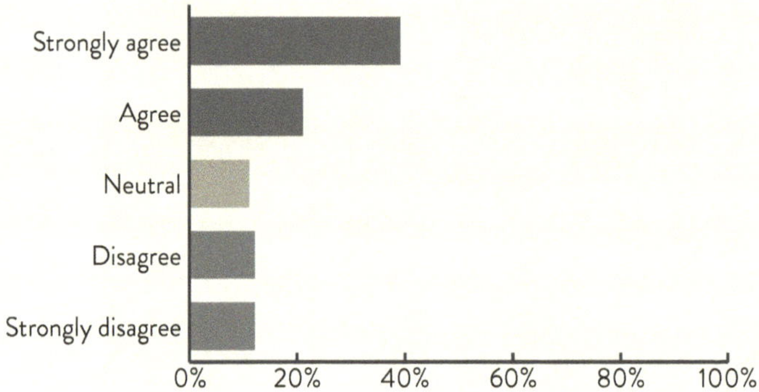

FIGURE 5.6. SHOULD FAMILY REUNIFICATION FORM A LARGER PART OF CANADA'S IMMIGRATION PROGRAM?

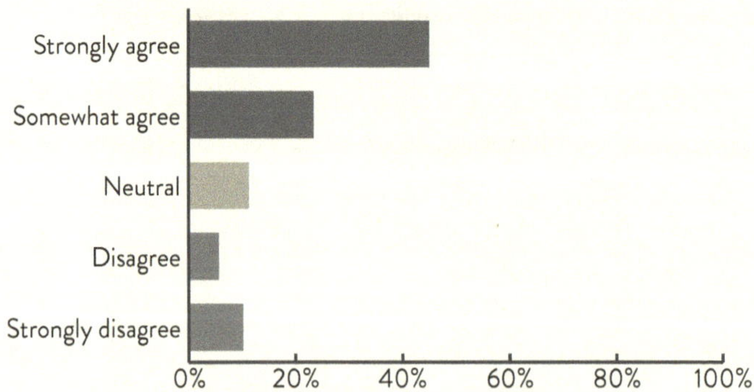

These results are not surprising and are consistent with other studies cited. Most immigration applicants are concerned with processing timelines, certainty of selection, employment opportunities, access to permanent residency, and family rights. Much work has been done toward achieving these ends, but we must now move boldly into the future. Our immigration program should not lose sight of the potential long-term contributions of certain applicants like family class applicants by only focusing on immediate ("economic") contribution.

Further, IRCC cannot embark on this journey alone. It requires the cooperation, vision, and assets of various stakeholders. IRCC over the past few years has markedly stepped up its stakeholder consultation. The nature of these consultations could benefit from even more broad-based consultation and when and who IRCC consults. For example, to ensure proper expression of all stakeholder interests, the details of lasting program changes should be tested and then fully rolled out for consultation in advance of parliamentary oversight and approval. The goal of such initiatives is to test and deliver an immigration program that has been carefully defined and debated; one that is efficient, responsive, and on par with global competition.

The possibility for a more measured, nuanced, and effective immigration delivery model is within reach. This is in part because of exciting retraining possibilities and technological innovations, as well as emerging international examples and program experience. A national immigration plan that is multi-tiered with new streams responsive to Canadian employer needs and the application of the *Service Fee Act* would be transformative when introduced in combination with effective retraining, leveraging of technology in an innovative, transparent, and responsible fashion, as well as the usage of plain language and the engagement of all stakeholders.

The next big test is how IRCC deals with the backlog that will not only identify our level of adherence to domestic and international legal obligations but will signal if we are embarking on radical disruption built on clear and convincing evidence we have gained from past missteps. If undertaken together, we can envision a future where we distance ourselves from disjointed tinkering, non-transparency, inaccessibility, delays, uneven processing, bias, and marginalization. If we put in the collective work now, pressing for thoughtful action through collaboration, oversight, transparency, and responsible implementation, we have the potential to become a world leader in the new age of AI-driven immigration delivery, law, and policy. One where our immigration program and platform are shining examples of innovative, real-time results that are applicant-centric guided by fairness and inclusion.

The future is bright if we find a new way but not forget our past. Above I set out what I believe are crucial steps moving forward to add to the conversation. There are many bright minds looking at these issues. We are well positioned. I remain optimistic. I also predict that the immigration delivery model of 2023 will change more in the next five to ten years than it has since inception. A bold prediction, but boldness is what we need going forward.

APPENDIX 1

Inadmissibility Provisions in the *Immigration and Refugee Protection Act* and Evidentiary Thresholds

Rules of interpretation

33 The facts that constitute inadmissibility under sections 34 to 37 include facts arising from omissions and, unless otherwise provided, include facts for which there are reasonable grounds to believe that they have occurred, are occurring or may occur.

Security

34(1) A permanent resident or a foreign national is inadmissible on security grounds for

(a) engaging in an act of espionage that is against Canada or that is contrary to Canada's interests;

(b) engaging in or instigating the subversion by force of any government;

(b.1) engaging in an act of subversion against a democratic government, institution or process as they are understood in Canada;

(c) engaging in terrorism;

(d) being a danger to the security of Canada;

(e) engaging in acts of violence that would or might endanger the lives or safety of persons in Canada; or

(f) being a member of an organization that there are reasonable grounds to believe engages, has engaged or will engage in acts referred to in paragraph (a), (b), (b.1) or (c).

(2) [Repealed, 2013, c. 16, s. 13]

Human or international rights violations

35 (1) A permanent resident or a foreign national is inadmissible on grounds of violating human or international rights for

(a) committing an act outside Canada that constitutes an offence referred to in sections 4 to 7 of the *Crimes Against Humanity and War Crimes Act*;

(b) being a prescribed senior official in the service of a government that, in the opinion of the Minister, engages or has engaged in terrorism, systematic or gross human rights violations, or genocide, a war crime or a crime against humanity within the meaning of subsections 6(3) to (5) of the *Crimes Against Humanity and War Crimes Act*;

(c) being a person, other than a permanent resident, whose entry into or stay in Canada is restricted pursuant to a decision, resolution or measure of an international organization of states or association of states, of which Canada is a member, that imposes sanctions on a country against which Canada has imposed or has agreed to impose sanctions in concert with that organization or association;

(c.1) having engaged in conduct that would, in the opinion of the Minister, constitute an offence under section 240.1 of the *Criminal Code*;

(d) being a person, other than a permanent resident, who is currently the subject of an order or regulation made under section 4 of the *Special Economic Measures Act* on the grounds that any of the circumstances described in paragraph 4(1.1)(c) or (d) of that Act has occurred; or

(e) being a person, other than a permanent resident, who is currently the subject of an order or regulation made under section 4 of the *Justice for Victims of Corrupt Foreign Officials Act (Sergei Magnitsky Law)*.

Clarification

(2) For greater certainty, despite section 33, a person who ceases being the subject of an order or regulation referred to in paragraph (1)(d) or (e) is no longer inadmissible under that paragraph.

Serious criminality

36 (1) A permanent resident or a foreign national is inadmissible on grounds of serious criminality for

(a) having been convicted in Canada of an offence under an Act of Parliament punishable by a maximum term of imprisonment of at least 10 years, or of an offence under an Act of Parliament for which a term of imprisonment of more than six months has been imposed;

(b) having been convicted of an offence outside Canada that, if committed in Canada, would constitute an offence under an Act of Parliament punishable by a maximum term of imprisonment of at least 10 years; or

(c) committing an act outside Canada that is an offence in the place where it was committed and that, if committed in Canada, would constitute an offence under an Act of Parliament punishable by a maximum term of imprisonment of at least 10 years.

Criminality

(2) A foreign national is inadmissible on grounds of criminality for

(a) having been convicted in Canada of an offence under an Act of Parliament punishable by way of indictment, or of two offences under any Act of Parliament not arising out of a single occurrence;

(b) having been convicted outside Canada of an offence that, if committed in Canada, would constitute an indictable offence under an Act of Parliament, or of two offences not arising out of a single occurrence that, if committed in Canada, would constitute offences under an Act of Parliament;

(c) committing an act outside Canada that is an offence in the place where it was committed and that, if committed in Canada, would constitute an indictable offence under an Act of Parliament; or

(d) committing, on entering Canada, an offence under an Act of Parliament prescribed by regulations.

Application

(3) The following provisions govern subsections (1) and (2):

(a) an offence that may be prosecuted either summarily or by way of indictment is deemed to be an indictable offence, even if it has been prosecuted summarily;

(b) inadmissibility under subsections (1) and (2) may not be based on a conviction in respect of which a record suspension has been ordered and has not been revoked or ceased to have effect under the *Criminal Records Act*, or in respect of which there has been a final determination of an acquittal;

(c) the matters referred to in paragraphs (1)(b) and (c) and (2)(b) and (c) do not constitute inadmissibility in respect of a permanent resident or foreign national who, after the prescribed period, satisfies the Minister that they have been rehabilitated or who is a member of a prescribed class that is deemed to have been rehabilitated;

(d) a determination of whether a permanent resident has committed an act described in paragraph (1)(c) must be based on a balance of probabilities; and

(e) inadmissibility under subsections (1) and (2) may not be based on an offence

- (i) designated as a contravention under the *Contraventions Act*,
- (ii) for which the permanent resident or foreign national is found guilty under the *Young Offenders Act*, chapter Y-1 of the Revised Statutes of Canada, 1985, or
- (iii) for which the permanent resident or foreign national received a youth sentence under the *Youth Criminal Justice Act*.

Organized criminality

37 (1) A permanent resident or a foreign national is inadmissible on grounds of organized criminality for

(a) being a member of an organization that is believed on reasonable grounds to be or to have been engaged in activity that is part of a pattern of criminal activity planned and organized by a number of persons acting in concert in furtherance of the commission of an offence punishable under an Act of Parliament by way of indictment, or in furtherance of the commission of an offence outside Canada that, if committed in Canada, would constitute such an offence, or engaging in activity that is part of such a pattern; or

(b) engaging, in the context of transnational crime, in activities such as people smuggling, trafficking in persons or laundering of money or other proceeds of crime.

Application

(2) Paragraph (1)(a) does not lead to a determination of inadmissibility by reason only of the fact that the permanent resident or foreign national entered Canada with the assistance of a person who is involved in organized criminal activity.

Health grounds

38 (1) A foreign national is inadmissible on health grounds if their health condition

(a) is likely to be a danger to public health;

(b) is likely to be a danger to public safety; or

(c) might reasonably be expected to cause excessive demand on health or social services.

Exception

(2) Paragraph (1)(c) does not apply in the case of a foreign national who

(a) has been determined to be a member of the family class and to be the spouse, common-law partner or child of a sponsor within the meaning of the regulations;

(b) has applied for a permanent resident visa as a Convention refugee or a person in similar circumstances;

(c) is a protected person; or

(d) is, where prescribed by the regulations, the spouse, common-law partner, child or other family member of a foreign national referred to in any of paragraphs (a) to (c).

Financial reasons

39 A foreign national is inadmissible for financial reasons if they are or will be unable or unwilling to support themself or any other person who is dependent on them, and have not satisfied an officer that adequate arrangements for care and support, other than those that involve social assistance, have been made.

Misrepresentation

40 (1) A permanent resident or a foreign national is inadmissible for misrepresentation

(a) for directly or indirectly misrepresenting or withholding material facts relating to a relevant matter that induces or could induce an error in the administration of this Act;

(b) for being or having been sponsored by a person who is determined to be inadmissible for misrepresentation;

(c) on a final determination to vacate a decision to allow their claim for refugee protection or application for protection; or

(d) on ceasing to be a citizen under

  (i) paragraph 10(1)(a) of the *Citizenship Act*, as it read immediately before the coming into force of section 8 of the *Strengthening Canadian Citizenship Act*, in the circumstances set out in subsection 10(2) of the *Citizenship Act*, as it read immediately before that coming into force,

  (ii) subsection 10(1) of the *Citizenship Act*, in the circumstances set out in section 10.2 of that Act, or

  (iii) subsection 10.1(3) of the *Citizenship Act*, in the circumstances set out in section 10.2 of that Act.

Application

(2) The following provisions govern subsection (1):

(a) the permanent resident or the foreign national continues to be inadmissible for misrepresentation for a period of five years following, in the case of a determination outside Canada, a final determination of inadmissibility under subsection (1) or, in the case of a determination in Canada, the date the removal order is enforced; and

(b) paragraph (1)(b) does not apply unless the Minister is satisfied that the facts of the case justify the inadmissibility.

Inadmissible

(3) A foreign national who is inadmissible under this section may not apply for permanent resident status during the period referred to in paragraph (2)(a).

Cessation of refugee protection — foreign national

40.1 (1) A foreign national is inadmissible on a final determination under subsection 108(2) that their refugee protection has ceased.

Cessation of refugee protection — permanent resident

(2) A permanent resident is inadmissible on a final determination that their refugee protection has ceased for any of the reasons described in paragraphs 108(1)(a) to (d).

Non-compliance with Act

41 A person is inadmissible for failing to comply with this Act

(a) in the case of a foreign national, through an act or omission which contravenes, directly or indirectly, a provision of this Act; and

(b) in the case of a permanent resident, through failing to comply with subsection 27(2) or section 28.

Inadmissible family member

42 (1) A foreign national, other than a protected person, is inadmissible on grounds of an inadmissible family member if

(a) their accompanying family member or, in prescribed circumstances, their non-accompanying family member is inadmissible; or

(b) they are an accompanying family member of an inadmissible person.

Exception

(2) In the case of a foreign national referred to in subsection (1) who is a temporary resident or who has made an application for temporary resident status or an application to remain in Canada as a temporary resident,

(a) the matters referred to in paragraph (1)(a) constitute inadmissibility only if the family member is inadmissible under section 34, 35 or 37; and

(b) the matters referred to in paragraph (1)(b) constitute inadmissibility only if the foreign national is an accompanying family member of a person who is inadmissible under section 34, 35 or 37.

Exception — application to Minister

42.1 (1) The Minister may, on application by a foreign national, declare that the matters referred to in section 34, paragraphs 35(1)(b) and (c) and subsection 37(1) do not constitute inadmissibility in respect of the foreign national if they satisfy the Minister that it is not contrary to the national interest.

Exception — Minister's own initiative

(2) The Minister may, on the Minister's own initiative, declare that the matters referred to in section 34, paragraphs 35(1)(b) and (c) and subsection 37(1) do not constitute inadmissibility in respect of a foreign national if the Minister is satisfied that it is not contrary to the national interest.

Considerations

(3) In determining whether to make a declaration, the Minister may only take into account national security and public safety considerations, but, in his or her analysis, is not limited to considering the danger that the foreign national presents to the public or the security of Canada.

Standards of Proof
(ss 34–37)

"Reasonable grounds to believe" is a bona fide belief in a serious possibility that a fact has been established based on credible evidence. Reasonable grounds to believe is more than suspicion. Some objective basis for the belief must exist. Put another way, the fact itself need not be proven; it is enough to show reasonable grounds for believing the allegation true. Information used to establish reasonable grounds should be specific, compelling, credible, and be received from a reliable source.[1]

"Balance of Probabilities" is a civil standard of proof used in administrative tribunals. It means that the evidence presented must show that the facts as alleged are more probable than not. The party having the burden of proof must demonstrate that the evidence presented outweighs any opposing evidence or arguments. It is a higher standard of proof than "reasonable grounds to believe" but is lower than the criminal standard of "beyond a reasonable doubt" used in criminal proceedings.[2]

APPENDIX 2

Population Growth Rates[1]

FIGURE 6.1. POPULATION GROWTH RATES OF G7, G20 COUNTRIES

Canada's population is growing at the fastest pace in the G7 and ranks seventh in the G20, 2016–2021.

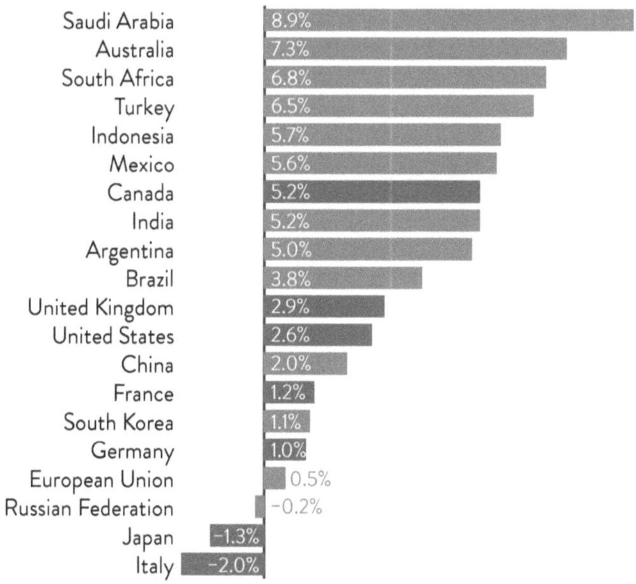

Source: Statistics Canada, World Bank

FIGURE 6.2. ALL RACIALIZED GROUPS IN CANADA HAVE BEEN GROWING FROM 2001 TO 2021, THOUSANDS

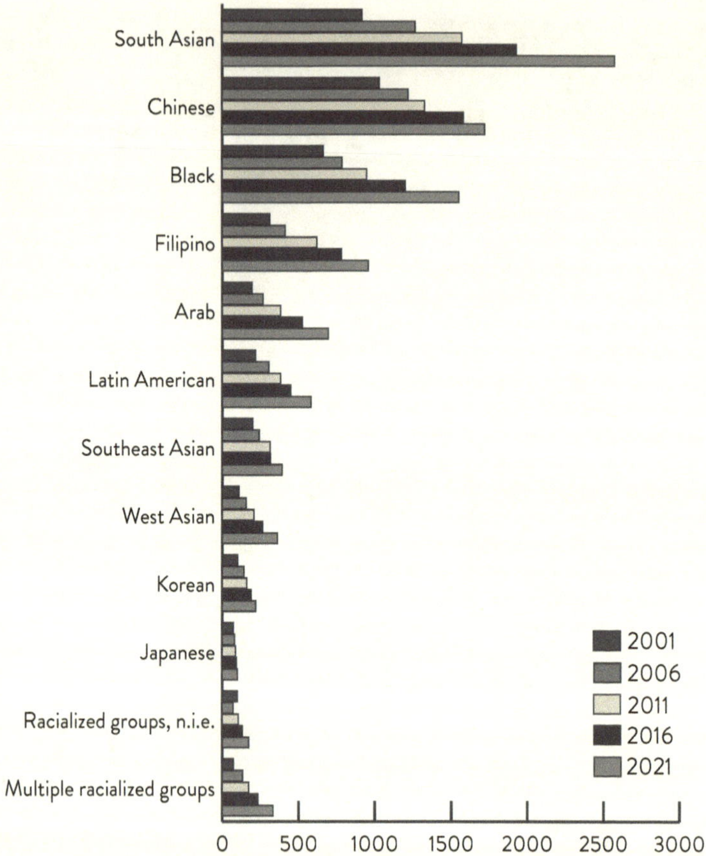

Note(s): In this chart, the concept of "racialized group" is derived directly from the concept of "visible minority." The *Employment Equity Act* defines visible minorities as "persons, other than Aboriginal peoples, who are non-Caucasian in race or non-white in colour." The abbreviation "n.i.e." means "not included elsewhere." This category includes people who provided written responses such as "Guyanese," "Pacific Islander," "Polynesian," "Tibetan" or "West Indian."

Source(s): Census of Population, 2001, 2006, 2016 and 2021 (3901), and National Household Survey, 2011 (5178).

Notes

CHAPTER ONE | Immigration: The Canadian Way

1 Archibald MacLeish, "Apologia" (1972) 85:8 *Harvard Law Review* 1505–11.
2 M. Parfit, "Human Migration" *National Geographic* (1998) at 6.
3 *Canada Past & Present: A Citizenship Education Guide*, *Historica Canada*, online: http://education.historicacanada.ca/en/tools/650.
4 *Ibid.*
5 A. Caldararu et al, *Canadian Settlement in Action: History and Future* (Open Education Alberta, 2021) at 17.
6 H. Troper, "Immigration to Canada" *The Canadian Encyclopedia* (2022), online: www.thecanadianencyclopedia.ca/en/article/immigration.
7 *Ibid.*
8 As amended by the *Constitution Act, 1982*, which came into force on 17 April 1982. The section originally read as follows: This Act may be cited as *The British North America Act, 1867*.
9 Margaret Young, *Immigration: Constitutional Issues* (revised October 1992), online: https://publications.gc.ca/Collection-R/LoPBdP/BP/bp273-e.htm.
10 L. Van Dyk (n.d.) *Canadian Immigration Acts and Legislation* (Canadian Museum of Immigration at Pier 21, retrieved 3 January 2023), online: https://pier21.ca/research/immigration-history/canadian-immigration-acts-and-legislation.
11 Caldararu et al, above note 5.
12 G. Dirks, "Immigration Policy in Canada" *The Canadian Encyclopedia* (23 October 2020), online: www.thecanadianencyclopedia.ca/en/article/immigration-policy.

13 Caldararu et al, above note 5.
14 SC 1885, c 71 plus amendments: 1887, 1892, 1900, 1903. See this chapter, at pages 12–14.
15 Caldararu et al, above note 5.
16 Van Dyk, above note 10.
17 *Ibid.*
18 V. Knowles, *Forging Our Legacy: Canadian Citizenship and Immigration, 1900–1977* (Ottawa, ON: Citizenship and Immigration Canada, 2000) at 160–61.
19 S. Schwinghamer, *The Colour Bar at the Canadian Border: Black American Farmers* (retrieved 13 January 2023), online: https://pier21.ca/research/immigration-history/black-american-farmers.
20 C. Anderson, "A Long-Standing Canadian Tradition: Citizenship Revocation and Second-Class Citizenship Under the Liberals, 1993–2006" (2008) 42:3 *Journal of Canadian Studies* 80–105.
21 *Act to Amend the Immigration Act*, SC 1919, c 25.
22 E. Winter, *Report on Citizenship Law: Canada* (EUDO Citizenship Observatory, 2015) at 4 [Winter, *Report*].
23 *Ibid.*
24 IRCC, "History of Citizenship Legislation" (6 July 2015), online: www.canada.ca/en/immigration-refugees-citizenship/corporate/publications-manuals/operational-bulletins-manuals/canadian-citizenship/overview/history-legislation.html.
25 *Ibid.*
26 *Ibid.*
27 *Ibid.*
28 *Ibid.*
29 *Ibid.*
30 A. Macklin, "Citizenship Revocation, the Privilege to Have Rights and the Production of the Alien" (2014) 40:1 *Queen's Law Journal* 1–54.
31 *Ibid.*
32 R. Joshee, "Citizenship and Multicultural Education in Canada: From Assimilation to Social Cohesion" in J.A. Banks, ed, *Diversity and Citizenship Education: Global Perspectives* (Hoboken, NJ: Jossey-Bass/Wiley, 2004) at 127–56.
33 *Ibid.*
34 *Ibid.*
35 H. Troper, "Canada's Immigration Policy Since 1945" (1993) 48:2 *International Journal* 255–81, online: https://doi.org/10.1177/002070209304800204.
36 IRCC, above note 24.
37 Caldararu et al, above note 5 at 30.

38 Troper, above note 6.

39 Canadian Museum of Immigration at Pier 21, *Immigration Act, 1976*, online: https://pier21.ca/research/immigration-history/immigration-act-1976.

40 Winter, *Report*, above note 22.

41 RSC 1985, c C-29.

42 For further information, please see: Labour Gazette, February 1908: *An Act to Restrict* and RSC 1885, c 71; *Internment of Persons of Ukrainian Origin Recognition Act*, SC 2005, c 52; *Canadian Race Relations Foundation Act*, SC 1991, c 8; Order In Council, PC 23 & 24, 7 January 1914; Order in Council, 8 January 1908; *An Act Respecting Immigration and Immigrants, 1906*, 6 Edw VII c 19, s 30; *An Act Respecting Immigration, 1910*, *Immigration Act, 1919*, 9-10 Geo V, c 25; *An Act to Amend the Immigration Act, 1919*, 9-10 Geo V, c 25, assented to 6 June 1919; *War Measures Act, 1914*, 5 Geo V, c 2; Statutes of Canada, *An Act Respecting Immigration, 1952*, 1 Elizabeth II, c 42, s 61(g)(i) [emphasis added] [*Immigration, 1952*].

43 Canadian Association for Community Living (CACL), *Inclusive Citizenship: It's Time* (November 2017), online: (pdf) www.ourcommons.ca/Content/Committee/421/CIMM/Brief/BR9256216/br-external/CanadianAssociationForCommunityLiving-e.pdf.

44 *Immigration, 1952*, above note 42, parts 1 and 5.

45 Prime Minister of Canada (24 December 24 2022), *Prime Minister Trudeau's Message on Christmas*, online: (retrieved 1 February 2023) https://pm.gc.ca/en/videos/2022/12/24/prime-minister-trudeaus-message-christmas.

46 Truth and Reconciliation Commission of Canada, *Canada's Residential Schools: The History, Part 1 Origins to 1939*, 1st ed (Montreal, QC: McGill-Queen's University Press, 2015) at 3.

47 E. Novic, *The Concept of Cultural Genocide: An International Law Perspective* (New York, NY: Oxford University Press, 2016).

48 Above note 46 at 110.

49 N. Angel, *Fragments of Truth: Residential Schools and the Challenge of Reconciliation in Canada* (Duke University Press, 2022) at 28.

50 H. Pellerin, "Indigenous Peoples in Canadian Migration Narratives: A Story of Marginalization" (2019) 8:1 *Aboriginal Policy Studies* at 7, online: https://doi.org/10.5663/aps.v8i1.29347.

51 Above note 46 at 106.

52 M. Moran & D. Dyzenhaus, *Calling Power to Account: Law, Reparations and the Chinese Canadian Head Tax Case* (Toronto, ON: University of Toronto Press, 2005).

53 *Ibid.*

54 *Ibid.*

55 S. Winter, "The Stakes of Inclusion: Chinese Canadian Head Tax Redress" (2008) 41:1 *Canadian Journal of Political Science* at 119–41, online: https://doi.org/10.1017/S0008423908080050 [Winter, "Stakes"].

56 *Ibid.*

57 *Ibid.*

58 *Ibid.*

59 Moran & Dyzenhaus, above note 52.

60 *Ibid.* See also the case: *R v Quong Wing*, 1914 CanLII 608, 49 SCR 440, online: https://canlii.ca/t/gdd3l.

61 Winter, "Stakes," above note 55.

62 *Ibid.*

63 *Ibid.*

64 *Ibid.*

65 Prime Minister of Canada, News Release, "Prime Minister Delivers Apology for the Internment of Italian Canadians During the Second World War" (27 May 2021), online: https://pm.gc.ca/en/news/news-releases/2021/05/27/prime-minister-delivers-apology-internment-italian-canadians-during; *War Measures Act, 1914*, 5 George V, c 2; *The Defence of Canada Regulations*, The Standing Interdepartmental Committee on Emergency Legislation was set up under the authority of a Minute of Council. PC 531, 14 March 1938.

66 News Release, *ibid.*

67 O. Stefanovich, "Reclaiming History" *CBC News* (23 May 2021), online: https://newsinteractives.cbc.ca/longform/italian-canadians-wwii-internment-apology/.

68 Citizenship and Immigration Canada, Columbus Centre, "Redress and Apology" *Italian Canadians as Enemy Aliens: Memories of World War II*, online: www.italiancanadianww2.ca/theme/detail/redress_apology.

69 The Canadian Encyclopedia, "Internment of Japanese Canadians (Plain-Language Summary)" (27 July 2022), online: www.thecanadianencyclopedia.ca/en/article/internment-of-japanese-canadians-plain-language-summary.

70 *Ibid.*

71 National Association of Japanese Canadians, *Internment Era Timeline*, online: https://bcredress.ca/internment-era-timeline/.

72 *Ibid.*

73 SC 2001, c 27.

74 Freda Hawkins, *Critical Years in Immigration: Canada and Australia Compared* (Montreal: McGill-Queen's University Press, 1991).

75 *House of Commons Debates* (35th Parl, 1st Sess) (22 September 1994).

76 *Ibid.*

77 F. Henry & C. Tator, *Discourses of Domination: Racial Bias in the Canadian English-Language Press* (Toronto, ON: University of Toronto Press, 2002).

78 *Ibid.*

79 *Ibid.*

80 *Ibid* at 165–67.

81 Citizenship and Immigration Canada, "Building on a Strong Foundation for the 21st Century: New Directions for Immigration and Refugee Policy and Legislation" (Ottawa, ON: Citizenship and Immigration Canada, 1998), online: https://publications.gc.ca/site/eng/9.660747/publication.html?wbdisable=true.

82 W. Chan, "Crime, Deportation, and the Regulation of Immigration in Canada" (2005) 44:2 *Crime, Law, and Social Change* at 153–80.

83 Canadian Museum of Immigration at Pier 21, *Immigration Act, 1952*, online: https://pier21.ca/research/immigration-history/immigration-act-1952.

84 N. LaViolette, "Coming Out to Canada: The Immigration of Same-Sex Couples Under the Immigration and Refugee Protection Act" (2004) 49 *McGill Law Journal* 969 at 971.

85 *Ibid.* Gay men and lesbians were permitted to seek exemptions to sponsor partners for a time pursuant to s 114 —humanitarian and compassionate grounds of the *1978 Immigration Act.* The decisions were discretionary.

86 *AP v Canada (MCI)*, 2020 FC 906, [2021] 1 FCR 3 at para 27.

87 Canadian Museum of Immigration at Pier 21 (1 January 2022), *Canadian Multiculturalism Policy, 1971*, online: https://pier21.ca/research/immigration-history/canadian-multiculturalism-policy-1971.

88 *Canadian Charter of Rights and Freedoms*, s 7, Part 1 of the *Constitution Act, 1982*, being Schedule B to the *Canada Act 1982* (UK), 1982, c 11.

89 J. Monpetit, "Historic Case in the Making as Quebec's Religious Symbols Ban Heads to Court" *CBC News* (1 November 2020), online: www.cbc.ca/news/canada/montreal/bill-21-quebec-secular-law-court-challenge-1.5784727.

90 J. Monpetit, "In Quebec Religious Symbols Decision, Canada Confronts Consequences of Controversial Constitutional Clause" *CBC News* (21 April 2021), online: www.cbc.ca/news/canada/montreal/notwithstanding-clause-secularism-law-religious-symbols-ban-1.5995738 [emphasis added].

91 *Ibid.*

92 SC 2014, c 22.

93 *Ibid.*

94 IRCC, "Immigration, Refugees and Citizenship Canada" (last modified 7 December 2023), online: www.canada.ca/en/immigration-refugees-citizenship.html.

95 *Ibid.*

96 *Ibid.*

97 Cato Institute, A.M. Baxter & A Nowrasteh, "A Brief History of U.S. Immigration Policy from the Colonial Period to the Present Day" (3 August 2021), online: www.cato.org/policy-analysis/brief-history-us-immigration-policy-colonial-period-present-day.

98 *Ibid.*

99 Migration Policy Institute, "U.S. Immigrant Population and Share over Time, 1850–Present" (1 January 2022), online: www.migrationpolicy.org/programs/data-hub/charts/immigrant-population-over-time. Migration Policy Institute (MPI) tabulation of data from US Census Bureau, 2010 and 2021 American Community Surveys (ACS), and 1970, 1990, and 2000 Decennial Census. All other data are from Campbell J. Gibson & Emily Lennon, "Historical Census Statistics on the Foreign-Born Population of the United States: 1850 to 1990" (Working Paper no 29, US Census Bureau, Washington, DC, 1999).

100 IRCC, "An Immigration Plan to Grow the Economy" (last modified 1 November 2022), online: www.canada.ca/en/immigration-refugees-citizenship/news/2022/11/an-immigration-plan-to-grow-the-economy.html.

101 *Ibid.*

102 Canadian Museum of Immigration at Pier 21 (1 January 2022), *Immigration Regulations, Order-in Council PC 1967-1616, 1967* (retrieved 7 February 2023), online: https://pier21.ca/research/immigration-history/immigration-regulations-order-in-council-pc-1967-1616-1967.

103 *Ibid.*

104 P.E. Trudeau (8 October 1971), *Federal Multicultural Policy* (retrieved 7 February 2023), online: https://wayback.archive-it.org/2217/20101208165216/http://www.abheritage.ca/albertans/speeches/trudeau.html.

105 *Ibid.*

106 Canadian Museum of Immigration at Pier 21, *Immigration Act, 1976*, online: https://pier21.ca/research/immigration-history/immigration-act-1976.

107 Statistics Canada, *Number and Proportion of Foreign-Born Population in Canada, 1871 to 2036* (27 September 2023), online: www.statcan.gc.ca/en/dai/btd/othervisuals/other006.

CHAPTER TWO | **Canadian Immigration Pathways**

1 See for example, *Patel v Canada (MCI)*, 2006 FC 224: "The current statutory and regulatory scheme does not say that a person's initial temporary purpose must remain constant and unchanged. The only requirement is the existence of a temporary purpose." See also *Stanislavsky v Canada (MCI)*, 2003 FC 835 and *Chandralingram v Canada (MCI)*, 2007 FC 282 at paras 8–12.

2 IRCC, "Submit an Express Entry Profile: Online Form" (last modified 23 August 2023), online: www.canada.ca/en/immigration-refugees-citizenship/services/immigrate-canada/express-entry/submit-profile.html.

3 IRCC, "Find Your National Occupation Classification (NOC)" (last modified 23 August 2023), online: www.canada.ca/en/immigration-refugees-citizenship/services/immigrate-canada/express-entry/eligibility/find-national-occupation-code.html.

4 IRCC, "Eligibility to Apply as a Federal Skilled Worker (Express Entry)" (last modified 13 September 2023), online: www.canada.ca/en/immigration-refugees-citizenship/services/immigrate-canada/express-entry/eligibility/federal-skilled-workers.html.

5 IRCC, "Eligibility to Apply for the Federal Skilled Trades Program (Express Entry)" (last modified 25 August 2023), online: www.canada.ca/en/immigration-refugees-citizenship/services/immigrate-canada/express-entry/eligibility/skilled-trades.html.

6 Government of Ontario, "Ontario Immigrant Nominee Program (OINP)," online: www.ontario.ca/page/ontario-immigrant-nominee-program-oinp.

7 *Ibid.*

8 *IRPR*, s 88(1).

9 IRCC, "Caregivers" (last modified 16 November 2023), online: www.canada.ca/en/immigration-refugees-citizenship/services/immigrate-canada/caregivers.html.

10 IRCC, "Canada to Reduce Work Experience Requirements for Caregivers and Provide Pathways to Permanent Residence" (last modified 10 February 2023), online: www.canada.ca/en/immigration-refugees-citizenship/news/2023/02/canada-to-reduce-work-experience-requirements-for-caregivers-and-provide-pathways-to-permanent-residence.html.

11 *IRPR*, s 117.

12 2019 FC 1286.

13 *Gonzalez v Canada (MCI)*, 2014 FC 201.

14 See Chapter 4 in this book.

15 *Laifatt v Canada (MCI)*, 2020 FC 365.

16 *Abdi v Canada (MCI)*, 2018 FC 475. The fifty-eight-year-old applicant was twenty-two years older than his spouse. The decision was set aside after the officer inappropriately questioned whether the spouse wanted to have children and if she didn't think it was too late to have children.

17 *Gill v Canada (MCI)*, 2010 FC 122. The officer noted that the wedding photos seemed staged and that the spouses seemed uncomfortable; the Federal Court noted that personal awkwardness may be expected in arranged marriages. The board must be careful not to apply western expectations of marriage in considering the genuineness of a relationship.

18 *Chen v Canada (MSEP)*, 2010 FC 584. The applicant had previously been sponsored by his wife. Upon arriving in Canada, he found her pregnant with another man's child and ended the relationship. When he later attempted to sponsor a new spouse as a permanent resident, he was declared inadmissible for misrepresenting his relationship as genuine. The Federal Court allowed his appeal as it was impossible for him to know that his relationship with his first spouse would not last.

19 *IRPR*, s 117(9).

20 *Ibid*, s 130(1).

21 *Ibid*, s 133(1).

22 *Ibid*, s 132(1).

23 *IRPA*, s 96.

24 *Tretsetsang v Canada (MCI)*, 2016 FCA 175. In theory, this "country of nationality" requirement could restrict Jewish persons from ever becoming a Convention refugee, due to Israel's Law of Return offering citizenship by birthright to any Jewish person. This problem was raised by a Russian claimant of Jewish heritage in *Katkova v Canada (MCI)*, 1997 CanLII 5166, 130 FTR 192 (FC). Justice McKeown noted that the Law of Return only applies to "every Jew who has expressed his desire to settle in Israel," and as the applicant stated she did not want to go to Israel, it should not be considered a country of nationality under s 96.

25 *Canada (Attorney General) v Ward*, [1993] 2 SCR 689 at 723, 103 DLR (4th) 1.

26 *Singh v Canada (MEI)*, [1985] 1 SCR 177, 17 DLR (4th) 422.

27 *Adjei v Canada (MEI)*, [1989] 2 FC 680, 57 DLR (4th) 153.

28 *Thirunavukkarasu v Canada (MEI)* (1993), 109 DLR (4th) 682, 1993 CanLII 3011 (FCA).

29 2014 FC 449.

30 *Ibid* at paras 4–5.

31 *IRPA*, s 101(1)–(2).

32 *Ibid*, s 101(1)(b).

33 IRCC, "AFGH — Response to Ukraine and Afghanistan — April 25, 2022" (last modified 22 August 2022), online: www.canada.ca/en/immigration-refugees-citizenship/corporate/transparency/committees/afgh-apr-25-2022/response-ukraine-afghanistan.html.

34 *Ibid*.

35 The Canadian Press, "1 in 3 Ukrainians with Visas Have Arrived in Canada as Applications Near 700K" *Global News* (22 November 2022), online: https://globalnews.ca/news/9298201/ukrainians-visas-canada.

36 IRCC, "#WelcomeAfghans: Key Figures" (last modified 5 December 2023), online: www.canada.ca/en/immigration-refugees-citizenship/services/refugees/afghanistan/key-figures.html.

37 Statistics Canada, 2022 (table), "Census Profile," 2021 Census of Population. Statistics Canada Catalogue no. 98-316-X2021001 (Ottawa), released 15 December 2022, online: www12.statcan.gc.ca/census-recensement/2021/dp-pd/prof/index.cfm?Lang=E (accessed 17 January 2023).

38 A. Fong & Z. Saar, "Canada Needs to Be as Welcoming to Afghan Refugees as It Is to Ukrainians" *The Conversation* (25 May 2022), online: https://theconversation.com/canada-needs-to-be-as-welcoming-to-afghan-refugees-as-it-is-to-ukrainians-182363.

39 B. Kaufmann, "Afghans Languish in Hotel Rooms While Ukrainian Refugees Are Quickly Settled: Advocate" *Calgary Herald* (11 October 2022), online: https://calgaryherald.com/news/local-news/afghans-languish-in-hotel-rooms-while-ukrainian-refugees-are-quickly-settled-advocate.

40 IRCC, "Applying for Permanent Residence from within Canada: Protected Persons and Convention Refugees [IMM 5205]" (last modified 24 July 2023), online: www.canada.ca/en/immigration-refugees-citizenship/services/application/application-forms-guides/guide-5205-applying-permanent-residence-within-canada-protected-persons-convention-refugees.html.

41 *Ibid*. See Part 8 — Refugee Classes of the *Immigration and Refugee Protection Regulations*, ss 138–158 — Pursuant to s 158:

> If the foreign national and their family members intend to reside in the Province of Quebec, the sponsor must meet the requirements for sponsorship that are provided by regulations made under *An Act respecting immigration to Québec*, R.S.Q., c.I-0.2, as amended from time to time. In such a case, the requirements of this Division, other than section 156, do not apply.

42 *Kanthasamy v Canada (MCI)*, 2015 SCC 61 at para 60 [*Kanthasamy*].

43 See, for example, *Mojica v Canada (MCI)*, 2014 FC 35 at para 44. Justice Russell notes that the applicant did not challenge the officer's conclusion that she could obtain a Parent and Grandparent Super Visa, which would enable her to remain in Canada for a two-year period. As this was an available option, it was "difficult to see how the Applicant would have to face unusual and undeserved or disproportionate hardship."

44 *Kanthasamy*, above note 42 at para 44.

45 *Ibid* at para 45.

46 Article 3.1 of the *Convention on the Rights of the Child*, Can TS 1992 No 3, provides: "In all actions concerning children, whether undertaken by public or private social welfare institutions, courts of law, administrative authorities or legislative bodies, *the best interests of the child shall be a primary consideration*." [Emphasis added.]

47 [1999] 2 SCR 817, 174 DLR (4th) 193.

48 *Ibid* at para 75.

49 *Kanthasamy*, above note 42 at para 59.

50 See, for example, *Sinniah v Canada (MCI)*, 2011 FC 1285 and *Moya v Canada (MCI)*, 2012 FC 971.

51 *Canada (MCI) v Legault*, [2002] 4 FC 358, 212 DLR (4th) 139 at para 19, Décary JA writes:

> In short, the Immigration Act and the Canadian immigration policy are founded on the idea that whoever comes to Canada with the intention of settling must be of good faith and comply to the letter with the requirements both in form and substance of the Act.... In this sense, the Minister is at liberty to take into consideration the fact that the humanitarian and compassionate grounds that person claims are the result of his own actions.

52 *De Vazquez v Canada (MCI)*, 2014 FC 530 at para 42.

53 See, for example, *Damian v Canada (MCI)*, 2019 FC 1158.

54 IRCC, "Permanent Residence Pathways for Hong Kong Residents: Who Can Apply" (last modified 5 January 2023), online: www.canada.ca/en/immigration-refugees-citizenship/services/immigrate-canada/hong-kong-residents-permanent-residence/eligibility.html.

55 IRCC, "Canada Doubles Immigration Program for Out-of-Status Construction Workers in the Greater Toronto Area" (last modified 15 August 2023), online: www.canada.ca/en/immigration-refugees-citizenship/news/2023/01/canada-doubles-immigration-program-for-out-of-status-construction-workers-in-the-greater-toronto-area.html.

56 IRCC, "Guide 0124 — Subsequent Temporary Public Policy to Continue to Facilitate Access to Permanent Resident Status for Out-of-Status Construction Workers in the Greater Toronto Area (GTA)" (last modified 1 December 2023), online: www.canada.ca/en/immigration-refugees-citizenship/services/application/application-forms-guides/guide-0124-out-of-status-construction-workers.html.

57 IRCC, "Guide 5069 — Temporary Public Policy: Temporary Resident to Permanent Resident Pathway (TR to PR Pathway)" (last modified 9 February 2023), online: www.canada.ca/en/immigration-refugees-citizenship/services/application/application-forms-guides/guide-5069-temporary-resident-permanent-resident-pathway.html.

58 For the full list of eligible occupations, see online: www.canada.ca/en/immigration-refugees-citizenship/services/immigrate-canada/tr-pr-pathway/who-can-apply.html.

59 *The Regularization of Non-Status Immigrants in Canada 1960–2004*, November 2004, online: www.kairoscanada.org/wp-content/uploads/2020/08/The-Regularization-of-NonStatus-Immigrants-in-Canada-1960-2004.pdf.

60 I. Inclan, "Migrants Call on Trudeau to Fulfill His Promise to Regularize the Undocumented" *NEW CANADIAN MEDIA* (22 January 2023), online: https://newcanadianmedia.ca/migrants-call-on-trudeau-to-fulfill-his-promise-to-regularize-the-undocumented/.

61 Prime Minister of Canada "Minister of Immigration, Refugees and Citizenship Mandate Letter" Government of Canada (16 December 2021), online: https://pm.gc.ca/en/mandate-letters/2021/12/16/minister-immigration-refugees-and-citizenship-mandate-letter.

62 Foreign nationals who have a condition that is maintained with medication are still considered to be "*in good health*."

63 IRCC, "Visitor Visa: Who Can Apply" (last modified 17 November 2023), online: www.canada.ca/en/immigration-refugees-citizenship/services/visit-canada/eligibility.html.

64 *IRPR*, ss 193, 183(1).

65 *IRPA*, s 3(1)(d).

66 IRCC, "Enhancements to the Super Visa Program for Parents and Grandparents Will Help Reunite Families More Easily and for Longer" (last modified 7 June 2022), online: www.canada.ca/en/immigration-refugees-citizenship/news/2022/06/enhancements-to-the-super-visa-program-for-parents-and-grandparents-will-help-reunite-families-more-easily-and-for-longer.html.

67 IRCC, "Ministerial Instruction Regarding the Parent and Grandparent Super Visa" (last modified 11 January 2021), online: www.canada.ca/en/immigration-refugees-citizenship/corporate/mandate/policies-operational-instructions-agreements/ministerial-instructions/other-goals/mi-super-visa.html.

68 IRCC, "Sponsor Your Parents and Grandparents: How to Apply" (last modified 24 October 2023), online: www.canada.ca/en/immigration-refugees-citizenship/services/immigrate-canada/family-sponsorship/sponsor-parents-grandparents/apply.html.

69 *IRPR*, s 196.1.

70 For a full list of LMIA exemptions through the International Mobility Program, refer to online: www.canada.ca/en/immigration-refugees-citizenship/corporate/publications-manuals/operational-bulletins-manuals/temporary-residents/foreign-workers/exemption-codes.html.

71 *Samra v Canada (MCI)*, 2020 FC 157 at paras 25 and 27: "The Respondent notes that the officer's duty of procedural fairness in this context is low, with the officer having no obligation to notify the applicant of deficiencies in the application or supporting documentation.... I am persuaded by the

Respondent's argument. There were no issues relating to credibility or accuracy of evidence, so no interview was required."

72 See *Portillo v Canada (MCI)*, 2014 FC 866 [*Portillo*]. The employer was a McDonald's restaurant, which advertised that no experience was needed, "although some previous experience in the fast-food industry would be preferred."

73 See *Ul Zaman v Canada (MCI)*, 2020 FC 268. The applicant of a sweet-making company did not speak English or French, only their native Urdu. However, the head sweet-maker was fluent only in Urdu, and twelve of the company's fourteen employees were bilingual (English and Urdu). The officer was found to have overemphasized the language requirement.

74 *Portillo*, above note 72.

75 *Liu v Canada (MCI)*, 2018 CarswellNat 4696; 2018 CarswellNat 5130 [*Liu*].

76 *Fredy's Welding Inc v Canada (MCI)*, 2017 FC 7.

77 *Liu*, above note 75.

78 IRCC, "Program Requirements for the Global Talent Stream" (last modified 24 November 2023), online: www.canada.ca/en/employment-social-development/services/foreign-workers/global-talent/requirements.html.

79 *Ibid.*

80 IRCC, "Find Out if You Need a Labour Market Impact Assessment (LMIA), and How to Hire a Temporary Foreign Worker" (last modified 11 December 2023), online: www.canada.ca/en/immigration-refugees-citizenship/services/work-canada/hire-temporary-foreign/find-need-labour-market-impact-assessment.html.

81 IRCC, "Program Requirements for Low-Wage Positions: Recruitment and Advertisement" (last modified 24 November 2023), online: www.canada.ca/en/employment-social-development/services/foreign-workers/median-wage/low/requirements.html#h2.9.

82 *Ibid.*

83 IRCC, "Program Requirements for High-Wage Positions" (last modified 24 November 2023), online: www.canada.ca/en/employment-social-development/services/foreign-workers/median-wage/high/requirements.html

84 *Ibid.*

85 *IRPR*, s 215(1)–(2).

86 *Ibid*, s 214.

87 *Ibid*, s 215(1).

88 *Adom v Canada (MCI)*, 2019 FC 26 at para 16.

89 See *Mahida v Canada (MCI)*, 2019 FC 423.

90 *IRPR*, s 188. For more information, refer to online: www.canada.ca/en/immigration-refugees-citizenship/services/study-canada/study-permit/eligibility.html.

91 Government of Canada, *International Education*, online: www.international.gc.ca/education/strategy-2019-2024-strategie.aspx?lang=eng.

92 "Sold a Lie" *CBC News* (11 October 2022), online: www.cbc.ca/news/fifthestate/sold-a-lie-1.6612702; CIMM Committee Report, "Differential Treatment in Recruitment and Acceptance Rates of Foreign Students in Quebec and in the Rest of Canada," online: www.ourcommons.ca/DocumentViewer/en/44-1/CIMM/report-8/page-30; Mario D. Bellissimo, "Canadian International Student Program 2022 & Beyond," House of Commons Canada (25 February 2022) online: www.ourcommons.ca/Content/Committee/441/CIMM/Brief/BR11713090/br-external/BellissimoLawGroupPC-1-e.pdf.

93 *IRPA*, s 24(1).

94 *IRPR*, s 183(4)–(5).

95 IRCC, "Temporary Resident Permits (TRPs): Eligibility and Assessment" (last modified 28 June 2019), online: www.canada.ca/en/immigration-refugees-citizenship/corporate/publications-manuals/operational-bulletins-manuals/temporary-residents/permits/eligibility-assessment.html.

96 *Donnellan v Canada (MCI)*, 2020 FC 227.

97 See, for example, *Farhat v Canada (MCI)*, 2006 FC 1275 at paras 22, 38, 40; *César Nguesso v Canada (MCI)*, 2015 FC 880 at paras 95–97; *Stordock v Canada (MCI)*, 2013 FC 16 at para 9; *Vaguedano Alvarez v Canada (MCI)*, 2011 FC 667 at para 36; and *Nasso v Canada (MCI)*, 2008 FC 1003 at paras 13–15.

98 See, for example, *Palmero v Canada (MCI)*, 2016 FC 1128 [*Palermo*] and *Krasniqi v Canada (MCI)*, 2018 FC 743.

99 *Palmero*, above note 98 at para 21.

100 2011 FC 1269.

101 *Ibid* at para 77.

102 2018 FC 1085.

103 See the *Constitution Act, 1867*, 30 & 31 Vict, c 3, s 95:

> In each Province the Legislature may make Laws in relation to … Immigration into the Province; and it is hereby declared that the Parliament of Canada may from Time to Time make Laws in relation … to Immigration into all or any of the Provinces; and any Law of the Legislature of a Province relative to … Immigration shall have effect in and for the Province as long and as far only as it is not repugnant to any Act of the Parliament of Canada.

104 *Québec Immigration Act*, CQLR c I-0.2.1.

105 A. Moosapeta, "Why Does Québec Have Its Own Immigration Policy?" CIC News (13 December 2022), online: www.cicnews.com/2022/12/why-does-Québec-have-its-own-immigration-policy-1230732.html.

106 *QIA*, s 1.

107 *Ibid*, ss 6–7.

108 *Ibid*, ss 8–9.

109 Government of Quebec, "Immigration," online: www.quebec.ca/en/immigration.

110 *QIA*, s 25.

111 *Québec Immigration Regulations*, CQLR c I-0.2.1, r 3, ss 23–24 (*QIR*).

112 *Ibid*, s 25.

113 *Ibid*, s 32.

114 *Ibid*, s 33.

115 *Ibid*, s 37.

116 *Ibid*, s 47.

117 *Ibid*, s 51.

118 *Ibid*, s 24.1.

119 *Ibid*, s 60.

120 *QIA*, s 34.

121 *QIR*, s 63.

122 *Ibid*, s 61.

123 *QIA*, s 17.

124 *QIR*, s 5.

125 *Ibid*, s 6.

126 *Ibid*, s 11.

127 *Ibid*, s 18

128 Legisinfo, "Budget Implementation Act 2008: Recorded Votes," online: www.parl.ca/LegisInfo/en/bill/39-2/C-50.

129 Wayne Dyer, www.drwaynedyer.com.

CHAPTER THREE | Canadian Immigration Inadmissibility

1 SC 2001, c 27 [*IRPA*].

2 See Appendix 1: Inadmissibility Provisions in the *Immigration and Refugee Protection Act* and Evidentiary Thresholds in this text.

3 *IRPA*, s 33.

4 *ENF 2, Evaluating Inadmissibility* at 8; *ENF 5, Writing 44(1) Reports*, Section 7.4 Standard of Proof at 16.

5 *ENF 5, Writing 44(1) Reports*, Section 7.3 Burden of Proof at 15.

6 Mario D. Bellissimo, *Canadian Citizenship and Immigration Inadmissibility Law*, 2d ed, ch 1, part II, section 1:2: A Brief History of Exclusion in Canadian Immigration Legislation at 1–2 [Bellissimo].

7 *Ibid*, ch 1, part II, section 1:3: Objectives of the *IRPA* at 1–5.

8 *IRPA*, ss 3(3)(a), 3(1)(h), and 3(1)(i).

9 *IRPA*, s 34(1).

10 *Special Economic Measures Act*, SC 1992, c 17.
11 *ENF 1, Inadmissibility* at 6.
12 *Ibid* at 8.
13 *Ibid* at 9.
14 *ENF 2, Evaluating Inadmissibility* at 22.
15 *Chiau v Canada (MCI)*, 2000 CanLII 16793 (FCA), [2001] 2 FC 297 at paras 57–59.
16 *Jalloh v Canada (PSEP)*, 2012 FC 317 at para 37.
17 *ENF 2, Evaluating Inadmissibility* at 23.
18 *Suresh v Canada (MCI)*, 2002 SCC 1 at para 90.
19 SC 2000, c 24 [*CAHWCA*].
20 *Ezokola v Canada (MCI)*, 2013 SCC 40 at paras 84–85.
21 *Ibid* at para 91.
22 *ENF 18, Human and International Rights Violations* at 11.
23 *Ibid* at 18.
24 *Ibid* at 17.
25 Bill S-8 (17 May 2022), online: www.parl.ca/DocumentViewer/en/44-1/bill/S-8/first-reading (Note: *IRPA* amended by SC 2023, c 19.)
26 SC 1992, c17, s 4, online: https://laws-lois.justice.gc.ca/eng/acts/s-14.5/page-1.html.
27 SC 2017, c 21, online: https://laws.justice.gc.ca/eng/acts/J-2.3/.
28 *IRPA*, ss 21(2), 25(1), 25.1(1), 42.1, and 101(f).
29 Bill S-8, s 7 enacting a new s 35.1(a)–(c). Note that the current s 35(1)(d) covers *SEMA* s 4(1.1)(c) and (d).
30 Bill S-8, s 1 amending s 4(2)(c) of the *IRPA*; s 2 amending s 21(2) of the *IRPA*; s 8 amending s 42(1) & (2) of the *IRPA*; s 9 amending s 55(3) of the *IRPA*, s 10 amending s 58(1)(c) of the *IRPA*; s 11 amending s 64(1) of the *IRPA*; s 16 amending s 24.1(1) of the *IRPR*, s 17 amending s 24.2 (1)(g) of the *IRPR*; s 18 amending s 65(b)(ii) of the *IRPR*; s 19 amending s 228(1)(f) of the *IRPR*; s 20 amending s 229(1)(b) of the *IRPR*; s 21 amending s 230(3) of the *IRPR.*
31 Bill S-8, s 7 enacting new s 35.1(2); s 12 amending s 101(1)(f). Standing Committee on Foreign Affairs and International Development, 1st Sess, 44th Parl Bill S-8, *An Act to amend the Immigration and Refugee Protection Act, to make consequential amendments to other Acts and to amend the Immigration and Refugee Protection Regulations*, May 31st, 2023. The Committee has submitted its report, with amendments: Committee Report No. 18 — FAAE (44-1) — House of Commons of Canada (ourcommons.ca).
32 *IRPR*, s19.
33 Bellissimo, above note 6, c 10, 10.4. Equivalency at 10–21.
34 *Brannson v Minister of Employment and Immigration*, [1981] 2 FC 141 (FCA).
35 *Hill v Canada* (1987), 1 Imm LR (2d) 1 (FCA).

36 *Li v Canada*, 1996 CanLII 4086, [1997] 1 FC 235 (FCA).

37 *Tran v Canada (MPSEP)*, 2017 SCC 50 at para 24.

38 IRCC, "Assessing Inadmissibility Due to Serious Criminality Following Tran v Canada" (last modified 14 November 2019), online: www.canada.ca/en/immigration-refugees-citizenship/corporate/publications-manuals/operational-bulletins-manuals/standard-requirements/tran.html.

39 CLEO, Steps to Justice, Glossary, "Hybrid offence," online: https://stepstojustice.ca/glossary/hybrid-offence.

40 *IRPA*, s 36(3)(a).

41 Bellissimo, above note 6, ch 1, part V, section 1:14: "Committing an Act" Provision of the *IRPA* at 1–36.

42 *IRPA*, s 36(3)(d).

43 *Ibid*, s 36(3)(e).

44 Bellissimo, above note 6, ch 1, part VI, section 1:15 at 1–38.

45 *ENF 2, Evaluating Inadmissibility* at 19.

46 *Ibid* at 20.

47 *IRPA*, s 37(2).

48 *IRPR*, s 30; IRCC, "Find Out if You Need a Medical Exam" (last modified 7 July 2022), online: www.canada.ca/en/immigration-refugees-citizenship/services/application/medical-police/medical-exams/requirements-temporary-residents/country-requirements.html.

49 *IRPA*, s 38(1)(a).

50 *Ibid*, s 38(1)(b).

51 *Ibid*, s 38(1)(c).

52 *Hilewitz v Canada (MCI); De Jong v Canada (MCI)*, 2005 SCC 57.

53 IRCC, "ARCHIVED — Temporary Public Policy Regarding Excessive Demand on Health and Social Services" (last modified 26 October 2022), online: www.canada.ca/en/immigration-refugees-citizenship/corporate/mandate/policies-operational-instructions-agreements/excessive-demand-june-2018.html and "Program Delivery Update: Public Policy Implementation for Excessive Demand and the Centralization of Files — June 1, 2018" (last modified 1 June 2018), online: www.canada.ca/en/immigration-refugees-citizenship/corporate/publications-manuals/operational-bulletins-manuals/updates/2018-excessive-demand.html.

54 IRCC, "Changes to the Medical Inadmissibility Policy of the Immigration and Refugee Protection Act Take Effect" (last modified 16 March 2022), online: www.canada.ca/en/immigration-refugees-citizenship/news/notices/changes-medical-inadmissibility-policy-irpa-take-effect.html.

55 2007 FCA 282.

56 2011 FCA 35.

57 2013 FCA 257.
58 *IRPR*, s 1(1) Definitions.
59 *Ibid.*
60 *Ibid.*
61 *IRPA*, s 38(2).
62 IRCC, "Proof of Funds — Skilled Immigrants (Express Entry)" (last modified 23 August 2023), online: www.canada.ca/en/immigration-refugees-citizenship/services/immigrate-canada/express-entry/documents/proof-funds.html.
63 IRCC, "Applications Under Family Classes: Assessing the Sponsor" (last modified 10 January 2023), online: www.canada.ca/en/immigration-refugees-citizenship/corporate/publications-manuals/operational-bulletins-manuals/permanent-residence/non-economic-classes/family-class-assessing-sponsor.html.
64 *IRPR*, s 133(4).
65 *IRPA*, s 39.
66 Bellissimo, above note 6, ch 5, part II, section 5:3: Obtaining Evidence at 5–7.
67 *ENF 2, Evaluating Inadmissibility* at 33.
68 *IRPA*, s 40(2).
69 Bellissimo, above note 6, ch 6, part II, section 6:3: subsection 40(1)(a) at 6–6.
70 *IRPA*, s 40(1).
71 *ENF 2, Evaluating Inadmissibility* at 30.
72 *Baro v Canada (MCI)*, 2007 FC 1299 at para 15 and *ENF 2, Evaluating Inadmissibility* at 32. *He v Canada (MCI)*, 2022 FC 112; *Vahora v Canada (MCI)*, 2022 FC 778; *Markar v Canada (MCI)*, 2022 FC 684; *Gautam v Canada (MCI)*, 2022 FC 550, and *Zhang v Canada (MCI)*, 2022 FC 197.
73 2022 FCA 50.
74 *IRPA*, s 42(1).
75 *IRPA*, s 42(2).
76 *ENF 5, Writing 44(1) Reports* at 17.
77 *Ibid*, Section 8.1 Limited discretion of officer at A44(1) at 17 as well as Section 9. A44(1) reports concerning foreign nationals, Sections 9.4 at 21, 9.6 at 22–24, and 9.7 at 24–25.
78 *ENF 6, Review of Reports Under A44(2)*, Section 7.2 Reviewing the A44(1) report at 16, Section 8.1 Minister's Delegate Options — Limited discretion of the MD at A44(2) at 21, and Section 15.6 Preparation of warning letter at 42–43.
79 *IRPA*, s 44(2).
80 Bellissimo, above note 6, ch 9, part III, Issuing Removal Orders: Temporary versus Permanent Residents at 9–10.
81 *IRPR*, s 223.
82 *Ibid*, ss 224–27.

83 Canada Border Services Agency (CBSA), "Arrests, Detentions, and Removals" (last modified 27 April 2023), online: www.cbsa-asfc.gc.ca/security-securite/rem-ren-eng.html. Refer also to *IRPA*, s 36(3)(c) & (d).

84 *IRPA*, s 56(1).

85 *Ibid*, s 45.

86 *IRPR*, s 48.

87 *ENF 20, Detention* at 33.

88 *IRPA*, s 57(1).

89 *Ibid*, s 57(2).

90 *Ibid*, s 173.

91 *Immigration Division Rules*, SOR/2002-229.

92 Bellissimo, above note 6, ch 8, part 8.3, section (c) Imposition of Detention at 8–16.

93 *Brown v Canada (MCI)*, 2020 FCA 130 at paras 122–23.

94 *Ibid* at paras 44 and 90–96.

95 *IRPA*, s 58(3).

96 IRB, "Chairperson Guideline 2: Detention," 3.2 Release Considerations, online: https://irb-cisr.gc.ca/en/legal-policy/policies/Pages/GuideDir02.aspx.

97 *Alvin Brown v Ministry of Public Safety*, 2016 ONSC 7760 at paras 30–31, 35, 106–7, and 109.

98 *ENF 20, Detention* at 27.

99 Part I of the *Constitution Act, 1982*, being Schedule B to the *Canada Act 1982* (UK), 1982, c 11.

100 2015 ONCA 700 at para 113 [*Chaudhary*].

101 Bellissimo, above note 6, ch 8, part 8.55, Habeas Corpus at 8–36.

102 2019 SCC 29.

103 *Chaudhary*, above note 100 at para 81.

104 *Ibid* at para 106.

105 Canadian Museum of Immigration, Pier 21, *Canadian Immigration Acts and Legislation*, online: https://pier21.ca/research/immigration-history/canadian-immigration-acts-and-legislation.

CHAPTER FOUR | **Challenging Canadian Immigration Inadmissibility**

1 *Immigration and Refugee Protection Act*, SC 2001, c 27 [*IRPA*].

2 Mario D. Bellissimo, *Canadian Citizenship and Immigration Inadmissibility Law*, 2d ed, ch 12, 12.5, Sample Inland H&C Submission at 12–19 [Bellissimo].

3 *Immigration and Refugee Protection Regulations*, SOR/2002-227 [*IRPR*].

4 2015 SCC 61 [*Kanthasamy*].

5 *Ibid* at para 33.

6 (1970), 4 IAC (IAB) at 350.

7 *Kanthasamy*, above note 4 at para 21.

8 IRCC, "Humanitarian and Compassionate Considerations: Assessment and Processing" (last modified 11 July 2017), online: www.canada.ca/en/immigration-refugees-citizenship/corporate/publications-manuals/operational-bulletins-manuals/permanent-residence/humanitarian-compassionate-consideration/processing.html.

9 IRCC, "Humanitarian and Compassionate Assessment: Hardship and the H&C Assessment" (last modified 2 March 2016), online: www.canada.ca/en/immigration-refugees-citizenship/corporate/publications-manuals/operational-bulletins-manuals/permanent-residence/humanitarian-compassionate-consideration/processing/assessment-hardship-assessment.html.

10 IRCC, "The Humanitarian and Compassionate Assessment: Reconsideration of a Negative H&C Decision" (last modified 24 July 2014), online: www.canada.ca/en/immigration-refugees-citizenship/corporate/publications-manuals/operational-bulletins-manuals/permanent-residence/humanitarian-compassionate-consideration/processing/assessment-reconsideration-negative-decision.html.

11 Sections 34, 35, and 37 render foreign nationals inadmissible for security, human, or international rights violations, and organized criminality, respectively.

12 *IRPA,* s 25.1(1) [emphasis added].

13 IRCC, "Humanitarian and Compassionate: Dealing with Inadmissibility" (last modified 11 July 2017), online: www.canada.ca/en/immigration-refugees-citizenship/corporate/publications-manuals/operational-bulletins-manuals/permanent-residence/humanitarian-compassionate-consideration/processing/dealing-with-inadmissibility.html.

14 *Shen v Canada (MCI)*, 2018 FC 620 at para 29. See also *Xia v Canada (MCI)*, 2022 FC 1414 at para 26.

15 *Kobita v Canada (MCI)*, 2012 FC 1479.

16 *IRPA*, s 25(1.3).

17 *Mulla v Canada (MCI)*, 2017 FC 445.

18 *Lemus v Canada (MCI)*, 2014 FCA 114 at para 40.

19 *Kanthasamy*, above note 4 at para 33.

20 *Ali v Canada (MCI)*, 2018 FC 824 at paras 17–19, citing *Cieslak v Canada (MCI)*, 2018 FC 579 at para 17 and *Marshall v Canada (MCI)*, 2017 FC 72 [emphasis added] [internal citations omitted].

21 *Yang v Canada (MCI)*, 2018 FC 780 at para 61.

22 *Shah v Canada (MCI)*, 2011 FC 1269 at para 58.

23 *Hinzman v Canada (MCI)*, 2010 FCA 177 at paras 39–40 [internal citations omitted].

24 *Gonzalez v Canada (MCI)*, 2015 FC 382 at para 55.

25 *Gonzalez v Canada (MCI)*, 2017 FC 448 at paras 24–25.

26 *Hawthorne v Canada (MCI)*, 2002 FCA 475 at para 5 [*Hawthorne*].

27 *Kanthasamy*, above note 4 at para 41.

28 *Akyol v Canada (MCI)*, 2014 FC 1252 at para 24 [internal citations omitted].

29 *Kaur v Canada (Immigration, Refugees and Citizenship)*, 2017 FC 549 at para 5 [internal citations omitted].

30 *IRPR*, s 2.

31 *Suleiman v Canada (MCI)*, 2017 FC 395.

32 *Naredo v Canada (MCI)*, 2000 CanLII 15973 at paras 20–21 (FC).

33 *Ramsawak v Canada (MCI)*, 2009 FC 636 at paras 19–20, citing MacKay J in *Swartz v Canada (MCI)*, 2002 FCT 268 and Mandamin J in *Yoo v Canada (MCI)*, 2009 FC 343.

34 *IRPA*, ss 36(1) & (2) and 38–42.

35 This bar does not apply in spousal sponsorships under the public policy in which the only inadmissibility is that the person is out of status.

36 IRCC, "Humanitarian and Compassionate: Intake and Who May Apply" (last modified 20 April 2021), online: www.canada.ca/en/immigration-refugees-citizenship/corporate/publications-manuals/operational-bulletins-manuals/permanent-residence/humanitarian-compassionate-consideration/intake-who-may-apply.html.

37 See, for example, *Brar v Canada (MCI)*, 2011 FC 691, in which the offence had been fifteen years prior to the H&C application. The minister's delegate's finding that "lack of new convictions does not in and of itself provide insight into a person's beliefs, morals or future plans" effectively means that the applicant's years of rehabilitation were given no weight (at para 56).

38 IRCC, "Humanitarian and Compassionate: Criminal Inadmissibilities — A36(1) and A36(2)" (last modified 24 July 2014), online: www.canada.ca/en/immigration-refugees-citizenship/corporate/publications-manuals/operational-bulletins-manuals/permanent-residence/humanitarian-compassionate-consideration/processing/dealing-with-inadmissibility/criminal-inadmissibilities-a36-1-a36-2.html.

39 *Singh v Canada (MCI)*, 2018 FC 744.

40 See *L (B) v Canada (MCI)*, 2012 FC 538, in which the officer determined that the applicant's sexual assault conviction outweighed any positive H&C factors and denied the application. Before conveying the decision to the applicant, the officer learned that the applicant had obtained a pardon. The officer removed all mentions of the sexual assault from the refusal, but did not alter the decision and provided no reasons as to why the applicant was still inadmissible for serious criminality. The application for judicial review was therefore allowed.

41 *Chieu v Canada (MCI)*, 1998 CanLII 9121, [1999] 1 FC 605 (CA) at para 18, endorsing *Ribic v Canada (MEI)*, [1985] IABD No 4 at para 4.

42 *Katwaru v Canada (MCI)*, 2010 FC 1277.

43 *Jones v Canada (MCI)*, 2018 FC 1070 at para 43.

44 *Avila v Canada (MCI)*, 2009 FC 13 at para 17

45 IRCC, "Humanitarian and Compassionate: Medical Inadmissibility A38(1)" (last modified 11 July 2017), online: www.canada.ca/en/immigration-refugees-citizenship/corporate/publications-manuals/operational-bulletins-manuals/permanent-residence/humanitarian-compassionate-consideration/processing/dealing-with-inadmissibility/medical-inadmissibility-a38-1.html.

46 *Fatt Kok v Canada (MCI)*, 2011 FC 741 at para 23. See also *Canada (MCI) v Khosa*, 2009 SCC 12 at para 61 and *Lupsa v Canada (MCI)*, 2009 FC 1054.

47 *Sittamplan v Canada (Citizenship and Immigration)*, 2009 FC 65.

48 *Wong v Canada (MCI)*, 2010 FC 569 at para 13.

49 *Kandhai v Canada (MCI)*, 2009 FC 656 at paras 24–26.

50 *IRPA*, above note 34.

51 *Owusu v Canada (MCI)*, 2004 FCA 38.

52 *IRPA*, above note 34.

53 *IRPA*, s 24(1).

54 Bellissimo, above note 2, ch 12, 12.7, Admissibility Requirements for TRPs at 12–40.

55 *IRPR*, s 199(d).

56 *Ibid*, s 215(1)(e).

57 *Ibid*, ss 64–65.

58 *IRPA*, s 65.

59 Bellissimo, above note 2, ch 12, 12.7, (f) TRPs: Subsequent Permits at 12–50.

60 IRCC, "Temporary Resident Permits (TRPs)" (last modified 22 July 2020), online: www.canada.ca/en/immigration-refugees-citizenship/corporate/publications-manuals/operational-bulletins-manuals/temporary-residents/permits.html.

61 *White (Litigation Guardian of) v Canada (MCI)*, 2011 FC 1043 at paras 49, 67.

62 *Lee v Canada (MCI)*, 2008 FC 236 at para 4, citing *Farhat v Canada (MCI)*, 2006 FC 1275 at paras 15, 17, 22–24 [*Farhat*] [internal citations omitted].

63 *Ramnanan v Canada (MCI)*, 2015 FC 632 at para 34. See also *Marques v Canada (MCI)*, 2010 FC 376 at para 13.

64 *Zlydnev v Canada (MCI)*, 2015 FC 604 at para 21. See also *Ali v Canada (MCI)*, 2008 FC 784, which states at para 10: "However, in this case, the Immigration Officer either simply had the material facts wrong or failed to consider material evidence. The department's own CIC Policy Manual directs officers to consider family ties as part of the consideration of personal circumstances."

65 *Stordock v Canada (MCI)*, 2013 FC 16 at para 11.

66 *Krasniqi v Canada (MCI)*, 2018 FC 743 at para 27 [internal citation omitted].

67 *Alabi v Canada (MCI)*, 2017 FC 294 at para 24.

68 *Farhat*, above note 62 at para 24; Immigration Manual, *OP 20, Temporary Resident Permits*, s 5.22.

69 *Vaguedano Alvarez v Canada (MCI)*, 2011 FC 667 at para 37.

70 *IRPA*, s 52(1).

71 *OP 1, Procedures* at 36.

72 *Ibid* at 37–38.

73 IRCC, "What Is a Record Suspension?" (last modified 19 October 2018), online: www.canada.ca/en/parole-board/services/record-suspensions/what-is-a-record-suspension.html.

74 IRCC, "Determining Your Eligibility for a Record Suspension or Pardon" (last modified 8 June 2022), online: www.canada.ca/en/parole-board/services/record-suspensions/determining-your-eligibility-for-record-suspension.html.

75 *IRPR*, ss 17–18.

76 *Tabban v Canada (MCI)*, 2018 FC 1279 at para 21; *De Campos Gregorio v Canada (MCI)*, 2020 FC 748 at paras 23–28; *Ramirez Velasco v Canada (MCI)*, 2019 FC 543 at paras 8–9.

77 *De Campos Gregorio*, above note 76 at para 27; *Lau v Canada (MCI)*, 2016 FC 1184 at para 24.

78 Bellissimo, above note 2, ch 4, part III, section 4:7: Procedural Fairness at 4–34.

79 *Ibid*, ch 6, part II, section 5:3.

80 *Hilewitz v Canada (MCI); De Jong v Canada (MCI)*, 2005 SCC 57 at paras 54–55.

81 Bellissimo, above note 2, ch 4, part IV, Responding to the PFL at 4–37.

82 *IRPA*, s 42(1).

83 *Agraira v Canada (MPSEP)*, 2013 SCC 36 at para 64.

84 *IRPR*, s 24.1(1).

85 CBSA, "Guide to Applying for a Declaration of Relief Under Subsection 42.1(1) of the *Immigration and Refugee Protection Act*" (last modified 28 November 2023), online: www.cbsa-asfc.gc.ca/travel-voyage/gadr-gddd-eng.html.

86 *Ibid.*

87 *Thomas v Canada (MPSEP)*, 2020 FC 164.

88 *Ibid* at para 21 citing *Douze v Canada (MCI)*, 2010 FC 1337; *Tameh v Canada (MPSEP)*, 2017 FC 288; and *Esmaeili-Tarki v Canada (MPSEP)*, 2010 FC 697.

89 *Canada (MPSEP) v Gaytan*, 2021 FCA 163 at paras 103 and 111.

90 *IRPA*, s 170(b)–(c); IRB, "About the Board — Divisions" (last modified 24 July 2023), online: https://irb.gc.ca/en/board/Pages/index.aspx#ab2.

91 A "quasi-judicial tribunal" refers to a body created by law with a mandate to settle matters in an impartial manner.

92 *IRPA*, s 45(d).
93 *Ibid*, s 173.
94 SOR/2002-229.
95 *IRPA*, s. 169.
96 *Immigration Division Rules*, r 7(1).
97 *IRPA*, s 64(1). One exception is convictions inside Canada that are punishable by a maximum term of imprisonment of at least ten years (*IRPA*, s 64(2)).
98 *IRPA*, s 64(3).
99 SOR/2022-277.
100 *IRPA*, s 67(1)(c).
101 *Ribic v Canada (MEI)*, [1985] IABD No 4; *Chieu v Canada (MCI)*, 2002 SCC 3 at para 40.
102 Bellissimo, above note 2, ch 10, 10.3, Appeals of Removal Orders at 10–2.
103 IRB, *Immigration Appeals* (18 March 2022), online: https://irb.gc.ca/en/information-sheets/Pages/FactIadSai.aspx.
104 2012 CanLII 92747 (CA IRB).
105 *Ibid* at paras 15–17.
106 2007 CanLII 67256 (CA IRB).
107 *Ibid* at para 38.
108 2008 CanLII 77226 (CA IRB).
109 *Federal Courts Act*, RSC 1985, c F-7, s 17(1).
110 *Ibid*, s 17(3)(b).
111 *Ibid*, s 18.1.
112 *IRPA*, s 72.
113 Bellissimo, above note 2, ch 11, 11.3, Application for Judicial Review at 11–5.
114 *Villanueva v Canada (MCI)*, 2023 FC 66 at para 15.
115 Federal Court of Appeal, "What Is the Mandate of the Federal Court?" (10 April 2023), online: www.fct-cf.gc.ca/en/pages/representing-yourself/faq#:~:-text=The%20Federal%20Court%20is%20Canada's,challenges%20to%20federal%20government%20decisions.
116 *IRPA*, s 74(d).
117 *Ibid*, s 87.01(1).
118 *Torre v Canada (MCI)*, 2016 FCA 48 at para 3 [internal citations omitted].
119 2019 FCA 262.
120 2020 FCA 202.
121 2003 FC 1085.
122 *Federal Courts Act*, s 52(b).
123 *Hawthorne*, above note 26.
124 2016 FCA 96.
125 2022 FCA 50.
126 2020 FCA 130 at paras 122–23.

127 [1999] 2 SCR 817, 174 DLR (4th) 193.

128 2019 SCC 65.

129 *Kanthasamy*, above note 4.

130 *B010 v Canada (MCI)*, 2015 SCC 58.

131 *Ibid* at para 68. See also para 60: the *Smuggling Protocol* defines migrant smuggling as the procurement of illegal entry "in order to obtain, directly or indirectly, a financial or other material benefit."

132 World Justice Project, *Global Scores & Rankings*, online: https://worldjusticeproject.org/our-work/wjp-rule-law-index/wjp-open-government-index/global-scores-rankings.

CHAPTER FIVE | The Future of Canadian Immigration Delivery

1 Wayne Dyer, online: www.drwaynedyer.com/blog/success-secrets.

2 The Right Honourable Prime Minister Trudeau's PC MP, Mandate Letter to then Minister of Citizenship and Immigration John McCallum (12 November 2015), online: *Prime Minister of Canada*, https://pm.gc.ca/en/mandate-letters/2015/11/12/archived-minister-immigration-refugees-and-citizenship-mandate-letter:

- Lead government-wide efforts to resettle 25,000 refugees from Syria in the coming months.
- As part of the Annual Immigration Levels Plan for 2016, bring forward a proposal to double the number of entry applications for parents and grandparents of immigrants to 10,000 a year.
- Give additional points under the Express Entry system to provide more opportunities for applicants who have Canadian siblings. Increase the maximum age for dependants to 22, from 19, to allow more Canadians to bring their children to Canada.
- Bring forward a proposal regarding permanent residency for new spouses entering Canada.
- Develop a plan to reduce application processing times for sponsorship, citizenship, and other visas.
- Fully restore the Interim Federal Health Program that provides limited and temporary health benefits to refugees and refugee claimants.
- Establish an expert human rights panel to help you determine designated countries of origin and provide a right to appeal refugee decisions for citizens from these countries.
- Modify the temporary foreign workers program to eliminate the $1,000 Labour Market Impact Assessment fee to hire caregivers and work with

provinces and territories to develop a system of regulated companies to hire caregivers on behalf of families.

- Lead efforts to facilitate the temporary entry of low-risk travellers, including business visitors, and lift the visa requirement for Mexico.
- Work with the Minister of Justice and the Minister of Public Safety and Emergency Preparedness to repeal provisions in the *Citizenship Act* that give the government the right to strip citizenship from dual nationals.
- Eliminate regulations that remove the credit given to international students for half of the time that they spend in Canada and regulations that require new citizens to sign a declaration that they intend to reside in Canada.

3 IRCC, "Key Highlights — 2016 Immigration Levels Plan" (last modified 8 August 2016), online: www.canada.ca/en/immigration-refugees-citizenship/news/2016/03/key-highlights-ndash-2016-immigration-levels-plan.html.

4 M. Carbert, "Canada on Track to Welcome More Than 300,000 Immigrants in 2016" *Globe and Mail* (8 March 2016), online: www.theglobeandmail.com/news/politics/ottawa-seeks-to-bring-more-than-300000-newcomers-this-year/article29069851.

5 IRCC, "Action Plan for Faster Immigration Producing Real Results" Government of Canada (26 March 2013), online: www.canada.ca/content/dam/ircc/migration/ircc/english/pdf/pub/2013-03-28.pdf.

6 CBC News, "Retirement Income Changes Won't Be Sudden, Government Says" *CBC* (27 January 2012), online: www.cbc.ca/news/canada/retirement-income-changes-won-t-be-sudden-government-says-1.1267790.

7 K. El-Assal & S. Thevenot, "IRCC's Application Backlog Grows Beyond 2.1 Million People" *CIC News* (10 May 2022), online: www.cicnews.com/2022/05/irccs-application-backlog-grows-beyond-21-million-people-0525204.html#gs.ta977a.

8 IRCC, "An Immigration Plan to Grow the Economy" (last modified 1 November 2022), online: www.canada.ca/en/immigration-refugees-citizenship/news/2022/11/an-immigration-plan-to-grow-the-economy.html; A. Fostik & N. Galbraith, "Changes in Fertility Intentions in Response to the COVID-19 Pandemic" (1 December 2021), Statistics Canada, online: www150.statcan.gc.ca/n1/en/catalogue/452800012021001000041.

9 This is germane given the long shadow of disturbing Canadian demographics, including a 1.5 percent declining fertility rate. Much of any future population growth signalled above will be the direct result of immigration. A. Fostik & N. Galbraith, "Changes in Fertility Intentions in Response to the COVID-19 Pandemic [ARCHIVED]" (14 December 2023), Statistics Canada, online: www150.statcan.gc.ca/n1/en/catalogue/452800012021001000041.

10 Government of Canada, "A Plan to Grow Our Economy and Make Life More Affordable" (2022), online (pdf): https://budget.gc.ca/2022/home-accueil-en.html.

11 *Ibid.*

12 Statistics Canada, "The Canadian Census: A Rich Portrait of the Country's Religious and Ethnocultural Diversity" Government of Canada (26 October 2022), online: www150.statcan.gc.ca/n1/daily-quotidien/221026/dq221026b-eng.htm.

13 *Ibid.*

14 *Ibid.*

15 *Ibid.*

16 *Ibid.*

17 *Ibid.*

18 *Ibid.*

19 *Ibid.*

20 *Ibid.*

21 *Ibid.*

22 Statistics Canada, "Immigrants Make Up the Largest Share of the Population in Over 150 Years and Continue to Shape Who We Are as Canadians" Government of Canada (26 October 2022), online: www150.statcan.gc.ca/n1/daily-quotidien/221026/dq221026a-eng.htm.

23 J. Gordon, "Canada's Population Surges from 2016–2021 on Immigration — Official Data" (9 February 2022), Reuters, online: www.reuters.com/world/americas/canadas-population-surges-2016-2021-immigration-official-data-2022-02-09.

24 Statistics Canada, above note 22.

25 *Ibid.*

26 See Chapter 2.

27 Parliament of Canada, "Canadian Multiculturalism" Library of Parliament (15 September 2009), online: https://lop.parl.ca/sites/PublicWebsite/default/en_CA/ResearchPublications/200920E#:~:text=As%20a%20sociological%20fact%2C%20multiculturalism,celebration%20of%20Canada's%20cultural%20diversity.

28 A. Cheatham, "What Is Canada's Immigration Policy?" Council on Foreign Affairs (9 February 2022), online: www.cfr.org/backgrounder/what-canadas-immigration-policy.

29 Statistics Canada, "Jobs in Canada: Navigating Changing Local Labour Markets" Government of Canada (30 November 2022), online: www150.statcan.gc.ca/n1/daily-quotidien/221130/dq221130b-eng.htm.

30 *Ibid.*

31 Statistics Canada, "In the Midst of High Job Vacancies and Historically Low Unemployment, Canada Faces Record Retirements from an Aging Labour Force: Number of Seniors Aged 65 and Older Grows Six Times Faster than Children 0-14" Government of Canada (27 April 2022), online: www150.statcan.gc.ca/n1/daily-quotidien/220427/dq220427a-eng.htm (accessed 15 February 2023).

32 Statistics Canada, "Population Projections for Canada, Provinces, and Territories, 2021 to 2068, 2022" Government of Canada (22 August 2022), online: www150.statcan.gc.ca/n1/daily-quotidien/220822/dq220822b-eng.htm.

33 *Ibid.*

34 *Ibid.*

35 IRCC, "2022 Annual Report to Parliament on Immigration" Ottawa: Government of Canada (31 December 2022), online: www.canada.ca/en/immigration-refugees-citizenship/corporate/publications-manuals/annual-report-parliament-immigration-2022.html at 10.

36 *Ibid* at 34.

37 Government of Canada, "An Immigration Plan to Grow the Economy" (1 November 2022), online: www.canada.ca/en/immigration-refugees-citizenship/news/2022/11/an-immigration-plan-to-grow-the-economy.html.

38 Statistics Canada, above note 12.

39 *Ibid.*

40 Statistics Canada, above note 32.

41 *Ibid.*

42 IRCC, "Notice — Supplementary Information for the 2023–2025 Immigration Levels Plan" Ottawa: Government of Canada (1 November 2022), online: www.canada.ca/en/immigration-refugees-citizenship/news/notices/supplementary-immigration-levels-2023-2025.html.

43 Government of Canada, above note 10.

44 *Ibid.*

45 Statistics Canada, "Asian Heritage Month ... by the Numbers" Government of Canada (6 January 2023), online: www.statcan.gc.ca/en/dai/smr08/2022/smr08_262.

46 R. Houle & H. Maheux, "150 Years of Immigration in Canada — ARCHIVED" Statistics Canada (17 May 2018), online: www150.statcan.gc.ca/n1/en/catalogue/11-630-x/11-630-x2016006.

47 Government of Canada, above note 10.

48 *Ibid.*

49 Global Affairs Canada, "Canada Launches Indo-Pacific Strategy to Support Long-Term Growth, Prosperity, and Security for Canadians" Government of Canada (27 November 2022), online: www.canada.ca/en/global-affairs/

news/2022/11/canada-launches-indo-pacific-strategy-to-support-long-term-growth-prosperity-and-security-for-canadians.html.

50 D. Burman, "3 in 10 Young Immigrants May Leave Canada in 2 Years: Survey" *CityNews* (5 April 2022), online: https://toronto.citynews.ca/2022/04/05/3-in-10-young-immigrants-may-leave-canada-in-2-years-survey.

51 Statistics Canada, "Reasons for Staying in Canada Cited By Immigrants Who Plan to Settle Here Permanently, by Immigration Category" Government of Canada (1 January 2005), online: www150.statcan.gc.ca/n1/pub/11-008-x/2007000/t/4097873-eng.htm.

52 A. Oliveira, "NYC Migrants Are Moving to Canada! Eric Adams Is Giving Disgruntled Asylum Seekers Free Bus Tickets to Canadian Border" *Daily Mail* (6 February 2023), online: www.dailymail.co.uk/news/article-11717237/Disgruntled-NYC-asylum-seekers-looking-better-quality-life-Canada.html.

53 Department of Finance Canada, "Measuring What Matters: Toward a Quality of Life Strategy for Canada" (19 April 2021), online: www.canada.ca/en/department-finance/services/publications/measuring-what-matters-toward-quality-life-strategy-canada.html.

54 *Ibid.*

55 *Ibid.*

56 *Ibid.*

57 Statistics Canada, above note 51.

58 OECD, "Better Life Index" (1 January 2022), online: www.oecdbetterlifeindex.org/countries/canada.

59 K. Frank, F. Hou & G. Schellenberg, "Life Satisfaction Among Recent Immigrants in Canada: Comparisons with Source-Country Populations and the Canadian-Born" Statistics Canada (2014), online: www150.statcan.gc.ca/n1/en/pub/11f0019m/11f0019m2014363-eng.pdf?st=4wxsSqmW at 8.

60 *Ibid* at 13–14.

61 *Ibid* at 21–22.

62 *Ibid* at 21.

63 L. Scialabba, B. Chew, C. Widener & I. Jenkins, "Government Backlog Reduction: Five Ways Government Agencies Can Improve Services and Mission Delivery" Deloitte (6 May 2019), online: www2.deloitte.com/us/en/insights/industry/public-sector/government-backlog-reduction.html.

64 M. Bellissimo, "Should We Send Immigration Officers Back to School?" Bellissimo Law Group PC (3 August 2016), online: https://bellissimolawgroup.com/should-we-send-immigration-officers-back-to-school.

65 *Ibid.*

66 *Ibid.*

67 M. Bellissimo, "Canadian International Student Program 2022 & Beyond" Bellissimo Law Group PC (25 February 2022), online: www.ourcommons.ca/Content/Committee/441/CIMM/Brief/BR11713090/br-external/BellissimoLawGroupPC-1-e.pdf.

68 It may be best to outsource this project to a company outside of IRCC that has the expertise and objectivity to recommend how operations can be improved. If IRCC opts to take this approach, it is crucial that they take steps to protect and ensure applicant privacy.

69 *Ibid.*

70 *Ibid.*

71 Bill C-27, 1st Sess, 44th Parl, Part 1, cl 12–14.

72 N. Arora, A. Banerjee & M. Narasu, "The Role of Artificial Intelligence in Tackling COVID-19" *Future Virology* (October 2020), online: www.futuremedicine.com/doi/10.2217/fvl-2020-0130.

73 A. Keshavarzi Arshadi et al, "Artificial Intelligence for Covid-19 Drug Discovery and Vaccine Development" *Frontiers in Artificial Intelligence* (2020) at 3, online: www.frontiersin.org/articles/10.3389/frai.2020.00065/full.

74 K. Davidson, "CIFAR and the Ontario Government Support Major Breakthroughs in COVID-19 Research" CIFAR (16 December 2020), online: https://cifar.ca/cifarnews/2020/12/16/ontario-researchers-use-ai-to-diagnose-and-treat-covid-19.

75 Investissement Quebec, International, "Montreal's Artificial Intelligence Hub," online: www.investquebec.com/international/en/secteurs-activite-economique/technologies-information-communications/Montreal-s-Artificial-Intelligence-Hub.html.

76 E. Niiler, "Can AI Be a Fair Judge in Court? Estonia Thinks So" *Wired* (5 March 2019), online: www.wired.com/story/can-ai-be-fair-judge-court-estonia-thinks-so/.

77 T. Vasdani, "Robot Justice: China's Use of Internet Court" *The Lawyer's Daily* (5 February 2020).

78 Misha Benjamin et al, "Towards Standardization of Data Licenses: The Montreal Data License" arXiv (2019), online: www.arxiv-vanity.com/papers/1903.12262.

79 K. Huang, "Alarmed by A.I. Chatbots, Universities Start Revamping How They Teach" *The New York Times* (16 January 2023), online: www.nytimes.com/2023/01/16/technology/chatgpt-artificial-intelligence-universities.html.

80 New Zealand Government, "Algorithm Charter for Aotearoa New Zealand" (July 2020), online: https://data.govt.nz/assets/data-ethics/algorithm/Algorithm-Charter-2020_Final-English-1.pdf.

81 *Ibid.*

82 European Commission, "Ethics Guidelines for Trustworthy AI" (8 April 2019), online: https://digital-strategy.ec.europa.eu/en/library/ethics-guidelines-trustworthy-ai.

83 J. Cox & B. Siu, "AI, Machine Learning, & Big Data Laws and Regulations 2023 Australia" *Global Legal Insights* (2023), online: www.globallegalinsights.com/practice-areas/ai-machine-learning-and-big-data-laws-and-regulations/australia#:~:text=Australia%20does%20not%20have%20specific,implementation%20of%20these%20emerging%20technologies.&text=Case%20law%20can%20also%20be%20relevant.

84 *Ibid.*

85 The White House, "What Is the Blueprint for an AI Bill of Rights?" (22 October 2022) online: www.whitehouse.gov/ostp/ai-bill-of-rights/what-is-the-blueprint-for-an-ai-bill-of-rights/.

86 *Ibid.*

87 *Blueprint for an AI Bill of Rights: Making Automated Systems Work for the American People*, The White House, 2022 at 23.

88 *Ibid* at 31.

89 *Ibid* at 30.

90 *Ibid.*

91 *Ibid* at 41.

92 *Ibid.*

93 *Ibid* at 5.

94 J. Liew & P. Molnar, "Clear Safeguards Needed Around Technology Planned for Border Checkpoints" *CBC News* (5 May 2021), online: www.cbc.ca/news/opinion/opinion-technology-border-canada-1.6005907.

95 The Conversation, "Canada Should Be Transparent in How It Uses AI to Screen Immigrants" (28 April 2021) (accessed 25 November 2022), online: https://theconversation.com/canada-should-be-transparent-in-how-it-uses-ai-to-screen-immigrants-157841.

96 RNZ, "Immigration NZ Pilot Described as Racial Profiling" YouTube (5 April 2018), online: www.youtube.com/watch?v=nfqPCrQmVKs&t=149s&ab_channel=RNZ.

97 New Zealand Government, above note 80.

98 *Ibid.*

99 *Ibid.*

100 IRCC, "Info Source: Personal Information Banks" (last modified 26 June 2019), online: www.canada.ca/en/immigration-refugees-citizenship/corporate/transparency/access-information-privacy/info-source/personal-information-banks.html.

101 Bill C-27, Part 1, cl 12–14.

102 *Ibid*, Part 3, cl 8.

103 Patrick McEvenue & Michelle Mann, "Case Study: Developing Guidance for the Responsible Use of Artificial Intelligence in Decision Making at Immigration, Refugees and Citizenship Canada" Law Society of Ontario, Special Lectures 2019 (2019).

104 Bill C-27, Part 1, cl 11.

105 *Ibid*, Part 3, cl 4.

106 A key finding from the reports as it pertains to the workings of the two systems is that both systems, while not making any ineligibility determinations, do "sort" applications by eligibility. A stark contrast between the two reports, however, lies in the fact that the former accounts for the system's explainability by relying on the fact that the impact of temporary resident visa (TRV) refusals on applicants is "temporary," whereas the latter is slightly more sensitive to the unforeseen negative impacts the system can have, such as bias and discrimination, and acknowledges that IRCC will need to be proactive in identifying those negative impacts and mitigate them. It is noted that the latter report was released about seven months after the former report, and thus this contrast represents a positive trend in IRCC's acknowledgement of the need for system transparency and explainability. For further information, please see IRCC, "Algorithmic Impact Assessment — Spouse or Common-Law Partner in Canada Advanced Analytics Pilot," Government of Canada, online: https://open.canada.ca/data/en/dataset/d41f9ec2-bf01-4b2a-bd8d-1b3a8424f534.

107 *Ibid*.

108 D. Lyon, "Social Sorting" in D. Lyon (ed) *Surveillance as Social Sorting: Privacy, Risk, and Digital Discrimination* (London UK: Routledge, 2003) at 13–28.

109 European Commission, above note 82.

110 *Ibid.*

111 Bill C-27, Part 1, cl 9.

112 Department of Home Affairs, "Immigration and Citizenship" *Australian Government* (2022), online: https://immi.homeaffairs.gov.au.

113 Government of Canada, above note 10.

114 El-Assal & Thevenot, above note 7.

115 IRCC, "Check Processing Times" (last modified 13 December 2023), online: www.canada.ca/en/immigration-refugees-citizenship/services/application/check-processing-times.html.

116 Bellissimo, above note 67.

117 *Ibid*, n 13.

118 SC 2017, c 20, s 451.

119 IRCC, "2017 to 2018 Fees Report" (last modified 11 July 2019), online: www.canada.ca/en/immigration-refugees-citizenship/corporate/publications-manuals/fees-report/2017-2018.html.

120 *Ibid.*

121 *Ibid.*

122 IRCC, "New Policy on Remissions When Service Standards Are Not Met in Some IRCC Programs" (last modified 31 March 2021), online: www.canada.ca/en/immigration-refugees-citizenship/news/notices/service-fee-act-remissions-policy-2021.html.

123 *Ibid.*

124 IRCC, "Learn About Representatives" (last modified 17 October 2023), online: www.canada.ca/en/immigration-refugees-citizenship/services/immigration-citizenship-representative/learn-about-representatives.html.

125 SC 2001, c 27, 87.3(5).

126 *Tabingo v Canada (MCI)*, 2014 FCA 191; *IRPA*, s 87.4(1).

127 Bellissimo Law Group PC, 2022–2023 Internal Survey to Facebook and Twitter followers.

APPENDIX 1 | **Inadmissibility Provisions in the *Immigration and Refugee Protection Act* and Evidentiary Thresholds**

1 *ENF 5, Writing 44(1) Reports*, Section 7.4 Standard of Proof at 16.

2 *Ibid.*

APPENDIX 2 | **Population Growth Rates**

1 Two charts: J. Gordon, "Canada's Population Surges from 2016–2021 on Immigration-Official Data" Reuters (9 February 2022) (retrieved 1 February 2023), online: www.reuters.com/world/americas/canadas-population-surges-2016-2021-immigration-official-data-2022-02-09 and "The Canadian Census: A Rich Portrait of the Country's Religious and Ethnocultural Diversity" (retrieved 1 February 2023), online: www150.statcan.gc.ca/n1/daily-quotidien/221026/dq221026b-eng.htm.

Table of Legal and Policy Instruments

An Act Respecting Immigration and Immigrants, 1906, 6 Edw VII, c 19, s 30
An Act Respecting Immigration, 1910, 9–10 Edw VII, c 27
An Act to Amend the Immigration Act, SC 1919, c 25

BELLISSIMO, MARIO D., *Canadian Citizenship and Immigration Inadmissibility Law*, 2d ed (Toronto: Thomson Reuters) (loose-leaf)

———. "Canadian International Student Program 2022 & Beyond" (25 February 2022), online (pdf): *House of Commons Canada* www.ourcommons.ca/Content/Committee/441/CIMM/Brief/BR11713090/br-external/BellissimoLawGroupPC-1-e.pdf

Bill C-27, *Digital Charter Implementation Act, 2022*, 1st Sess, 44th Parl, 2021

Bill S-8 (17 May 2022), online: www.parl.ca/DocumentViewer/en/44-1/bill/S-8/first-reading

CANADIAN ASSOCIATION FOR COMMUNITY LIVING (CACL). *Inclusive Citizenship: It's Time* (November 2017), online (pdf): www.ourcommons.ca/Content/Committee/421/CIMM/Brief/BR9256216/br-external/CanadianAssociationForCommunityLiving-e.pdf

Canadian Race Relations Foundation Act, SC 1991, c 8

CBSA. "Arrests, Detentions, and Removals" (last modified 27 March 2023), online: www.cbsa-asfc.gc.ca/security-securite/rem-ren-eng.html

CBSA. "Guide to Applying for a Declaration of Relief Under Subsection 42.1(1) of the *Immigration and Refugee Protection Act*" (last modified 28 November 2023), online: www.cbsa-asfc.gc.ca/travel-voyage/gadr-gddd-eng.html

CARBERT, M., *Canada on track to welcome more than 300,000 immigrants in 2016*, *Globe and Mail* (8 March 2016), online: www.theglobeandmail.com/news/politics/ottawa-seeks-to-bring-more-than-300000-newcomers-this-year/article29069851

Chinese Immigration Act, SC 1885, c 71, plus amendments: 1887, 1892, 1900, 1903

CIMM COMMITTEE REPORT. *Differential Treatment in Recruitment and Acceptance Rates of Foreign Students in Quebec and in the Rest of Canada*, online: www.ourcommons.ca/DocumentViewer/en/44-1/CIMM/report-8/page-30

Citizenship Act, RSC 1985, c C-29

CITIZENSHIP AND IMMIGRATION CANADA. (1998) *Building on a Strong Foundation for the 21st Century: New Directions for Immigration and Refugee Policy and Legislation*, online: https://publications.gc.ca/site/eng/9.660747/publication.html

CLEO, Steps to Justice, Glossary, *Hybrid offence*, online: https://stepstojustice.ca/glossary/hybrid-offence

Convention on the Rights of the Child, Can TS 1992 No 3, Article 3.1

Crimes Against Humanity and War Crimes Act [*CAHWCA*], SC 2000, c 24

DEPARTMENT OF CITIZENSHIP AND IMMIGRATION. *Government Response to the Eighth Report of the House of Commons Standing Committee on Citizenship and Immigration Entitled "Differential Treatment in Recruitment and Acceptance Rates of Foreign Students in Quebec and in the Rest of Canada,"* online (pdf): www.ourcommons.ca/content/Committee/441/CIMM/GovResponse/RP11946588/441_CIMM_Rpt08_GR/DepartmentOfCitizenshipAndImmigration-e.pdf

DEPARTMENT OF FINANCE CANADA (19 April 2021). *Measuring What Matters: Toward a Quality of Life Strategy for Canada*, online: www.canada.ca/en/department-finance/services/publications/measuring-what-matters-toward-quality-life-strategy-canada.html

DEPARTMENT OF HOME AFFAIRS: IMMIGRATION AND CITIZENSHIP (2022). *Australian Government.* online: https://immi.homeaffairs.govau

ENF 1, Inadmissibility

ENF 2, Evaluating Inadmissibility

ENF 20, Detention

ENF 5, Writing 44(1) Reports

ENF 6, Review of reports under A44(2)

FEDERAL COURT OF APPEAL. *What Is the Federal Court of Appeal?* (5 July 2023), online: www.fca-caf.ca/en/pages/about-the-court/what-is-the-federal-court-of-appeal

GIBSON, CAMPBELL J. & EMILY LENNON, "Historical Census Statistics on the Foreign-Born Population of the United States: 1850 to 1990" (Working Paper no 29, US Census Bureau, Washington, DC, 1999)

GLOBAL AFFAIRS CANADA (27 November 2022). *Canada launches Indo-Pacific Strategy to support long-term growth, prosperity, and security for Canadians*. Government of Canada, online: www.canada.ca/en/global-affairs/news/2022/11/canada-launches-indo-pacific-strategy-to-support-long-term-growth-prosperity-and-security-for-canadians.html

GOVERNMENT OF CANADA, *International Education*, online: www.international.gc.ca/education/strategy-2019-2024-strategie.aspx?lang=eng

GOVERNMENT OF CANADA (2022) *A Plan to Grow Our Economy and Make Life More Affordable*, online (pdf): www.budget.canada.ca/2022/home-accueil-en.html

GOVERNMENT OF ONTARIO, *Ontario Immigrant Nominee Program (OINP)*, online: www.ontario.ca/page/ontario-immigrant-nominee-program-oinp

GOVERNMENT OF QUÉBEC, *Immigration*, online: www.quebec.ca/en/immigration

Immigration Act, 1919. 9-10 Geo V, c 25; *An Act to Amend the Immigration Act*, 1919, assented to 6 June 1919

Immigration Act, RSC 1952, c 325

Immigration and Refugee Protection Act [*IRPA*], SC 2001, c 27

Immigration Appeal Division Rules, SOR/2022-277

Immigration Division Rules, SOR/2002-229

Immigration, Refugees and Citizenship Canada (IRCC), online: www.canada.ca/en/immigration-refugees-citizenship.html

Internment of Persons of Ukrainian Origin Recognition Act, SC 2005, c 52

IRB, *Chairperson Guideline 2: Detention*, 3.2 Release considerations, online: https://irb-cisr.gc.ca/en/legal-policy/policies/Pages/GuideDir02.aspx

———. *Immigration Appeals* (18 March 2022), online: https://irb.gc.ca/en/information-sheets/Pages/FactIadSai.aspx

IRCC, "#WelcomeAfghans: Key figures" (last modified 5 December 2023), online: www.canada.ca/en/immigration-refugees-citizenship/services/refugees/afghanistan/key-figures.html

———. "2017 to 2018 Fees Report" (last modified 11 July 2019), online: www.canada.ca/en/immigration-refugees-citizenship/corporate/publications-manuals/fees-report/2017-2018.html

———. "AFGH — Response to Ukraine and Afghanistan — April 25, 2022" (last modified 22 August 2022), online: www.canada.ca/en/immigration-refugees-citizenship/corporate/transparency/committees/afgh-apr-25-2022/response-ukraine-afghanistan.html

———. "Algorithmic Impact Assessment — Spouse or Common-Law Partner in Canada Advanced Analytics Pilot," *Government of Canada*, online: https://open.canada.ca/data/en/dataset/d41f9ec2-bf01-4b2a-bd8d-1b3a8424f534

———. "An Immigration Plan to Grow the Economy" (last modified 1 November 2022), online: www.canada.ca/en/immigration-refugees-citizenship/news/2022/11/an-immigration-plan-to-grow-the-economy.html

———. "Applications under family classes: Assessing the sponsor" (last modified 10 January 2023), online: www.canada.ca/en/immigration-refugees-citizenship/corporate/publications-manuals/operational-bulletins-manuals/permanent-residence/non-economic-classes/family-class-assessing-sponsor.html

———. "Applying for Permanent Residence from within Canada: Protected Persons and Convention Refugees [IMM 5205]" (last modified 24 July 2023), online: www.canada.ca/en/immigration-refugees-citizenship/services/application/application-forms-guides/guide-5205-applying-permanent-residence-within-canada-protected-persons-convention-refugees.html

———. "ARCHIVED — Temporary Public Policy Regarding Excessive Demand on Health and Social Services" (last modified 26 October 2022), online: www.canada.ca/en/immigration-refugees-citizenship/corporate/mandate/policies-operational-instructions-agreements/excessive-demand-june-2018.html

———. "Assessing inadmissibility due to serious criminality following Tran v. Canada" (last modified 14 November 2019), online: www.canada.ca/en/immigration-refugees-citizenship/corporate/publications-manuals/operational-bulletins-manuals/standard-requirements/tran.html

———. "Canada doubles immigration program for out-of-status construction workers in the Greater Toronto Area" (last modified 20 January 2023), online: www.canada.ca/en/immigration-refugees-citizenship/news/2023/01/canada-doubles-immigration-program-for-out-of-status-construction-workers-in-the-greater-toronto-area.html

———. "Canada to reduce work experience requirements for caregivers and provide pathways to permanent residence" (last modified 10 February 2023), online: www.canada.ca/en/immigration-refugees-citizenship/news/2023/02/canada-to-reduce-work-experience-requirements-for-caregivers-and-provide-pathways-to-permanent-residence.html

———. "Caregivers" (last modified 16 November 2023), online: www.canada.ca/en/immigration-refugees-citizenship/services/immigrate-canada/caregivers.html

———. "Changes to the medical inadmissibility policy of the Immigration and Refugee Protection Act take effect" (last modified 16 March 2022), online: www.canada.ca/en/immigration-refugees-citizenship/news/notices/changes-medical-inadmissibility-policy-irpa-take-effect.html

———. "Check processing times" (last modified 16 March 2023), online: www.canada.ca/en/immigration-refugees-citizenship/services/application/check-processing-times.html

———. "Determining your Eligibility for a Record Suspension or Pardon" (last modified 8 June 2022), online: www.canada.ca/en/parole-board/services/record-suspensions/determining-your-eligibility-for-record-suspension.html

———. "Eligibility to apply as a Federal Skilled Worker (Express Entry)" (last modified 25 August 2023), online: www.canada.ca/en/immigration-refugees-citizenship/services/immigrate-canada/express-entry/eligibility/federal-skilled-workers.html

———. "Eligibility to apply for the Federal Skilled Trades Program (Express Entry)" (last modified 16 November 2022), online: www.canada.ca/en/immigration-refugees-citizenship/services/immigrate-canada/express-entry/eligibility/skilled-trades.html

———. "Enhancements to the super visa program for parents and grandparents will help reunite families more easily and for longer" (last modified 7 June 2022), online: www.canada.ca/en/immigration-refugees-citizenship/news/2022/06/enhancements-to-the-super-visa-program-for-parents-and-grandparents-will-help-reunite-families-more-easily-and-for-longer.html

———. "Find out if you need a Labour Market Impact Assessment (LMIA), and how to hire a temporary foreign worker" (last modified 11 December 2023), online: www.canada.ca/en/immigration-refugees-citizenship/services/work-canada/hire-temporary-foreign/find-need-labour-market-impact-assessment.html

———. "Find out if you need a medical exam" (last modified 7 July 2022), online: www.canada.ca/en/immigration-refugees-citizenship/services/application/medical-police/medical-exams/requirements-temporary-residents/country-requirements.html

———. "Find your National Occupation Classification (NOC)" (last modified 23 August 2023), online: www.canada.ca/en/immigration-refugees-citizenship/services/immigrate-canada/express-entry/eligibility/find-national-occupation-code.html

———. "Guide 0124 — Subsequent temporary public policy to continue to facilitate access to permanent resident status for out-of-status construction workers in the Greater Toronto Area (GTA)" (last modified 1 December 2023), online: www.canada.ca/en/immigration-refugees-citizenship/services/application/application-forms-guides/guide-0124-out-of-status-construction-workers.html

———. "Guide 5069 — Temporary public policy: Temporary Resident to Permanent Resident Pathway (TR to PR Pathway)" (last modified 9 February 2023), online: www.canada.ca/en/immigration-refugees-citizenship/services/application/application-forms-guides/guide-5069-temporary-resident-permanent-resident-pathway.html

———. "History of citizenship legislation" (last modified 6 July 2015), online: www.canada.ca/en/immigration-refugees-citizenship/corporate/publications-manuals/operational-bulletins-manuals/canadian-citizenship/overview/history-legislation.html

———. "Humanitarian and compassionate assessment: Hardship and the H&C assessment" (last modified 2 March 2016), online: www.canada.ca/en/immigration-refugees-citizenship/corporate/publications-manuals/operational-bulletins-manuals/permanent-residence/humanitarian-compassionate-consideration/processing/assessment-hardship-assessment.html

———. "Humanitarian and compassionate considerations: Assessment and processing" (last modified 11 July 2017), online: www.canada.ca/en/immigration-refugees-citizenship/corporate/publications-manuals/operational-bulletins-manuals/permanent-residence/humanitarian-compassionate-consideration/processing.html

———. "Humanitarian and compassionate: Criminal inadmissibilities — A36(1) and A36(2)" (last modified 24 July 2014), online: www.canada.ca/en/immigration-refugees-citizenship/corporate/publications-manuals/operational-bulletins-manuals/permanent-residence/humanitarian-compassionate-consideration/processing/dealing-with-inadmissibility/criminal-inadmissibilities-a36-1-a36-2.html

———. "Humanitarian and compassionate: Dealing with inadmissibility" (last modified 11 July 2017), online: www.canada.ca/en/immigration-refugees-citizenship/corporate/publications-manuals/operational-bulletins-manuals/permanent-residence/humanitarian-compassionate-consideration/processing/dealing-with-inadmissibility.html

———. "Humanitarian and compassionate: Intake and who may apply" (last modified 20 April 2021), online: www.canada.ca/en/immigration-refugees-citizenship/corporate/publications-manuals/operational-bulletins-manuals/permanent-residence/humanitarian-compassionate-consideration/intake-who-may-apply.html

———. "Humanitarian and compassionate: Medical inadmissibility A38(1)" (last modified 11 July 2017), online: www.canada.ca/en/immigration-refugees-citizenship/corporate/publications-manuals/operational-bulletins-manuals/permanent-residence/humanitarian-compassionate-consideration/processing/dealing-with-inadmissibility/medical-inadmissibility-a38-1.html

———. "Info Source: Personal Information Banks" (last modified 26 June 2019), online: www.canada.ca/en/immigration-refugees-citizenship/corporate/transparency/access-information-privacy/info-source/personal-information-banks.html

———. "Key Highlights — 2016 Immigration Levels Plan" (last modified 8 August 2016), online: www.canada.ca/en/immigration-refugees-citizenship/news/2016/03/key-highlights-ndash-2016-immigration-levels-plan.html

———. "Labour market impact assessment (LMIA) exemption codes — International Mobility Program" (last modified 4 July 2023), online: www.canada.ca/en/immigration-refugees-citizenship/corporate/publications-manuals/operational-bulletins-manuals/temporary-residents/foreign-workers/exemption-codes.html

———. "Learn about representatives" (last modified 17 November 2023), online: www.canada.ca/en/immigration-refugees-citizenship/services/immigration-citizenship-representative/learn-about-representatives.html

———. "Ministerial Instruction regarding the Parent and Grandparent Super Visa" (last modified 11 January 2021), online: www.canada.ca/en/immigration-refugees-citizenship/corporate/mandate/policies-operational-instructions-agreements/ministerial-instructions/other-goals/mi-super-visa.html

———. "New policy on remissions when service standards are not met in some IRCC programs" (last modified 31 March 2021), online: www.canada.ca/en/immigration-refugees-citizenship/news/notices/service-fee-act-remissions-policy-2021.html

———. "Permanent residence pathways for Hong Kong residents: Who can apply" (last modified 15 August 2023), online: www.canada.ca/en/immigration-refugees-citizenship/services/immigrate-canada/hong-kong-residents-permanent-residence/eligibility.html

———. "Program delivery update: Public policy implementation for excessive demand and the centralization of files — June 1, 2018" (last modified 1 June 2018), online: www.canada.ca/en/immigration-refugees-citizenship/corporate/publications-manuals/operational-bulletins-manuals/updates/2018-excessive-demand.html

———. "Program requirements for high-wage positions" (last modified 24 November 2023), online: www.canada.ca/en/employment-social-development/services/foreign-workers/median-wage/high/requirements.html

———. "Program requirements for the Global Talent Stream" (last modified 24 November 2023), online: www.canada.ca/en/employment-social-development/services/foreign-workers/global-talent/requirements.html

———. "Proof of funds — Skilled-immigrants (Express Entry)" (last modified 23 August 2023), online: www.canada.ca/en/immigration-refugees-citizenship/services/immigrate-canada/express-entry/documents/proof-funds.html

———. "Recruitment and advertisement" (last modified 24 November 2023), online: *Program requirements for low-wage positions* www.canada.ca/en/employment-social-development/services/foreign-workers/median-wage/low/requirements.html#h2.9

———. "Sponsor your parents and grandparents: How to apply" (last modified 24 October 2023), online: www.canada.ca/en/immigration-refugees-citizenship/services/immigrate-canada/family-sponsorship/sponsor-parents-grandparents/apply.html

———. "Study permit: Who can apply" (last modified 12 September 2023), online: www.canada.ca/en/immigration-refugees-citizenship/services/study-canada/study-permit/eligibility.html

———. "Submit an Express Entry profile: Online form" (last modified 23 August 2023), online: www.canada.ca/en/immigration-refugees-citizenship/services/immigrate-canada/express-entry/submit-profile.html

———. "Temporary public policies: Temporary resident to permanent resident pathway — Who can apply" (last modified 6 November 2021), online: www.canada.ca/en/immigration-refugees-citizenship/services/immigrate-canada/tr-pr-pathway/who-can-apply.html

———. "Temporary resident permits (TRPs): Eligibility and assessment" (last modified 28 June 2019), online: www.canada.ca/en/immigration-refugees-citizenship/corporate/publications-manuals/operational-bulletins-manuals/temporary-residents/permits/eligibility-assessment.html

———. "Temporary resident permits (TRPs)" (last modified 22 July 2020), online: www.canada.ca/en/immigration-refugees-citizenship/corporate/publications-manuals/operational-bulletins-manuals/temporary-residents/permits.html

———. "The humanitarian and compassionate assessment: Reconsideration of a negative H&C decision" (last modified 24 July 2014), online: www.canada.ca/en/immigration-refugees-citizenship/corporate/publications-manuals/operational-bulletins-manuals/permanent-residence/humanitarian-compassionate-consideration/processing/assessment-reconsideration-negative-decision.html

———. "Visitor visa: Who can apply" (last modified 17 November 2023), online: www.canada.ca/en/immigration-refugees-citizenship/services/visit-canada/eligibility.html

———. "What is a record suspension?" (last modified 19 October 2018), online: www.canada.ca/en/parole-board/services/record-suspensions/what-is-a-r ecord-suspension.html

———. (26 March 2013). *Action Plan for Faster Immigration Producing Real Results*. Government of Canada, online: www.canada.ca/content/dam/ircc/migration/ircc/english/pdf/pub/2013-03-28.pdf

———. (31 December 2002) *2022 Annual Report to Parliament on Immigration* (Ottawa: Government of Canada), online: www.canada.ca/en/immigration-refugees-citizenship/corporate/publications-manuals/annual-report-parliament-immigration-2022.html

———. (1 November 2022). *Notice — Supplementary Information for the 2023–2025 Immigration Levels Plan* (Ottawa: Government of Canada), online: www.canada.ca/en/immigration-refugees-citizenship/news/notices/supplementary-immigration-levels-2023-2025.html

Justice for Victims of Corrupt Foreign Officials Act (Sergei Magnitsky Law), SC 2017, c 21, online: https://laws.justice.gc.ca/eng/acts/J-2.3/

LEGISINFO. "Budget Implementation Act 2008: Recorded Votes," online: www.parl.ca/LegisInfo/en/bill/39-2/C-50

MIGRATION POLICY INSTITUTE. *US Immigrant Population and Share over Time, 1850–Present*, online: www.migrationpolicy.org/programs/data-hub/charts/immigrant-population-over-time

MIGRATION POLICY INSTITUTE (DATA HUB), Immigrants in the US, 1850–Present, published: 4 November 2020,updated: 6 October 2023, online: https://public.tableau.com/app/profile/mpi.data.hub/viz/ImmigrantsintheU_S_-1850-2015/NumberofImmigrantsandTheirShareoftheTotalU_S_Population1850-2012

MIGRATION POLICY INSTITUTE (MPI) tabulation of data from US Census Bureau, 2010 and 2021 American Community Surveys (ACS), and 1970, 1990, and 2000 Decennial Census.

NEW ZEALAND GOVERNMENT (July 2020) *Algorithm Charter for Aotearoa New Zealand*, online: www.data.govt.nz/toolkit/data-ethics/government-algorithm-transparency-and-accountability/algorithm-charter

OP 1, Procedures

OP 20, Temporary Resident Permits

Order in Council, 8 January 1908

Order in Council, PC 23 & 24, 7 January 1914

Parliament Canada (1994) *House of Commons Debates* (35th Parl, 1st Sess) (Ottawa: Canadian Government Publishing)

PARLIAMENT OF CANADA (15 September 2009) *Canadian Multiculturalism*, Library of Parliament, online: https://lop.parl.ca/sites/PublicWebsite/default/en_CA/ResearchPublications/200920E#:~:text=As%20a%20sociological%20fact%2C%20multiculturalism,celebration%20of%20Canada's%20cultural%20diversity

Special Economic Measures Act (*SEMA*), SC 1992, c 17, s 4, online: https://laws-lois.justice.gc.ca/eng/acts/s-14.5/page-1.html

STATISTICS CANADA. (29 June 2016). 150 years of immigration in Canada, Statistics Canada (retrieved 1 February 2023), online: www150.statcan.gc.ca/n1/pub/11-630-x/11-630-x2016006-eng.htm

Steps to Justice: Your guide to law in Ontario, online: https://stepstojustice.ca/glossary/hybrid-offence/

The British North America Act, 1867

The Canadian Charter of Rights and Freedoms, Part I of the *Constitution Act, 1982*

The Constitution Act, 1982, which came into force on 17 April 1982

The Defence of Canada Regulations, The Standing Interdepartmental Committee on Emergency Legislation was set up under the authority of a Minute of Council. PC 531, 14 March 1938

War Measures Act, 1914, 5 Geo V, c 2

World Justice Project, *Global Scores & Rankings*, online: https://worldjusticeproject.org/our-work/wjp-rule-law-index/wjp-open-government-index/global-scores-rankings

Table of Cases

Index

About the Author

Mario D. Bellissimo is a graduate of Osgoode Hall Law School and is a certified specialist in citizenship and immigration law and refugee protection. He is the founder of Bellisimo Law Group PC and the principal lawyer with a practice focused on citizenship, immigration, protected person litigation, and inadmissibility law. Mr. Bellissimo has appeared before all levels of immigration tribunals and courts, including the Supreme Court of Canada. He is the past Chair of the Canadian Bar Association National Immigration Law Section, serves as an appointed member of the Federal Court Rules Committee, and participates on multiple stakeholder committees involving the Federal Courts; the Immigration and Refugee Board; Immigration, Refugees and Citizenship Canada; the Canada Border Services Agency; Employment and Social Development Canada; and the Department of Justice.

Mr. Bellissimo has testified before parliamentary and Senate committees on several proposed amendments to immigration law over the years. He has been the lead on policy papers, legal analysis, and proposed recommendations to government on behalf of immigration advocacy associations and in his personal capacity.

Mr. Bellissimo acts on a *pro bono* basis for Toronto's SickKids Hospital and Pro Bono Law Ontario and as the National Immigration

Law and Policy Advisor for COSTI Immigration Resettlement Services. He and his team represent clients from all over the world, and Bellissimo Law Group PC is exclusively committed to Canadian citizenship, immigration, and refugee matters. Bellissimo Law Group PC handles hundreds of files each year and represents clients at every stage of the immigration process.

Mr. Bellissimo has authored several legal publications, including *Canadian Citizenship and Immigration Inadmissibility Law*, 2d ed; *Labour Market Impact Assessments, Compliance and Enforcement: A Practical Guide*; *Canadian Citizenship and Immigration Inadmissibility: Criminal Law Edition*; *Practical Guide to Canadian Citizenship and Immigration Inadmissibility Law: Corporate Edition*; *Practical Guide to Canadian Citizenship and Immigration Inadmissibility Law: Refugee Law Edition*; and *Practical Guide to Canadian Citizenship and Immigration Inadmissibility Law: Immigration Practitioner's Edition.* He is the editor-in-chief of *ImmQuest* and the *Immigration Law Reporter*. Mr. Bellissimo has taught several immigration law courses, speaks across Canada, and appears frequently in the media on breaking citizenship, immigration, and refugee stories.

About the Editor

Gregory Tardi, BCL, LLB, DJur, is the general editor of the Understanding Canada Collection. He is a member of the Barreau du Québec and serves both as president of the Institute of Parliamentary and Political Law and as editor of the *Journal of Parliamentary and Political Law*. He has served as legal counsel with Elections Canada and at the House of Commons. He has taught at McGill, York, and Queen's universities and is the author of several books, including *The Theory and Practice of Political Law* and *Anatomy of an Election*.

FSC
www.fsc.org
MIX
Papier | Fördert
gute Waldnutzung
FSC® C083411

Zeitfracht Medien GmbH
Ferdinand-Jühlke-Straße 7
99095 Erfurt, Deutschland
produktsicherheit@kolibri360.de